*The Sierra Club Naturalist's Guides*

The Deserts of the Southwest
The North Woods of Michigan, Wisconsin, Minnesota, and
    Southern Ontario
The Sierra Nevada
The Southern Rockies: The Rocky Mountain Regions of
    Southern Wyoming, Colorado, and Northern New Mexico

# THE DESERTS
# OF THE SOUTHWEST

# THE DESERTS
# OF THE SOUTHWEST

A Sierra Club Naturalist's Guide
*Second Edition*

Peggy Larson and Lane Larson

FOREWORD BY EDWARD ABBEY

DRAWINGS BY LYNN LARSON

SIERRA CLUB BOOKS     *San Francisco*

The Sierra Club, founded in 1892 by John Muir, has devoted itself to the study and protection of the earth's scenic and ecological resources—mountains, wetlands, woodlands, wild shores and rivers, deserts and plains. The publishing program of the Sierra Club offers books to the public as a nonprofit educational service in the hope that they may enlarge the public's understanding of the Club's basic concerns. The point of view expressed in each book, however, does not necessarily represent that of the Club. The Sierra Club has some sixty chapters coast to coast, in Canada, Hawaii, and Alaska. For information about how you may participate in its programs to preserve wilderness and the quality of life, please address inquiries to Sierra Club, 85 Second Street, San Francisco, CA 94105.

www.sierraclub.org/books

GRATEFUL ACKNOWLEDGMENT is made for permission to reprint material from the following sources: E. F. Adolph and Associates, *Physiology of Man in the Desert* (N.Y.: Interscience Publishers, Inc.). Copyright © 1947 by Interscience Publishers, Inc. / Mary Austin, *The Land of Little Rain* (Boston: Houghton Mifflin Co.). Copyright © 1903 by Mary Austin. / Joseph Wood Krutch, *The Forgotten Peninsula* (N.Y.: William Sloane Associates). Copyright © 1961 by Joseph Wood Krutch. / Joseph Wood Krutch, *The Voice of the Desert* (N.Y.: William Sloane Associates). Copyright © 1954, 1955 by Joseph Wood Krutch. / Forrest Shreve and Ira L. Wiggins, *Vegetation and Flora of the Sonoran Desert* (Stanford, Calif.: Stanford University Press). Copyright © 1964 by the Board of Trustees of the Leland Stanford Junior University.

Published by Sierra Club Books, in conjunction with Crown Publishers, New York, New York. Member of the Crown Publishing Group.

Random House, Inc., New York, Toronto, London, Sydney, Auckland
www.randomhouse.com

SIERRA CLUB, SIERRA CLUB BOOKS, and Sierra Club design logos are registered trademarks of the Sierra Club.

Maps by Stephen Bahre
Printed in the United States of America

Library of Congress Cataloging-in-Publication Data
Larson, Peggy Pickering
    The deserts of the Southwest: a Sierra Club naturalist's guide / by Peggy Larson and Lane Larson; foreword by Edward Abbey; drawings by Lynn Larson—rev. and updated
    Rev. ed. of: Sierra Club naturalist's guide to the deserts of the Southwest, © 1997.
    Includes bibliographical references.
    1. Desert biology—Southwestern States. 2. Desert biology—Mexico. 3. Deserts—Southwestern States. 4. Deserts—Mexico. I. Larson, Lane II. Larson, Peggy Pickering, Sierra Club naturalist's guide to the deserts of the Southwest. III. Title.

QH88.L37                    2000
578.754'0979—dc21           99-056996

ISBN 1-57805-052-9
10 9 8 7 6 5 4 3 2
Second Edition

For our favorite desert denizens
**Ryan and Aaron,**
sons, grandsons, nephews
—*L.D.L, P.A.L., L.A.L.*

# FOREWORD

WHY GO INTO THE DESERT? That sun, roaring at you all day long. The fetid tepid vapid little waterholes slowly evaporating—full of cannibal beetles, spotted toads, hairworms, liver flukes—and down at the bottom, invariably, the pale drowned cadaver of a ten-inch centipede. Those pink rattlesnakes down in The Canyon, those diamondback monsters thick as a catskinner's wrist that lurk in shady places along the trail, those unpleasant solpugids and unnecessary Jerusalem crickets that scurry on dirty feet across your face at night. Why? The rain that comes down like lead shot and wrecks the trail before you, those sudden rockfalls of obscure origin that crash like thunder ten feet behind you in the heart of a dead-still afternoon. Why? The ubiquitous vultures, so patient—but only *so* patient. The ragweed, the tumbleweed, the jimsonweed, the snakeweed. The scorpion in your shoe at dawn. The dreary wind that seldom stops, the manic-depressive mesquite trees waving their arms at you on moonlight nights. Sand in the soup du jour. Halazone tablets in your canteen. The barren hills that always go up, which is bad, or down, which is worse.

Why go to Starvation Creek, Poverty Knoll, Buzzard Gulch, Wolf Hole, Bitter Springs, Last Chance Canyon, Dungeon Canyon, Whipsaw Flat, Dead Horse Point, Scorpion Flat, Dead Man Draw, Stinking Spring, Camino del Diablo, Hell Hole Canyon, Jornado del Muerto . . . Death Valley? I think of a homemade sign I once saw at a fork in a rocky road somewhere in the boondocks of western Texas:

> Hartung's Road
> Take the Other

A good sign. One would have liked to meet Mr. Hartung. But I didn't. I respected his need for privacy. I share that need— as who doesn't these days?

Well then, why indeed go walking into the desert when you could be strolling along the golden beaches of California or camping by a stream of pure Rocky Mountain spring water in colorful Colorado or loafing through a laurel slick in the high blue misty hills of North Carolina?

Some time ago a friend and I took a walk around the base of a mountain up in Coconino County, Arizona. About halfway around this mountain, on the third or fourth day, we paused for a while—two days—by the side of a stream which the Navajos call Nasja, perhaps because of the strange amber color of the water. (Caused by juniper roots—the water seemed safe enough to drink.) On our second day there I walked down the stream, alone, to look at the canyon beyond. I entered the canyon and followed it for half the day, three or four miles maybe, until it became a gorge so deep, narrow and dark, full of water and the inevitable quagmires of quicksand, that I turned around and looked for a way out. A way different than the way I'd come, which was crooked and uncomfortable and buried. I wanted to see what was up on top of this world. I found a sort of chimney flue on the east wall, which looked feasible, and sweated and cursed my way up through that for an unreasonable distance until I reached a point where one could walk upright, like a human being. Another 300 feet of scrambling brought me to the rim of the canyon. No one, I felt certain, had ever departed Nasja Canyon by *that* route before.

But someone had. I found near the summit an arrow sign, three feet long, formed of stones and pointing off into the north, toward those same old purple vistas, so grand, immense and mysterious, of more canyons, more mesas and plateaus, more mountains, more cloud-dappled sun-spangled leagues of desert sand and rock, under the same old, same true wide and aching sky.

The arrow pointed "into" the north. But what was it pointing at? I looked at the sign closely and saw that those dark, desert-varnished stones had been in place for a long, long time; they rested in compacted dust. I followed the direction suggested and came promptly, within a hundred yards, to the rim of another canyon and a drop-off straight down of a good 500 feet. Not that way, surely. Across this canyon was nothing of any unusual interest that I could see—only more of the familiar sunblasted sandstone, a few scrubby clumps of black-brush and prickly pear, a few acres of nothing where only a lizard could graze surrounded by a few square miles of more nothingness of interest chiefly to horned toads. I returned to the arrow and checked again, this time with field glasses, looking away toward the north for 10, 20, 40 miles into the distance. I studied the scene with care, looking for an ancient Indian ruin, a significant cairn, perhaps an abandoned mine, a hidden treasure, the mother of all mother lodes . . .

But there was nothing out there. Nothing at all. Nothing but the desert. Nothing but the world.

That's why.

Edward Abbey
Tin Cup Mesa, Utah

# ACKNOWLEDGMENTS

We appreciate the assistance of many individuals in the new edition of this book. The expertise of Wanda Larson, Training Program Director, Arizona Emergency Medicine Research Center, University of Arizona, in the revision of the chapter on first aid was invaluable. Jude McNally, Managing Director of the Arizona Poison and Drug Information Center in Tucson, gave freely of his time and extensive knowledge regarding the desert's venomous creatures. Lynn Larson revised three of the maps to reflect changes in the borders of the Sonoran Desert. The staff members of the Arizona-Sonora Desert Museum were most helpful, and special thanks go to the museum's publication manager, Steve Phillips. Jim Cohee, Sierra Club editor of both the first and second editions, has been, always, patient and most helpful. And thanks to Merv, who, over the years, has taken us to distant desert corners, from the Sonoran to the Sahara.

We extend our gratitude to these individuals. Any errors contained herein are not theirs, however, but solely those of the authors.

# CONTENTS

# THE DESERTS
# OF THE SOUTHWEST

# CHAPTER I

# Rewarding Travel

"REWARDING TRAVEL in an unfrequented land," naturalist-author Joseph Wood Krutch called his journeys through the southwestern desert country. The same reward awaits the explorer of today who approaches the desert with an open, inquiring mind; who comes to the desert with a desire to be a closer, more integral, and harmonious part of the biota; and who also acknowledges, respects, and prepares for the particular conditions to which he or she may be subjected by the unique, noncompromising desert environment.

The desert holds a mystique, a subtle fascination, which is difficult to pinpoint and more difficult to describe. Not all people are so affected by it, but those who have experienced the desert in this way are the richer. Mary Austin—playwright, poet, essayist, novelist—wrote:

> If one is inclined to wonder at first how so many dwellers came to be in the loneliest land that ever came out of God's hands, what they do there and why stay, one does not wonder so much after having lived there. None other than this long brown land lays such a hold on the affections.

This "long brown land" is a land of beauty. But it does not display the traditional concept of beauty imposed upon us by an Anglo-Saxon cultural heritage. Except where drastically changed from its natural state by the introduction of exotic or fossil water, the desert displays no timbered green, no fruited plain, no amber waves of grain. Rather, it reveals bare ground, or shrub- and cactus-studded earth, sand, or rock. And, although the desert may have its mountains, they fall somewhat short of the traditional concept of purple mountains' majesties. Where, then, is the beauty to be found?

The elements of space and openness contribute importantly to desert beauty. Desert air is typically remarkably clear (though unfortunately it grows gradually less so with increasing pollution). Little moisture is held within it, little haze is produced, and under normal unpolluted conditions visibility stretches sixty or more miles. Thus, from an unobstructed location, the human observer can turn full circle, viewing a sixty-mile radius—and in most of the desert, the view is relatively unrestricted. Here and there, mountain ranges rear their rocky masses from the desert's floor, but the view often stretches from the observer to the horizon, where earth joins sky. Nor do large trees or other heavy growth obstruct the vista.

Open space exists not only at eye level; much openness may be found at ground level, as well. With water limited, desert vegetation is sparse and widely spaced. Space and openness in the desert, above and below, result in easy viewing, easy walking, and a feeling of spaciousness—ankle and elbow room, so to speak, an increasingly rare commodity, but one we are learning is basic to human well-being.

Sky contributes to the desert expanse. Little obstructs the extensive view of the sky dome, which in the clear, arid atmosphere appears bluer by day and more brightly star-studded by night than do the skies over many moister regions. Sunsets often tend toward the magnificent, as do sunrises, and the displays of towering, snow-white, black-bottomed, thunder clouds that sweep across the summer sky are spectacular. So, too, are the manifestations of the storms these clouds produce—displays of brilliant lightning, resounding thunder, and occasional drowning deluges in a normally dry land.

The desert's anatomy lies exposed. No complete vegetative cloak covers its naked geology; its geological history is varied, and the composition and relationships of its components are more easily observed and more readily studied and appreciated than those in most other climates. The North American deserts are geologically young; their surfaces have not yet been worn down to monotonousness. Angular, jagged, sharp lines and rough textures—rather than smooth, soft, rounded, cloaked ones—characterize much of the desert's surface. The visible geology, indeed the total visible aspect of the desert, has the character of a handsomely rugged, virile individualist.

The physical components of the desert and the living

things which dwell there abound with texture, form, and color. Much of the variety is derived from the very obvious ground surface—the rocks, sand, gravel, and soil. From the black and reddish volcanic flows, which solidified as they once sludged across the landscape, to the occasional greens and blues of mineral deposits, to the beige-yellow sands, the base of the desert displays a wide range of color, as well as of form and texture. The plants exhibit particularly various forms. Unlike other habitats, the desert is seldom dominated by one ecological life form. Shrubs, cacti, bushes, trees, small ground-hugging annuals—to a certain degree all dissimilar from one another in form and appearance—share the role of dominance in the desert, whereas dominance in other habitats is often restricted to a single growth type—for example, conifers, or grasses, or deciduous hardwood trees. The desert's plant variety provides interest in viewing, comparing, and touching. The animals, too, provide variety in color, form, and texture. Consider the patterning, glossiness, and glassy smoothness of the snake's scales; the shine of the beetle's carapace; the flash of the hummingbird's color and iridescent sheen; the coyote's beige-yellow-gray fur; or the black of the feather-slick raven against the summer sky. The color of most desert animals serves to blend into their background of browns and grays. Spots of vivid color do occur in the desert, most of them brief in tenure—flowers, butterflies, some other insects such as beetles, a male lizard in courting display, an occasional bird. For the most part, however, one receives from the desert as a whole a color impression of subdued variations on a theme of gray, brown, black, beige, green, blue, purple, and subtle combinations of these hues.

The desert light, producer of the colors, seems almost a physical entity. Its long rays, warm and almost caressing on an early summer morning, shift to a hard, hot, flat, white glare at noon, then gradually recede to the warm red and pink of the sunset sky; in the waning evening light, cool blues and purples color the distant mountains. Indeed, while much of the coloring of the adjacent desert is in the brown range, the distances are painted in hues of purple. Far mountain ranges in the fluctuating desert light are transposed from a flat-surfaced, grayish-brownish-blue at the sun's daily zenith to sculptured surfaces colored by shades of amethyst and lilac as the sun lies closer to the morning or evening horizons. Particularly at sunset, one may view as many as three or four sets of desert mountain peaks ranged one beyond another, their colors varying from the dark purple of the closest to the lighter shades of the more distant, and all shifting in degree of coloration, minute by minute, as the sun drops. The subtle, constantly changing coloration of the desert is one of its most striking beauties.

The environment of the desert is also harsh and demanding. It does not coddle. Therefore those plants and animals which make it their home often display adaptations of form, function, behavior, or all of these, which allow them to survive and often prosper under the climatic conditions imposed upon them. These adaptations have produced singularly unique and fascinating living things—cacti fifty feet tall, boojums resembling seventy-foot inverted carrots, mice that never drink, snakes that move forward by traveling sideways. The economy of the desert is normally exceedingly frugal, particularly from the standpoint of water. At certain times in the desert, the line between life and death is very tenuous for plants and animals. (For the human species, when unprepared, the line may also prove tenuous.) The desert's nature is open and visible, and its climatic conditions are stringent; probably in no other biome are the relationships of living things to the physical aspects of their environment and to one another so obvious and observable as they are in the desert. A rewarding understanding of the special beauty of adaptation, the tenacity and strength of the force of life, and, by extrapolation, a deeper appreciation of all things living awaits the human desert explorer who looks, learns about, and seriously considers the desert biota.

The deserts represent one of the last North American areas in which large tracts remain relatively uninhabited. The arid wilderness has been slower to "develop" in the usual sense than areas more amenable to settlement and exploitation through agriculture and industry—a magnificent beneficence insofar as desert and wilderness aficionados are concerned.

Space between people is one of the desert's most pleasing aspects for those who would explore it.

Surely to meet and enjoy a challenge must be basic to human nature. Adventurers have long accepted the challenge of the mountain, the jungle, and the sea, and tested themselves against them. Fewer have recognized the challenge of the desert; today, increasing numbers are realizing that challenge, wilderness, and rewards also exist in the arid habitat. Just as the mountaineer, sailor, or jungle explorer must recognize the special conditions imposed by the environment he or she seeks to know, so must the desert enthusiast understand desert conditions and how best to cope with them in order to understand and enjoy desert exploration—whether by foot, on horseback, or by winged or wheeled transport. The desert can be a difficult, even deadly land for living things. Many plants and animals have physically adapted to its special conditions over spans of time. Man has not adapted physically, and cannot, but to some extent, as have certain animals, he can adapt behaviorally. Mankind possesses technology and the ability to think on a high level. Common sense demands the use of these two factors for the safe, intelligent enjoyment of the desert in a nondisruptive manner, and the derivation of the many recreational, spiritual, and humanly renewable benefits the desert can afford. Man must understand the components in the desert biome and their interrelationships and the intelligent ways in which the desert lands may be explored and appreciated.

Krutch's travels in an "unfrequented land" rewarded him with a very special feeling for the desert:

> Long before I ever saw the desert I was aware of the mystical overtones which the observation of nature made audible to me. But I have never been more frequently or more vividly aware of them than in connection with the desert phenomena.

In expressing his feelings, Krutch coined an appropriate term; he spoke for a good many of us who experience a deep affection for desert beauty, desert life, and desert wilderness when he readily acknowledged that, indeed, a "desert phenomenon" exists.

# CHAPTER II

# Define Desert

DEFINE DESERT. Seemingly, almost as many definitions of the term arise as there are definers. The simplest definition holds that a desert is an area receiving an average of ten or fewer inches of precipitation annually. This definition is far from complete. Some areas receive less than ten inches rainfall annually, yet are not considered deserts. Some authorities would place the desert-defining figure at a five-inch limit; however, some areas receiving in excess of five inches precipitation annually are, nonetheless, deserts. Many factors influence the value plants derive from moisture they receive; hence, these factors are instrumental in determining the type of habitat established. A gentle soaking rain benefits the vegetation more than a violent cloudburst, which results in rapid runoff and moisture loss. Several well-spaced showers are more valuable than a single rain, even though the same total precipitation may be produced. Moisture received in summer heat will be more readily evaporated than that received during cool weather; conversely, moisture received in hot weather may be greatly needed by the vegetation for survival in that particular stressful period.

Portions of the North American desert receive very limited rainfall. The record for lowest average annual precipitation for North America is held by Bataques, Mexico, located in the Sonoran Desert, with a fourteen-year average of 1.2 inches. That record is followed closely by the one for Death Valley, California, in the Mohave Desert, with an average of 1.8 inches. Toward the opposite end of the scale lies Tucson, Arizona, considered to be in the Sonoran Desert, yet receiving an average of approximately 12 inches annual precipitation.

The figure of ten inches or less annual precipitation, as used in the desert definition, is an *average* figure. However, the erratic nature of its occurrence is a basic characteristic of desert precipitation. For example, in one study Yuma, Arizona, was reported to have a mean annual precipitation of 3.39 inches. However, extreme annual precipitation records for Yuma included one year of 11.42 inches and another year when a mere .28-inch total was received. An extreme example of the irregularity of desert rainfall is provided by Bagdad, California, in the Mohave Desert, which has an average annual rainfall of approximately 2¼ inches. Death Valley is reported to have no rainfall in two years out of fifty. However, Bagdad holds the record for the longest dry period in the United States, having undergone 767 days—from October 3, 1912, to November 8, 1914—without precipitation!

More than water, or the lack of it, is involved in producing desert. Temperature, too, plays a vital role. High temperatures compound the effects of moisture shortage. *Evapotranspiration* is defined as the total loss of water from the soil both by evaporation from the soil surface and by transpiration from the plants growing in that soil. Certainly temperature in conjunction with air movements exerts the major influence on the rates at which evaporation and transpiration occur. Evapotranspiration rates are determined by comparing precipitation (P) received to potential evapotranspiration (PET). The potential evaporation rate is considered to be approximately 60 percent of the water that evaporates from an exposed, wide pan of water. Factoring in P and a 60 percent estimate for PET, scientists determine a PET/P ratio. Dr. Mark Dimmitt of the Arizona-Sonora Desert Museum states that the ratio for Tucson, Arizona, which is located in the Arizona Upland Division of the Sonoran Desert, is 4.3. An area with a ratio higher than 3.0 is considered semiarid. He also reports that the area around Yuma, Arizona has a PET/P ratio of 30, and the interior Sahara Desert's is a mighty 600! Yet another definition of desert is that it is an area in which potential evapotranspiration exceeds precipitation.

The high-temperature record for the Western Hemisphere is an impressive 134° F. on July 10, 1913, in Death Valley, California. This temperature is exceeded by only one world record—136.4° F.—reported in 1922 at El Azizia, Libya. Death Valley is also reported to have the hottest summers in

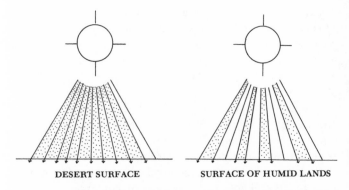

**DESERT SURFACE**    **SURFACE OF HUMID LANDS**

FIG. 1.    With little atmospheric humidity or plant cover to impede its passage to their surfaces, deserts receive approximately nine-tenths of possible solar radiation, whereas the surfaces of humid lands receive approximately two-fifths.

the Western Hemisphere, with an average daily (not maximum) temperature of 98° F. And although Death Valley holds the extreme high record for the North American desert, it is not an isolated example; many of the other desert localities report record temperatures in the 120°-plus range. High summer maximum temperatures are often sustained over long periods in the southwestern deserts. Thus Dr. Forrest Shreve, one of the foremost early desert ecologists, noted that periods of ninety consecutive days with a maximum of at least 100° F. are not exceptional for portions of the Sonoran Desert.

Just as the extremes of precipitation play a very determining role with regard to survival by living things in the desert, so also are temperature extremes important. These extremes are often very great in the desert, where lack of moisture results in air of low humidity and formation of only limited cloud cover. A very high percentage of possible sunlight is therefore received. In one recent year, for example, Yuma, Arizona, received 93 percent of possible sunshine; that same year, Norfolk, Virginia, received 31 percent. With little water vapor in the air and little cloud cover or plant growth to deflect the sun's rays, approximately 90 percent of the solar radiation possible reaches the ground surface and lower air layer

**DESERT SURFACE**          **SURFACE OF HUMID LANDS**

FIG. 2.   In the desert, approximately nine-tenths of the day's accumulated heat is reradiated back toward the sky; approximately one-half of the day's accumulated heat is lost at night in humid climates. Desert country displays a wide range of daily temperatures; humid lands show a much lesser range.

in the desert, resulting in very high air and ground-surface temperatures. Temperatures at the ground surface in sunlight often range thirty to fifty degrees higher than the accompanying official air temperature taken under standardized conditions. Humid areas receive approximately 40 percent of the solar radiation possible, 60 percent being deflected before it reaches the ground and lower air levels.

After sundown in the desert, heat is rapidly and easily radiated back toward the sky, with approximately 90 percent escaping unimpeded. In moister climates, the heat gained at lower levels during the day is less easily lost, with approximately 50 percent of it escaping and the remainder being deflected downward and held by growth as well as by clouds, water, and dust in the air. Thus in moist climates temperatures fluctuate only moderately from day to night, but in the desert the range between daytime highs and nighttime lows is extreme. The difference is often fifty degrees or more. Similarly there is a very great range between the low and high temperature records over the period of a year or several years. For example, Yuma, Arizona, reported for one particular year a maximum temperature in August of 116 degrees and a minimum temperature in December of 30 degrees, a difference of eighty-six degrees. This is not unusual for this region. Records over a period of years, as compiled by Dr. R. Logan for Yuma, showed an all-time maximum temperature of 123.08 degrees and an all-time minimum of 22.1 degrees, or a difference of approximately 101 degrees. Elko, Nevada, in the northern Great Basin Desert has records of –43 to 107 degrees Fahrenheit, a remarkable 150-degree range.

Snow occurs in the North American deserts, primarily in the more northern parts, but also as far south as Tucson, Arizona, which receives at least traces almost every winter and is occasionally the recipient of 2- to 4-inch snowfalls. Also, incongruous as it may seem, a limited amount of dew occurs in the North American deserts. The amount of water vapor contained in the air at any one time compared to the amount it is capable of containing is known as the *relative humidity,* and is expressed as a percentage. Warm air is capable of holding more vapor than cool air before it reaches the saturation point. Thus although desert air often has a very low relative humidity during the day, as the night air cools rapidly it may reach the saturation point, resulting in excess moisture being deposited on ground and plant surfaces in the form of dew.

Heat and aridity spawn characteristics typical of deserts. Plants are widely spaced due to lack of moisture. Very occasional areas may be totally without vegetation. Shreve estimated that in the parts of the arid Mohave Desert which support small creosote bushes, only 3 percent of the ground surface was covered. And, in the more "lush" portions of the Sonoran Desert, the percentage of ground covered is considerably higher, although even there much of the desert's surface lies exposed, subject to erosion by both wind and water. Paucity of vegetation results in soil low in humus. Shreve reported humus in soils of the Colorado and Mohave deserts as ranging from 0.25 to 0.65 percent, compared to a range of 3 to 5 percent in soils of more humid regions. Desert soils have acquired relatively large amounts of sodium and potassium salts as well as other water soluble minerals due to the high rates of mineralization in these areas. In more moist regions, minerals present tend to be leached downward through the soil as abundant moisture soaks through it. Not so in the desert, where water is insufficient to soak the soil to any great depth; there, minerals in suspension may even be sucked upward through the soil by capillary action and pulled to the surface to be deposited as the moisture carrying them is evaporated. Depending upon the minerals present and the amounts, desert soils may vary from those exceedingly rich in plant growth to those which inhibit or even prevent it.

Winds are frequent in the desert. These desert winds are caused by general atmospheric patterns, as an accompaniment to storms, or in some cases by local topography. They are also often caused by the rapid heating and cooling of the air near the ground surface. Winds, due to their frequency and to the air they circulate, which is often dry and hot, constitute a powerful evaporative force as they sweep across the soil and over the living things in their paths. They also contribute greatly to erosion of the desert's surface. Winds carrying dust and sand act as agents of abrasion, sandblasting rocks and objects over which they move. The winds also act as agents of deflation and deposition, moving loose material such as soil, dust, sand, and dead plants from one site to deposit it in another.

Steady winds of one or more days' duration are commonplace in the southwestern desert, particularly in the late winter and spring. These winds only occasionally reach or exceed 35 miles per hour in speed, although, due to the openness of the terrain through which they move relatively unimpeded, their speed is often estimated to be greater. Gusts of wind moving at much higher speeds sometimes accompany storms, particularly in the summer months. *Dust devils,* or whirlwinds—rotating air currents occasionally as much as several hundred feet in height and carrying dust, sand, and debris—are of common occurrence on hot still days; often several at a time may be seen moving across the landscape. These whirlwinds are caused when extreme heating of the ground surface results in columns of upflowing air. Surrounding air rushes into this vacuum and diverts to one side or the other of the rising air, causing a strong, uprising, whirling column. Although dust devils occasionally topple poorly supported block patio walls, they are rarely dangerous in the North American desert.

Unlike the potentially very destructive tornadoes—whirling masses of air reaching downward from clouds—the dust devils rotate upward from the ground surface. They can be exceedingly annoying to the person caught afoot or driving through the dusty center of one.

Frequent winds and open ground surface cause occasional desert sand and dust storms. These storms are relatively infrequent; one study determined that in most of the North American desert not more than three or four, and more often a maximum of one to two, occur annually in any one locality. Over most of our desert terrain, winds must reach approximately 35 miles per hour or higher in order to initiate and maintain such storms. Minor storms may last only a few hours; major ones often persist twelve to thirty-six hours. Sand, being heavier than dust, is rarely carried by the winds to any height much greater than three feet above the ground. However, the lighter dust may be carried to heights of many hundred feet in the air. The North American desert has only relatively limited areas of sand, estimated at 1 percent or less of its total area, primarily but not solely limited to the area around the head of the Gulf of California.

Sand storms in the North American deserts are rarely dangerous for human beings, as compared to some of the storms in the Old World deserts, such as the Arabian and Sahara, where much more extensive areas of sand and vast sweeps of open desert contribute to the devastating force. North American sand storms do occasionally damage automobiles, sandblasting paint and windshields, and may also damage other objects, such as wooden power poles. Dust storms in the North American desert can be devastating, however, particularly in conjunction with vehicular traffic; they may suddenly obscure vision, causing serious accidents. Dust storms are intensified where man has removed all plant cover preparatory to planting crops; such areas are often near highways where the mix of dust storm and traffic may prove fatal.

Strangely, however, the most important erosional factor in the desert is not wind, but water. The effects of water are everywhere apparent in this land where the sight of water itself is for the most part a rarity. Precipitation is often received through violent cloudbursts accompanied by rapid runoff. Even when precipitation is received in a less violent manner, its absorption may be somewhat impeded, for much of the desert's surface is rock or gravel, or exhibits other factors of a low or nonabsorptive character. Also, the geologically young North American deserts have many rocky, low, but precipitous mountain ranges, which often receive much of the desert's precipitation, but down which much of this water rapidly flows. In the desert the ground surface, more bare than covered, lies vulnerable to these occasional, but highly effective and destructive water forces.

Water, as it falls on the desert mountains, often first runs in a broad, shallow, sheet flow, then collects in normally dry watercourses. It carries with it boulders, rocks, gravel, and finer materials. As the flood debouches onto the lower levels of the hills, its speed diminishes; gradually, the material it carries is dropped, spread out in a fan shape, graded from the heavier material higher up the slope to the lightest at the bottom. A subsequent heavy runoff may follow the same channel, but as the lower levels are blocked by material from the previous storm, its rock-carrying water will be diverted to one side or the other of the blockage to create its own alluvial fan adjacent to the previous fan. A large number of contiguous alluvial fans, which eventually coalesce with one another, is known as a *bajada.* Desert mountain ranges gradually being buried by debris derived from their upper limits and delivered primarily by water flow to their lower levels are a characteristic feature of the desert.

Much of the North American desert displays a topography referred to as *basin and range,* signifying numerous mountain ranges separated from one another by intermountain basins. The most northern of the deserts is called the Great Basin. Actually, it consists of numerous basins, rather than a single one. Much of the North American desert country, then, gives one an overall impression of generally low, roughly parallel mountain ranges, many of which are skirted at their bases by alluvial fans, or bajadas, which slope gently to low basins, or valleys, between the ranges. The slopes and intervening basins are marked by *dry washes,* or *arroyos*—normally dry streambeds occasionally carrying heavy, brief streamflow, which drains toward the basin centers. Many of these basin centers—known as *sinks,* or *bolsons*—are undrained, so that water from a storm not otherwise absorbed into the ground or evaporated before reaching the low point of the basin collects in an ephemeral lake from which it eventually evaporates, leaving behind the minerals carried in suspension. On these *playas,* or *dry lakes,* the buildup of minerals may be extreme, inhibiting plant growth or supporting a special vegetative community of plants known as *halophytes* (plants capable of growing in a salty soil). Very occasionally in the desert, sufficient water accumulates to form permanent lakes. These lakes tend to be highly saline, with water constantly evaporating from them, concentrating their mineral content. The Great Salt Lake in the Great Basin Desert is a prime example.

Other basins have the potential for being drained through connections to major streamways. With precipitation severely limited, however, this occurrence is often more potential than fact. Some rivers do flow, at least part-time, through the desert and may eventually deliver water, primarily to the Gulf of California. However, such rivers usually carry water derived mainly from outside the desert; they simply move this water through the arid land, receiving minor contributions during the desert sojourn. One major river which traverses the North American desert and once delivered water year-round to the sea is the Colorado, whose water is primarily derived from the Rocky Mountains, and whose remaining water, if any after man has taken a heavy toll for his use, is finally delivered to the head of the Gulf of California. Similarly, the Rio Grande flows through the Chihuahuan Desert and then far beyond it, finally reaching the Gulf of Mexico. Such rivers as these, crossing the desert but carrying water largely derived from sources outside it, are known in the deserts through which they pass as *exotic rivers.*

Dry washes are a dominant feature of the desert land; their rough courses cut into the earth to various depths and are readily visible on the open, sparsely vegetated surface. As recipients of runoff, their borders support a heavier, more extensive vegetation than that of the surrounding area. The

THE DESERTS OF THE SOUTHWEST

wash, or stream, margins may be marked by the heavy growth of large cottonwoods, mesquites, and other species of plants where receipt of sufficient water makes this possible. But even the edges of the smallest washes often display a slightly greener, more favored vegetational aspect, particularly apparent when viewed from the air.

Occasionally in washes, *tanks, tinajas,* or deep holes, will be worn in rock in the streambed, especially at the base of a sudden drop in the wash. Some tanks are quite large and may hold water for considerable periods following their last flooding. This water serves as a valuable supply for the animals of the area—as it once did and occasionally still does for man. Much of the runoff received by the washes soaks into their beds and may lie rather close to the surface in favored areas. Thirsty animals, such as coyotes, sometimes dig holes in the gravel wash bottoms; into these holes seep small amounts of water—relished by animal excavators and nonexcavators alike.

Flash floods are a desert phenomenon of the rivers and washes. Localized, often violent, rainstorms accompanied by thunder and lightning are common in summer in parts of the desert. These storms may produce up to several inches of rain in a brief period of time. Vast amounts of runoff quickly collect in the washes, where, constricted by the banks of the wash and pressed forward by continuing heavy inflow, the water may form an actual wall, or advancing front, varying from a few inches to, rarely, a few feet in height. This moves with tremendous force down the previously dry streambed, roiling dirt, rocks, and debris with it. Such floods may flow for miles, moving into areas which originally received no part of the storm. The flood may thus startle or even drown the unwary and the unwarned caught in its path. Death by drowning in the desert seems an incongruity but is an actuality each year. Fatalities probably occur most frequently when drivers cross a wash just as the water strikes that point or when they attempt to drive through a flooding wash, deceived as to the depth or force of the water, or both, so that vehicle and occupants are swept downstream.

As flash floods sometimes produce water where it is not ex-

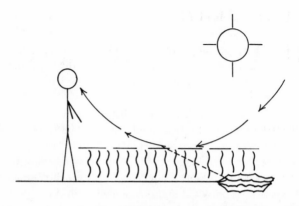

FIG. 3. A common desert mirage is produced when a ray of light, coming from above the horizon, passes through dense cool air, then strikes a layer of hot, shimmering air lying near the ground surface. The light is then bent upward. To the eye of the observer, the image of the sky thus produced appears to be rippling water in the distance.

pected, another phenomenon, the *mirage,* promises water where none exists. Mirages occur in the desert on hot, still days. They are caused by refracted light; light waves from above strike a layer of intensely heated air near the ground surface and are then bent upward into the denser air above. The image of the sky is produced; most often, it appears as distant rippling water, although irregularities in the image may at times produce supposed trees or other shimmering objects.

That *desert* is not easily, specifically defined is apparent. However, certain characteristics of the North American desert can be listed: low and often irregular patterns of precipitation; prolonged high temperatures; extreme temperature fluctuations; low humidity; a high percentage of possible sunlight received; soil high in minerals and low in humus; and extreme erosion of the ground surface by wind and water. Obviously such conditions exert a profound influence on those living things—plant and animal, including the animal called man—who seek to make the desert their home.

# CHAPTER III

# The Deserts of North America

DESERTS COVER approximately one-seventh of the earth's land surface, or about eight million square miles. (Semi-arid lands cover an additional one-seventh, another eight million square miles.) The North American desert covers approximately 500,000 square miles. The world's largest desert is the Sahara in northern Africa, whose 3.5 million square miles stretch from the Atlantic Ocean on the west to the Red Sea on the east. Second in size is the Australian Desert of approximately 1.3 million square miles. The Arabian Desert covers approximately one million square miles. Smaller than the North American desert are the Kara Kum of Turkmenistan; the Kyzyl Kum of Kazakhstan and Uzbekistan; the Patagonian of Argentina; India's Thar; southern Africa's Kalahari and Namib; China's Takla Makan; the Iranian; and the Atacama-Peruvian of South America.

Although all share certain characteristics in common—the overriding characteristic of aridity in particular—each desert is distinctive. Even the four deserts comprising the North American desert are each quite distinctive from one another; their causes, their appearances, their overall characters, and their biotas are pleasingly varied. Indeed, the variations (particularly among the biota) developed in each desert in response to the theme of aridity make the deserts of the world one of the most fascinating of ecological studies.

Deserts are not scattered haphazardly over the earth; the pattern of their occurrence is shaped by the factors that produce them. The major world deserts occur in two discontinuous belts ringing the globe. In both the Northern and Southern Hemispheres, this desert country occurs largely between 15 and 35 degrees latitude. Thus, in the Northern Hemisphere, the desert belt is roughly centered over the Tropic of Cancer; in the Southern Hemisphere, it is centered over the Tropic of Capricorn. Because more land surface occurs in the Northern Hemisphere in the latitudes defined, more desert occurs in the Northern than in the Southern Hemisphere. Centered along the desert belt in the Northern Hemisphere are the North American deserts and the Sahara, Arabian, Indian, and Iranian deserts; somewhat to the north of these on the Eurasian continent are the Kara Kum, Kyzyl Kum, Takla Makan, and Gobi. Along the Tropic of Capricorn in the Southern Hemisphere are the Australian, the Kalahari and Namib of Africa, and the Atacama-Peruvian and Patagonian of South America; the Patagonian stretches far south of the Tropic of Capricorn.

Desert formation in these particular latitudes is primarily due to complex global air-circulation patterns caused by the rotation of the earth on its axis (so that the earth is moving at great speed at the equator and very slowly near the poles), the seasonal tilting of the earth in relationship to the sun, and other factors. In very general terms, air is heated at the equator, ascends, and is replaced by inrushing air. As the heated air moves upward, it is gradually cooled. Cool air, with a lower saturation point, is capable of holding less moisture within it than warm air. As the air cools, it releases the excess moisture it contains, helping to produce the moist tropics. The ascending air, in the area of low atmospheric pressure over the equator, then flows from that point toward the poles. The air becomes heated as it descends in the subtropical zones of high pressure near the Tropics of Cancer and Capricorn. As the temperature of the air increases, so also does the air's ability to absorb and retain moisture, producing aridity of varying degrees. To the north and south of these desert latitudes, the air once again ascends, producing moisture for the land; finally, over the poles, the air again descends.

Some deserts are caused partially or wholly by mountains; the arid land lies in the *rain shadow* cast by the mountains. In these cases, moisture-laden air encounters a mountain mass and is forced upward. The ascending air is cooled and releases moisture on the windward side of the range. Once over the summit, the air descends the lee side of the range, warming as it does so, and hence increasing its evaporative power. Thus the windward side of the mountain range may support a heavy, well-watered forest, while the lee side and the area far beyond it, robbed of moisture, are occupied by a desert or steppe plant community.

Yet another cause of desert formation is remoteness from oceanic moisture sources. Areas lying deep within a continent may become desert simply because air currents reaching them have already traversed vast land distances; by the time they arrive over the deserts, these currents have already lost the moisture they once carried.

Cold ocean currents flowing from the poles toward the equator, in conjunction with onshore winds, may produce deserts where the currents wash close to shore. Air moving across the frigid currents is cooled to a low temperature; thus the air holds little moisture when it arrives over land, where it may produce mist and fog, but rarely rain. Two of the most extreme of the world's deserts, the Namib and the Atacama, are so influenced; the Atacama is, in fact, the world's most arid desert, averaging less than one-half inch annual precipitation. One site within it—Iquique, Chile—is generally accepted as having the world's record for the longest rainless period: fourteen consecutive years!

All these climatic, desert-producing factors—descending, drying air currents; mountain-produced rain shadows; distance from oceanic moisture sources; and cold ocean currents—are instrumental, sometimes singly, more often in combination, as primary forces producing the four North American deserts or distinctive individual portions of these. Various authorities cut the North American desert into four, or occasionally more, distinctive deserts. To draw precise boundaries for the North American desert in general, or for its individual parts, is often difficult, except in those locations where desert meets mountain, sea, or some similar sharp desert-delimiting factor. Along much of their boundaries, the North American deserts grade gradually into an adjoining environment, desert grassland, for instance, or *chaparral*. In some areas, one desert grades gradually into another.

Desert boundaries bear little or no relationship to political boundaries, and often only a partial relationship to geographical features. With only one small exception, we have chosen to follow the boundaries and divisions of the North American desert into its individual deserts as set up half a century ago by the eminent desert ecologist Dr. Forrest Shreve. He divided the North American desert into four individual deserts—the Great Basin, the Mohave, the Chihuahuan, and the Sonoran—dependent largely on the basis of their vegetation. He then divided the Sonoran Desert into seven vegetational subdivisions. Within the last twenty years ecologists have reclassified one of these subdivisions and no longer consider it desert; we follow this one change that has been made in Shreve's classification.

Other systems for drawing the boundaries of the North American deserts have been proposed. In 1957 Dr. Edmund C. Jaeger proposed adding a fifth major desert, the Painted Desert. In 1979 Dr. James MacMahon drew his scientific interpretation of North American desert boundaries, taking both plant and animal distributions into account. MacMahon's boundaries do not extend as far north in Oregon and Idaho, and his Chihuahuan Desert area is expanded beyond that of Shreve's.

A small discontinuous portion of desert country exists in the Columbia River Basin in eastern Washington State. Desert country flows southward from central and eastern Oregon and southern Idaho, covering almost all of Nevada and much of Utah, extends an arm into Wyoming, touches western Colorado, then covers southeastern California and portions of northern, and much of central, southern, and western Arizona. It covers much of the Lower, or Baja, California Peninsula and most of the northern Mexican state of Sonora. The most northern region of this desert country constitutes the Great Basin Desert. The Mohave is located primarily in southeastern California, entering the southern tip of Nevada and touching western Arizona. The Sonoran sections lie in southern Arizona, extreme southeastern California, Baja California, and Sonora.

This one large sweep of desert country is separated from the Chihuahuan Desert by desert grassland on the very low elevations of the southern United States Continental Divide in eastern Arizona and western New Mexico, and increased elevations to the south in Mexico. The Chihuahuan Desert encompasses a small portion of southern New Mexico and a part of western Texas; it then extends far south into Mexico through eastern Chihuahua, over most of Coahuila, then into eastern Durango, northern Zacatecas, western Nuevo León, and northern San Luis Potosí. Small detached areas of Chihuahuan Desert also occur farther south in the states of Hidalgo and Puebla.

The most northern of the North American deserts, the Great Basin, is caused primarily by the rain-shadow effect of the Cascade and Sierra Nevada mountains. Lying to the west of the Great Basin, these tall, vast mountain chains wring most of the moisture from the air moving inland from the Pacific Ocean. To the east of this desert lie the Rocky Mountains, a barrier to moisture coming from the east; additionally, the Great Basin lies at a vast distance inland from an eastern moisture source.

The southern deserts lie more directly than does the Great Basin under the pattern of descending, warming air—one of the major desert-producing factors. Thus the air-lifting process, which would produce moisture, is absent or limited much of the time. However, the air circulating over these deserts is not totally lacking in moisture, as is obvious when it meets large mountain masses within a desert or at its borders, is lifted, cooled, and deposits precipitation on the mountain heights.

Additionally the southern reaches of the Sierra Nevadas and other mountains lie to the west of the Mohave and portions of the Sonoran Desert, producing a rain-shadow effect for these areas. This rocky, mountainous backbone extends even into northern Baja California, where on this very narrow peninsula it is a factor in producing an elongated strip of extreme desert between the mountains and the eastern, Gulf-bordering coast of the peninsula.

Off the west coast of northern and central Baja California, the cold California Current flows. In conjunction with onshore winds, this current produces a special foggy, coastal desert of the same general type as the Atacama along the west

FIG. 4. The North American Desert is composed of four separate deserts: the Great Basin, the Mohave, the Sonoran, and the Chihuahuan.

THE DESERTS OF THE SOUTHWEST

coast of South America and the Namib on the west coast of Africa.

The Chihuahuan Desert, in addition to being located under the usually inhibiting high-pressure belt characterized by descending air, also lies between two major ranges of mountains, which serve to rob it of moisture. Much of the Mexican portion of this desert lies on an elevated intermountain plateau bounded partially on the west by the Sierra Madre Occidental and on the east by the Sierra Madre Oriental.

The figure of a half million square miles of North American desert is an approximation, dependent upon the scientist computing it and the method of determination used. In North America, desert spans approximately 27 degrees of latitude, from about 22 to 49 degrees. This range constitutes an approximate north-south distance of 2,300 miles. The farther one moves either north or south from the equator, the cooler the climate becomes. Obviously, with the latitudinal span of the North American desert, the more northern reaches will be considerably cooler than the southern.

The hottest and driest portion of the North American desert occurs in its more southern and lowest reaches. The hub of this area surrounds the head of the Gulf of California in Baja California and in Sonora, Mexico. It extends into extreme southwestern Arizona and southeastern California, then runs northward up a low trough which includes Death Valley in its northern extremity. Average annual rainfall for this area is five or fewer inches, with the emphasis on fewer. Bataques, Mexico, with the record low annual precipitation rate for North America of 1.2 inches, lies in this area; many other nearby sites report averages of approximately two inches per year. Included, too, in this area is Bagdad, California, with the record for a rainless period in the United States. In this area, also, the highest sustained summer temperatures occur in Death Valley and the world's second highest maximum temperature has been recorded. Moving outward from this extreme desert core, precipitation gradually increases, with much of the Great Basin and Chihuahuan Deserts receiving five to ten inches precipitation annually.

Temperatures gradually decrease as one moves to the east and north from this arid hub, due to two primary factors: increasing elevation of the desert's floor in these directions and movement into higher latitudes. A general rule is that temperature drops approximately one degree Fahrenheit for each 300-foot rise in elevation. Also, an increase of 1,000 feet in elevation is considered roughly equivalent to a 300-mile move nearer to the closest pole. The altitudinal range of the North American desert as a whole extends from 282 feet below sea level in Death Valley, the lowest point in the Western Hemisphere, to 5,000 feet above sea level, with occasional locations even higher. Thus the more northern desert, the Great Basin, for the most part lies at elevations of 4,000 feet or above; the most eastern, the Chihuahuan, lies mainly above 3,500 feet.

In addition to a general increase in elevation of the desert's surface, mountains rise from the desert base; the desert flora reach to various altitudinal levels on these mountains, depending upon the specific conditions present. Mountains bordering the desert may reach great elevations, as do the Sierra Nevadas; some ranges occurring within the desert may also extend to heights which preclude the presence of desert vegetation on their upper limits. The effects of the mountains on the surrounding or adjoining desert are many and varied. For example, some ranges, such as the Sierra Nevadas, may cause formation of a rain shadow; others occurring within the desert may cause limited air lifting, resulting in precipitation on their flanks, a portion of which drains into the desert below; or cool air from the upper limits of some ranges may drain down canyons into the desert at their bases, affecting temperature and moisture extremes, and thereby the biota, in these limited locations.

Latitude, in conjunction with altitude, affects temperature extremes, which, in turn, dictate season length. Thus summer in the northern Great Basin Desert may last two or three months, but endure up to seven or eight months in the southern Sonoran Desert. The Great Basin undergoes prolonged periods of freezing temperatures, whereas portions of the southern Sonoran Desert, along the Gulf and Pacific coasts, are frost free.

Large portions of the southern Sonoran Desert border the Gulf of California and the Pacific Ocean. Shreve indicates that more than half of the Sonoran Desert lies within fifty miles of tidewater. Large bodies of water affect, to varying degrees, the land lying adjacent to them—these effects occur in terms of temperature levels, decreased temperature fluctuations, humidity levels, and winds. The Pacific Ocean, with its cold California Current, strongly influences the limited desert land immediately adjacent to it in Baja California in the Sonoran Desert. However, the much more extensive Sonoran Desert area lying like a horseshoe around the upper Gulf of California is only very slightly affected by the waters of this almost landlocked, relatively stable body of water. Shreve states that the Gulf's influence is so negligible as to only slightly lower the air temperature over the land, and then only within 100 meters of the shore during the day. Therefore, the climate of most of the Sonoran Desert, and the climate of all the other three deserts, is of the continental type.

Precipitation patterns over the North American deserts are varied. In general, winter precipitation is the rule in the northern and western portions of the North American desert lands, including the Great Basin, Mohave, and western Sonoran. This winter precipitation is derived from storms from the northwest sweeping in off the Pacific Ocean over the land. Conversely, the eastern and southern desert lands receive most of their precipitation, derived from the Gulf of Mexico and Gulf of California, during the summer months. Additionally, occasional severe, late summer or early fall storms, known as *chubascos* (Spanish, squalls), strike the southern Sonoran Desert. These tropical hurricanes originate off the west coast of Mexico and move northwesterly. They often move out over the Pacific before reaching the desert latitudes, strike over the Gulf of California waters, or are dissipated before reaching the desert. However, at times they do bring high winds and heavy precipitation to the southern Sonoran Desert.

Thus, the eastern-lying Chihuahuan Desert receives approximately 70 to 80 percent of its precipitation in summer; the northern-lying Great Basin receives approximately 60 percent of its precipitation in winter; and the western-lying Mohave receives almost all of its limited precipitation in the winter. The winter rain pattern overlaps on its eastern margins with the summer rainfall pattern, so that some portions of the most centrally located desert, the Sonoran, receive both winter and summer precipitation. The western Sonoran receives primarily winter rainfall, whereas the eastern and southern portions receive both summer and winter precipitation. Tucson, Arizona, located near the eastern border of the Sonoran Desert, is thus favored with two "rainy" seasons, receiving approximately half its annual average of twelve inches in winter, the other half in summer.

Winter storms tend to produce gentle, soaking, widespread rains, with the storms enduring for several hours or days. In the more northern latitudes and higher elevations, precipitation is often in the form of snow. Summer storms tend to be localized, often violent, brief thunderstorms.

Obviously, no one North American desert climate may be defined nor does a single characteristic desert exist. North American deserts, with their varied causes and the resulting diversity of physical and biotic features, are limited in square miles as compared to such vast deserts as the Sahara, Australian, or Arabian. The pleasing result is that nowhere else in the world is such a concentration of different types of deserts so readily accessible to the desert enthusiast as in North America.

CHAPTER IV

# Desert Plants: Adaptations

FACTS: (1) Water is the matrix of life, yet (2) the desert's most notable characteristic is shortage of water.

Problem: How does life exist and endure (even thrive) in the desert?

The solutions are numerous, sometimes surprising, and often complex.

Inasmuch as plants are the base upon which all animal life depends, with some animal species consuming plants directly and others occupying higher rungs on the consumer ladder, let us first consider the means whereby desert-inhabiting plants obtain and use the water supplies available to them.

Water is an essential component in all plant tissue; it is a vital ingredient of the basic protoplasm itself. Depending on the plant type, most plants are composed of approximately 80 to 90 percent water. Water not only provides the medium within the plant in which chemical reactions necessary for life take place, often entering into these reactions, but also provides a transport system to move minerals and other materials through the plant body. The individual plant cells are kept *turgid* (swollen or distended) by the water held within them; water thus provides vital support for the plant. Transpiration of water from the plant cools it by transferring absorbed heat out of the plant. And, finally, water is an essential ingredient in photosynthesis.

In the process of *photosynthesis,* carbohydrates are chemically formed from water and carbon dioxide by the action of chlorophyll through the plant's use of light energy. Water is absorbed by the plant, usually through its roots. Carbon dioxide enters the plant from the air through *stomates*—minute openings, often present in great numbers, located in the *epidermis* (superficial layer of cells) of leaves and stems; oxygen, a byproduct of photosynthesis, leaves the plant by way of the stomates. Through the process of photosynthesis the chlorophyll of green plants uses light energy to produce food, that is, chemical energy—usable by both plant and animal.

Each stomate consists of a pore bordered by two guard cells. When turgid with water, these cells swell and pull apart, thereby opening the stomate. When the water within the cells is insufficient, the cells draw together, closing the stomate. Not only are carbon dioxide and oxygen transferred through the stomates, but water, too, moves through them in the process of *transpiration*—the giving off of water vapor from the plant's surface to the atmosphere. *Stomatal transpiration* is that movement taking place through the stomates; much lesser amounts of transpiration take place directly through the outer surface of the plant in a process termed *cuticular transpiration.* Water is rather constantly circulating upward through a plant from root to leaf, serving various purposes on its journey. Ultimately much of it, up to 98 percent, is transpired, primarily through the stomates, either in the process of cooling the plant or when the stomates are open in conjunction with photosynthesis. As water is lost from the plant to the atmosphere, additional supplies are needed in the leaves; a pressure gradient initiated in the leaves is set up, and water is pulled up through the plant. The amount of water loss from the plant will vary depending upon many factors, including the type of plant, and is greatly dependent on environmental factors such as temperature, humidity, air movements, and light intensity.

Plants in general can be divided into three large groups according to their varying water needs. *Hydrophytes* are plants requiring an abundance of water, which grow in water or in soil too waterlogged for most other plants. *Mesophytes* are plants growing under medium conditions of moisture. *Xerophytes* are those plants adapted for life and growth with a limited water supply. Thus we are primarily concerned with xerophytic species as we discuss desert plants. The xerophytes display an astounding array of morphological, physiological, and/or behavioral adaptations to the desert environment.

Let us first survey a category of plants which occur in the desert, but, through the aspect of time or place, or both, avoid the extreme of desert conditions and are not truly xerophytes. One major group of these plants includes perennial plants growing in locations where water is rather readily available to them. Occasionally, streambeds emerging from canyons that drain higher mountains adjoining the desert may have limited running water several months of the year. In such locations, heavy water-users, such as cottonwood and sycamore trees, may line the stream banks for varying distances, tentatively pushing narrow fingers of green outward from the hills into

THE DESERTS OF THE SOUTHWEST

the desert to the point where the water supply dissipates. Along the few permanent rivers, such as portions of the Colorado, heavy plant growth may occur, but this growth belt extends back from the river only a very limited distance. Although not numerous, occasional oases occur in the desert, around which heavy water-users may cluster. Water in an oasis is often rather high in mineral content; palm trees, unlike many other plants, are capable of using this water and therefore occur in these locations. Tamarisk trees, introduced from the Eastern Hemisphere, are also capable of effectively using mineral-laden water. Since their introduction, tamarisks have flourished near waterways in the Southwest, such as the Salt River in Arizona—the river's name demonstrates the condition contributing to the tamarisk's virtual takeover in certain areas along its length.

To the casual observer, the abundance of greenery produced in these special locations with permanent or semipermanent water must seem to present the *climax,* or high point, of desert vegetation, in contrast to the surrounding, less abundant, smaller-statured, more drab array of desert plants. Not so, for this abundant vegetation is living in the desert under special, largely nondesert conditions. While pleasant to human observers and often life-sustaining to animal visitors, this type of vegetation is not coping with desert conditions on the same basic survival level as are the xerophytic, truly desert plants growing out on the arid desert plain or hillside.

Thus the cottonwoods, palms, and similar plants take advantage of place—propitious locations—for their growth. So a group of annuals take advantage of propitious but transitory times, largely in terms of moisture availability, for theirs. These plants, like oasis-hugging perennials, never meet the desert head-on, except as seeds; hence, they are referred to as *drought-escapers.* The "grasshoppers" of the plant world, these species endure in the desert for months or even years in their durable seed form, but when conditions favorable to their growth occur, they quickly germinate, rapidly grow, blossom, produce seed, and once again enter the long dormant wait. With speed of development an outstanding characteristic common to many of them, the term *annuals* seems almost extreme; hence they are often referred to as *ephemerals,* from the Greek for daily. Although their life span is certainly not limited to a single day, the plants may appear within three days after germination and finish their growth, blossoming, and seeding within a period of a very few weeks.

These ephemerals produce the showy arrays, the blankets of extravagant ground-covering flowers, which attract visitors and photographers to the desert, usually in the spring, but only in favorable years. To predict when and where these shows will occur is not easy, and desert newspapers regularly report the educated-guess possibilities for, and the actual occurrences of these masses of flowers. Predictability is difficult since more than simple availability of moisture is involved in their occurrence, as was determined through a classic series of scientific investigations regarding these ephemerals conducted over forty years ago by Dr. Frits Went. Went's experiments were conducted in Joshua Tree National Monument in the Mohave Desert of southeastern California. He concluded that the success of the ephemerals was based on "birth control," and he discovered some of the means whereby the ephemeral species practice this control.

Went found that in order for certain ephemeral seeds to germinate, rain of an amount minimal for the plant's successful growth and development must have fallen. Approximately .4 inch was insufficient, whereas a one-inch fall triggered germination. The seeds obviously had no means of measuring rainfall; Went theorized that the seeds of many ephemerals contained chemical inhibitors, which were leached away only by means of sufficient moisture. Such seeds, he found experimentally, could not be tricked into germination by water seeping upward from below by capillary action, for such water movement does not carry the inhibitory substances away from the vicinity of the seed. And if only small amounts of inhibitor are removed by insufficient amounts of moisture, he theorized, the seed replenishes the chemical lost, and the waiting period continues.

Not only the seeds of the ephemerals "plan ahead" hereditarily; many other desert plants use various means to do so. Seeds of the palo verde, ironwood, and smoke tree, which grow along desert washes, have extremely hard coats. These sheaths prevent germination until a strong force cracks their outer coverings. Lying in the bed of a wash, these seeds are caught up in the floods which occasionally move through the washes. Abraded by sand and bashed by rocks during the flood, the seed coat is cracked, germination occurs, and the growth of the plant is initiated under positive moisture conditions. Went reported that seeds of some plants have inhibitors which are removed by bacterial action which occurs only under conditions of prolonged moisture. He further stated that some seeds, particularly those of many grasses, delay germination after a rainfall for several days. If after that period of time the soil is still moist, signifying a rainfall of some magnitude, growth is begun. Many plants produce more than one type of seed—a portion of the seed crop is capable of germination soon after production, if favorable environmental conditions are available. Another portion is capable of germination only after the passage of a length of time. Such plants thus accomplish a dispersal of their seeds through time.

Went found additional factors which influenced ephemerals' germination. For example, two subminimal showers of .3 inch each, if they occurred within forty-eight hours of one another, would trigger germination; a torrential rain triggered fewer germinations than a gentle rain, although both produced the same amounts of rainfall, and rain in darkness did not have the same effect as rain during the day. In addition to moisture, Went found the most critical factor to be temperature. In the study area in the Mohave, widespread winter rains provided the major precipitation, but summer convectional storms also occurred in scattered localities. Went found four main groups of annual plant species growing there: (1) summer annuals, which germinate and produce seeds following the summer rains; (2) annuals germinating following the winter rains and blooming in the spring; (3) annuals germinating following the summer rains and blooming the next spring; (4) a small group of annuals germinating and growing whenever sufficient moisture was present and temperatures were not too low. All groups required sufficient moisture to initiate germination, but summer-germinating species also required high day and night temperatures; winter-germinating species required cool day and night temperatures. A five- to ten-degree differential separates the two groups; thus summer-germinating species will not be deceived into germinating after the winter rains, nor winter species after summer rains, and only a few species are sufficiently versatile to grow under both extremes of the temperature range.

As a consequence, a general east-west seasonal distribution of the growth and blossoming of the ephemerals occurs in our North American desert, dependent on the seasonal rainfall patterns. Annuals in the Chihuahuan Desert are more numerous in the summer; those in the far western desert areas are more plentiful in the early spring following the winter rains; and the central and eastern Sonoran, which have two rather equal winter and summer rainy seasons, produce two crops of annuals in favorable years, with certain species present in the spring and other species present in the summer.

In the Sonoran Desert, species which germinate in the fall and winter then flower in the spring are the most numerous and usually the showiest. Germination of these occurs in the interim marked by the passing of summer's heat and before the onset of winter temperatures. During this time of moderated temperatures there must be at least one soaking shower which brings a minimum of one inch of rain. For many species germination produces rosettes of leaves that lie close to the ground surface. This aids in keeping the plants warm and here they slowly grow through the winter. When temperatures rise in the spring the plants quickly grow, flower, and produce seeds. A second group of annuals in the Sonoran Desert are those that germinate, grow, and blossom as a response to summer rains. And a third group consists of a few species that are capable of germinating following sufficient rainfall at any time of the year.

Dr. Mark A. Dimmitt of the Arizona-Sonora Desert Museum notes that the annual habit serves very successfully those desert plants which employ it and that the more arid the habitat in North America, the greater will be the proportion of annual species occurring there. He states that half of the

Sonoran Desert's flora is made up of annual species and that in its driest habitats, such as in the sand dunes near Yuma, Arizona, up to 90 percent of the plants are annuals.

It has been determined that a very basic physiological difference exists between many of the winter and summer annuals. One group is termed the $C_4$ plants, referring to the four-carbon molecules in the product produced by photosynthesis. The second group is referred to as $C_3$ plants, in which photosynthesis produces a three-carbon chemical. $C_3$ plants germinate during cool periods; $C_4$ plants germinate at higher temperatures, conduct photosynthesis more efficiently, use water more efficiently, and produce more plant material than do $C_3$ plants under extreme environmental conditions.

Some perennial plants also cope with aridity by avoiding it, not as seeds, but as bulbs, or fleshy roots or rootstalks that remain hidden underground. When favorable conditions prevail, these produce aboveground parts.

The season during which an ephemeral grows influences its characteristics greatly. The summer ephemerals tend to have short lives, speeding through their life cycles during the hot time of year. Winter annuals, in lower temperatures, develop slowly and are often small in size. And in some cases ephemerals that germinate in the summer and continue growing through the winter rains tend to be large, since they benefit from both rainy seasons.

A minimal amount of water for probable success in growth, flowering, and seeding often will initiate germination; however, once growth starts, a plant may be further aided by additional showers, in which case it may grow to a large size for its species and produce quantities of seeds; conversely, in some cases a plant may receive no additional moisture and must subsist on that initially present, or die, or it may be submitted to other extenuating circumstances. An outstanding characteristic of many desert ephemerals is their capability to mature very rapidly when necessary, under drought, heat, cold, or other unfavorable conditions, yet produce some seeds, even though the plant has matured at an unnaturally small size—in some cases when only one-thousandth the species' normal mature size.

Whereas the drought-escapers avoid the desert's most extreme aridity, many perennial plant species endure, even prosper, in vegetative form, through moderate to extreme aridity. Their means of doing so are many, far from completely understood, and somewhat open for scientific controversy. These plants include succulents, which basically are water-savers, and those known as drought-resisters or drought-tolerators.

Succulents are very efficient at obtaining and storing water. These include all cacti and some additional plants such as agaves and euphorbias. Cacti have root systems that are wide-reaching and located near the soil surface, which allow them to obtain water quickly following a shower. Many succulents, including cacti and agaves, are capable of sprouting new "rain roots" within a few hours after a shower to further increase the plants' water-absorbing capabilities. Once water has been obtained and stored within the plant, succulents display a number of adaptations for conserving it. The surfaces of many are covered by a waxy cuticle which prevents dehydration when their stomates are closed. Cacti have no leaves, thus reducing the area for possible water loss. Their spines provide a measure of cooling shade and aid in protecting the plant from animals who might otherwise break into them, providing an avenue for moisture loss. Also water in succulents is often held in compounds that impede its release. However, one of the most outstanding adaptations to aridity that is employed by cacti and some other plants is that of crassulacean acid metabolism, known as CAM. The usual plant practice consists of photosynthesis conducted during daylight hours when temperatures may be high and water loss through transpiration from the open stomates great. Instead, plants using CAM open their stomates at night when it is cooler and then store received carbon dioxide as an organic acid. During the day the stomates remain closed while photosynthesis occurs within the plant using the stored carbon dioxide. Under conditions of extreme stress, the stomates will remain closed both day and night and, within the plant, a low level of gas exchange continue with some recycling of oxygen and carbon

THE DESERTS OF THE SOUTHWEST

FIG. 5. Prickly pear cacti, *Opuntia* spp., are among the most common of the cacti and are found in many areas outside the desert. The flattened fleshy stems store moisture. In times of prolonged drought, the water-depleted pads become wrinkled and shrunken. The fruits are edible.

dioxide occurring; this slowed-down state is referred to as CAM-idling.

The water-savers, cautious xerophytes that they are, achieve survival yet pay a price for their safety. With the more frequent and prolonged closure of their stomates, extremely moderate expenditure of water, and less expansive surfaces to bear stomates and to receive light energy, the water-savers, in general, have a very slow growth rate. If the ephemerals are the "grasshoppers" of the plant world, certainly the savers are the "tortoises."

Basically, any plant may suffer from moisture stress if the soil contains insufficient water for the plant's use, if water is being transpired from the plant more rapidly than it can be supplied through the roots, or if the mechanisms regulating water transport and transpiration within the plant are malfunctioning. Regardless of the cause, moisture stress, depending on its severity, may cause injury or death to the plant. Stress may ultimately result in direct strain on the plant, such

FIG. 6.   The saguaro cactus is composed of an inner ring of woody ribs embedded in a fleshy pith. Because its outer surface is accordion-pleated, the saguaro expands or contracts in relationship to the amount of moisture stored within its fleshy interior.

as decrease of turgor, resulting in mechanical injury to the plant as evidenced by wilting. Stress may also result in the disruption of various of the plant's vital metabolic processes, such as photosynthesis, and therefore failure to produce organic materials needed for maintenance and growth. Plants that are drought-tolerators employ many means to obtain, retain, and efficiently use the water available to them to prevent problems accompanying moisture stress.

The stomates of these plants may be open only briefly each day and are capable of rapid closure. The stomates of some are sunk below the surface level of the leaf, or are surrounded by hairs thought to be, at least in some cases, an aid to moisture conservation. Some have a lower cuticular transpiration rate than mesophytes. The leaves may be covered with a deposit of lipids, producing a waxy layer that reduces moisture evaporation from their surfaces. Certain plants are capable of moving their leaves so that during the hottest time of day only their narrow edges are directed toward the sun; others roll or fold their leaves, thereby reducing surface area and exposure of the stomates. Leaves may be partially or completely dropped during drought, as may entire branches, resulting in a "partial death"; any moisture resources available are then used to maintain life in the remaining portions of the plant. This physiological independence of one part of a plant from another—that is, death occurring in one part with life strongly maintained in another portion—is a strong adaptation to drought stress. In some cases the proportion of root to visible portions of the plant is great, supplying water from a large soil area for a relatively small aboveground portion. The tolerators tend to have deeper roots than do the succulents and absorb water that reaches their depth brought by storms delivering a substantial amount of rainfall, and the tolerators are capable of absorbing water from much drier soil than can the succulents.

Some tolerators have an increased ability to undergo drought and yet avoid or tolerate metabolic strain, such as that produced by starvation, or avoid or tolerate direct strain, such as that produced to the plant body from wilting. Certain of these plants exhibit the ability to maintain a high osmotic pressure within the cells, thus increasing the plant's ability to absorb water from the soil and to resist loss of moisture to the atmosphere. Rather fundamental changes on the cellular level may be present in some of these species, including a small cell size, which helps prevent tearing of the protoplasm during desiccation and later rehydration. Changes may also occur in the physical properties and strengths of the cell walls. For example, xerophytes wilt only after the loss of 30 to 40 percent of their water content, whereas some shade plants wilt after a loss of only 1 to 2 percent. Even the basic metabolism of various plant species is thought to vary, with some drought-adapted plants having a low rate of metabolism, which aids them in surviving under a regime of low photosynthetic activity, thus allowing them to keep their stomates closed a large percentage of the time.

The most drought-tolerant perennial plant and the most common plant in the Sonoran, Mohave, and Chihuahuan deserts is the creosote bush. This evergreen shrub has many stems, which arise at an angle from the ground and reach up to six feet in height. It bears small dark green leaves, and at times has small yellow flowers followed by a whitish, woolly, ball-shaped fruit. During drought the plant's mature leaves are shed, as are whole twigs and branches; however the new, small, partly developed leaves are retained and one study

FIG. 7. The creosote bush, *Larrea tridentata*, is the most abundant and widespread shrub of the Sonoran, Mohave, and Chihuahuan deserts. It is extremely drought-resistant and ranges from the southern deserts of North America far south into South America. Growth consists of slender branches arising from the crown of the root.

showed that these new leaves can survive a reduction in water content to less than 50 percent of their dry weight, and a saturation deficit of at least 77 percent. Yet even at these extremes the leaves are still metabolically active. Therefore when moisture again becomes available, these leaves are able to take immediate advantage of its presence. The widespread water-seeking roots of the creosote bush inhibit the growth of the roots of some plant species in their immediate area, and its roots produce a germination inhibitor which prevents the growth of its own seeds within the parent roots' range.

Rather amazingly, creosote bush is among the longest-lived plants. A single stem may live for one or two hundred years, but new stems are produced from the edge of the root crown, as older, center stems die and decay. Dr. Mark Dimmitt of the Arizona-Sonora Desert Museum reports that as centuries pass the ring of growth slowly expands and breaks into separate bushes, these all clones, due to the fact that they descended from a single original plant.

Dr. Dimmitt also documents this plant's extreme drought

THE DESERTS OF THE SOUTHWEST

FIG. 8.    Junco, all spine, or crucifixion thorn, *Koeberlinia spinosa,*
is a spreading shrub 3 to 4½ feet in height with rigid, spine-pointed
branches. This species is essentially without functional leaves; as an
adaptation to aridity, the yellow-green branches have taken over the
normal leaf functions.

tolerance. Rainfall diminishes from 12 inches near Tucson,
Arizona, to 3 inches near the mouth of the Colorado River;
along this path the number of perennial plant species decreases from more than 300 to fewer than 12. In the drier portions there are valleys with only creosote bush and white
bursage on the flats, and in extreme cases, even the bursage is
absent. He states that creosote bush can live for at least 2
years with no rain, losing its leaves and some branches to reserve the plant's resources.

When environmental stresses build, animals and man can
crawl, walk, run, or fly to reach the most amenable environmental conditions available; not so the rooted, immobile
plants, which must meet sun, wind, heat, and aridity where
they stand. In the desert, where moisture supplies tend to be
limited and environmental stresses tend to be extreme, the
plants, in order to survive, must be capable of operating with
a low margin of error where high demand and low supply of
water is concerned. Ranging from cacti to creosote bush to
boojum tree, those plants that have been successful in meeting this challenge make up one of the most highly adapted,
unusual, and interesting of the world's floras. We will consider
many of these hardy, desert members of the plant kingdom as
we survey individual North American deserts.

# CHAPTER V

# Desert Animals: Adaptations

LIMITED RESOURCES applied in an economy characterized by parsimony is the theorem of the desert—nowhere else on earth can so little count for so much. This theorem is as applicable to animals as to plants. A few drops of water, a small patch of shade, an underground retreat—all are small things in themselves, but they may provide a life-saving edge for the desert animal which is adapted in some way to make the most advantageous use of one or more of them. Many desert adaptations displayed by animals have to do with handling temperature and moisture stresses. Moisture stresses are often present normally but are compounded by heat stress, which, in turn, is ameliorated by increased loss of body water, and hence increased moisture stress. Other adaptations for desert life occurring in some species aid them in use of a particular habitat—for example, sand. Some animals have adapted morphologically or physiologically, or both, to desert conditions. Primarily, however, body adaptations consist not of new mechanisms but rather of the evolutionary enhancement and increased development and use of characteristics common to the animal's basic group—that is, quantitative rather than qualitative changes. To an even greater degree, however, most desert animals have adapted to their environment behaviorally.

The so-called desert world is actually a mosaic of smaller worlds, and the environmental conditions present in any one of these small worlds are often strikingly different from those of another area which may be located only a few feet or even inches away. These smaller pieces of the habitat, or *microhabitats,* in general each has its own microclimate. The microhabitat composed of an area under a cottonwood tree growing along an intermittent desert stream often has a cooler, moister microclimate than does the microhabitat under a sparsely leafed creosote bush on a nearby desert plain. So, too, a vast difference is apparent between the small world under an insulating rock on the desert floor and that of the ground surface next to it. A north-facing slope presents different climatic conditions than does a south-facing one. The temperature five feet above ground among the mesquite leaves is considerably lower than that found only a few feet away in the sun at the ground surface. Use of favorable microclimates is one of the very important ways in which animals adjust to desert environmental stresses.

Studies conducted by Dr. Knut Schmidt-Nielsen revealed that while summer daytime air temperatures in the desert often are in the 104°-to-113° F.-and-higher range, the temperature of the soil surface at that same time may exceed 158° F. Conversely, at night, if radiation to the sky from the surface is unimpeded, the surface temperature may fall to a level far below that of the night air, and register as much as 122 Fahrenheit degrees lower than the daytime high surface temperature. Due to the insulative quality of the soil, however, temperatures underground are much ameliorated and stabilized. Schmidt-Nielsen stated that at a depth of .5 meter (approximately 19.7 inches) in the soil, the daily temperature fluctuation is less than 33.8 Fahrenheit degrees; no fluctuation occurs at one meter (39.4 inches). Obviously, to prevent being broiled, a low-statured ant, snake, or small rodent must be able to escape such extremes as those found at certain times on the ground surface. These animals and a good many others escape the surface heat by entering underground burrows, which provide favorable microclimatic conditions under stressful surface conditions. Such burrows are among the most important means used by the animals to avoid heat and dehydration. Studies of the temperatures of the burrows of a kangaroo rat and of a pack rat determined that the *highest* summer temperature within the two burrows was a comfortable, life-saving 87.8° F.

Some animal groups are, due to their makeup, physically predisposed in many ways to succeed under desert conditions. Certain of the arthropods are included in this group. Some of the arthropod species lose moisture rapidly through their integument and must remain in moist surroundings; they are therefore not well adapted to dry environments. But many of the species, including many insects, are covered by an almost impervious, waxy-layered integument which prevents or greatly impedes desiccation of the body. However, even in these species, small amounts of moisture may be lost from the animal's body through elimination of waste products and by means of the spiracles through which the insect breathes.

Other factors, in addition to the near-impervious integument, can then play a role in effecting a moisture savings. Foremost among these factors is the use of favorable microclimates, primarily those found underground. Thus some arthropods, particularly insects, are especially adapted for burrowing. This adaptation is particularly noticeable among species evolved for life in sand. In some cases their bodies may be flattened and sharp-edged, allowing them to bury themselves quickly in the loose sand with alternate sideways movements. Others may have "fringed" feet, giving them traction on the sand and increased burrowing power. The fringes also may aid them in "sand-swimming"—that is, moving through the sand just below its surface.

FIG. 9. The back feet of the fringe-toed lizard, *Uma notata* (body size without tail 2¾ to 4½ inches), are equipped with lateral fringes of long, pointed scales, an adaptation providing increased foot surface for running on sand and also aiding the lizard in pushing its way under the sand.

Ants, for example, use underground microclimates to great advantage. Even termites, soft-bodied and seemingly totally unfitted for the desert, may be found in large numbers. They provide their own highly favorable microclimate, either through galleries excavated in the soil or within highly protective, aboveground earthen tunnels of their own construction. Grasshoppers and some other insects have long legs which lift the major portion of the insect's body into a slightly cooler air layer than that found at ground surface. Other insects rest several inches or a few feet above the ground in vegetation. The wings of insects can be a valuable asset. As the winged insect becomes heated near the ground, it can make short vertical flights upward or longer horizontal flights in the higher, cooler, air layers.

Arthropods often employ diurnal or seasonal cycles which favor their desert survival. During the summer, many emerge only at night, when temperatures are lowered and humidity heightened. Some change their daily cycle on a seasonal basis. Thus many desert ants are active at midday under mild winter temperatures; as daily temperatures rise, the same species forages in early morning and late afternoon. Finally in the summer their foraging may be conducted largely at dawn, dusk, and into the nighttime hours as daily heat levels become extreme. Some arthropods may enter seasonal resting stages during unfavorable times. The adults may simply retire underground or to some other protected location and wait out the unfavorable season. Often, the adults may die, and the species endures as eggs, larvae, or pupae in the soil or plants. Some arthropods possess the ability to enter a state of *diapause*—somewhat of a "holding" or resting state marked by a temporary stoppage of growth, reduced metabolism, and often an enhanced resistance to such climatic factors as drought, heat, or cold. Diapause works as a timing mechanism, particularly valuable in an inconstant environment, which the desert often is, allowing the arthropod to wait out unfavorable periods and to take quick advantage of favorable conditions once they again prevail. Arthropods enduring through eggs, immature stages, and diapause are reminiscent

FIG. 10. Honey ants represent an adaptation of a few species to aridity and seasonally limited availability of food. Certain members of the colony become "repletes," hanging from the ceiling of their underground nests. These repletes, with their greatly extended abdomens, are living containers of sweet plant juices, which they regurgitate to normal colony members when other food is not available.

in many ways of some desert plants, particularly the ephemeral species which survive unfavorable conditions through the plant's most resistant phase, the seed.

Granted, many arthropods are extremely frugal regarding their bodies' water. But how is the water originally obtained, and how are the small amounts lost replaced? A certain amount of metabolic water is produced by living cells as a byproduct of the oxidative metabolism of food. Also, a percentage—often a surprisingly high percentage—of the plant body is composed of water. Even quite dry plant material absorbs water, such as dew from its surface. Dew itself is sometimes available to arthropods which forage early in the day and consume the dew-decked vegetation. And many arthropod species are carnivorous; since the bodies of most living animals are roughly two-thirds water, those arthropods consuming animal prey may derive sufficient water for their needs.

Additionally, some arthropods have the ability to withstand

THE DESERTS OF THE SOUTHWEST

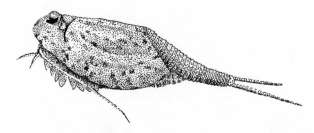

FIG. 11. Tadpole shrimp, a crustacean, is a denizen of temporary rain pools. The species endures in egg form once the pool dries; the young hatch when water is again present. Adult size is approximately 1 inch or less.

rather high heat and severe desiccation levels. Certain beetle species seem particularly able to withstand elevated temperatures, and beetles are among the most commonly represented successful desert insects. The eggs of the fairy and tadpole shrimp are outstanding in withstanding desiccation. Some of these small, freshwater crustaceans are only a few millimeters long; the fairy shrimp are usually more than one-third inch in length and may range up to approximately four inches. These creatures are not restricted to the desert habitat but are found there in temporary rain pools for brief periods as adults. As the water begins to evaporate, these crustaceans produce eggs; the eggs remain in the mud, then finally are preserved in the sun-baked soil of the pool's bottom long after the water is gone and the aquatic adults have perished. Such eggs are known to endure the extreme conditions of the desert's surface for several months; they may endure for as long as twenty-five years or more, until pools once again form in those locations and the cycle is quickly reinitiated.

Not only temperature and moisture stresses must often be endured by desert animals. Food shortages, too, may plague them. Many arthropods, again, score high on their ability to endure such shortages; some are able to survive prolonged fasting. Their small size precludes the necessity for large quantities of food. In the dry desert, vegetable matter is slow to decay or fails to do so altogether; some becomes buried in drifting sand and soil and is later uncovered, or is discovered by subterranean dwellers. In fact, in some severely stark Old World desert areas, a largely subterranean arthropod fauna is thought to survive primarily on plant matter carried there by the winds.

Reptiles are the animal form popularly associated with deserts. True, their species are well represented, but the reptiles are certainly not a special desert creation. Certain species have simply been able to capitalize on particular reptilian characteristics as avenues to desert success.

In mammals the urinary wastes carrying the body's chief nitrogen excretion, urea, must be kept in solution in order for elimination from the body to be achieved. Insects, birds, and reptiles, however, have the ability to precipitate uric acid from the wastes; the birds and reptiles ultimately discharge the uric acid along with the feces as a semisolid whitish mass. Thus they achieve a great saving in the moisture required for excretion.

Reptiles are *poikilothermic*—that is, their bodies display a variable temperature usually just slightly higher than the temperature of their environment. The reptile at rest in a favorable microclimate maintains a body temperature which needs support only a moderate or reduced metabolic level, demanding only limited water and food. The reptile's temperature during the colder, winter months also drops, and its body has few metabolic demands placed upon it as it endures the waiting period. Additionally, air in an underground burrow, the resting site of many reptiles, tends to have a high relative humidity. If a mammal with a temperature considerably higher than the burrow air temperature exhales warmed air from its lungs into the burrow, moisture is absorbed by the air from the animal's respiratory system and is expelled into the surrounding air, for warm air (that from the respiratory tract) is capable of holding more moisture than cool air (that inhaled from the burrow). Therefore the warm animal tends to lose moisture to the atmosphere. However, for the reptile with a body temperature very close to the burrow air temperature, this saturation deficit is much reduced or does not occur; hence respiratory moisture loss is very small.

Even when maintained at like temperatures, the basic

THE DESERTS OF THE SOUTHWEST

FIG. 12. The desert tortoise, *Gopherus agassizii,* may reach 14 inches in length. These tortoises are vegetarians; they survive even in some of the very arid North American deserts. They escape summer heat and winter cold by entering underground retreats.

metabolic rates of reptiles are much lower, approximately one-seventh those of equal-size *homeotherms* (animals having a relatively uniform body temperature maintained nearly independent of the environmental temperature).

Most, although not all, desert reptiles are carnivorous, obtaining needed moisture from the bodies of their prey. However, a few subsist on vegetation sufficiently water-filled to sustain them. Additionally, although some moisture is lost through their scale-covered skin, the reptiles' tough outer covering serves to prevent undue moisture loss.

An interesting member of the desert reptile group—a vegetarian, well-protected from dehydration by a heavy skin and shell—is the desert tortoise, *Gopherus agassizii* (also known as *Xerobates agassizii*), which may reach fourteen inches in length and is found even in some of the very arid portions of the Sonoran and Mohave Deserts. Unlike most desert reptiles, which obtain much or all of their moisture from animal prey, this tortoise derives food and water from its vegetation diet, consuming grass, cacti, and other low-growing plants. The desert tortoise often will drink water when it is available, as following a rain; individuals have been recorded to increase 41 to 43 percent in weight by drinking. However, one investigator reported successfully keeping hatchlings for three years without water; when they were at last offered water, they drank very little. Water is stored within the urinary bladder of the animal; as a water-saving measure, large quantities of waste in the form of solid urates can be stored for long periods in the bladder without ill effect, and the animal is able to endure considerable dehydration. The desert tortoise is active approximately six months of the year during the more favorable plant-growth periods. The remainder of the year is spent in dormancy in sometimes long (up to thirty-five feet), horizontal burrows or dens, which the tortoises excavate. Under certain conditions the desert tortoise may enter a period of summer estivation or torpor, as well as hibernation during colder months. During their active foraging months, they retreat to shorter burrows or natural rock shelters for rest or protection from high environmental temperatures.

Reptiles are not capable of enduring prolonged high temperatures. Reptile species vary in their heat tolerance, with snakes proving less tolerant as a group than the lizards. The spiny lizard, *Sceloporus magister,* a desert-dwelling species, has a lethal body temperature of approximately 109 degrees Fahrenheit. An outstanding desert dweller is the desert iguana, *Dipsosaurus dorsalis,* which has a lethal body temperature of approximately 122 degrees Fahrenheit. The latter are known to be active even when the air temperature reaches 115 degrees. Lethal body temperatures for some desert snake species considered in one study were approximately 110 degrees. Although reptiles are able to achieve some evaporative cooling of their bodies through the respiratory tract, they prevent overheating and consequent death primarily through behavioral means. They often retreat to shade or burrows during heat. Active only during favorable seasons and becoming dormant during others, they forage when the most favorable temperatures prevail. Reptile activity is severely reduced or nonexistent during the cooler months in the desert. In warmer periods, the lizards tend in general to be diurnal, although they may vary their activity from midday in cooler weather to early morning and late afternoon hours during days of higher temperatures. Snakes tend to be more nocturnal, although diurnal species certainly exist, and some may vary between diurnal and nocturnal activity in response to the environmental temperature.

Even though poikilothermic, reptiles are by no means completely at the mercy of their environment, for many of them actively seek to keep their temperature at a rather stable level when active. Thus they may bask in the sunlight, even flattening their bodies to some extent to expose a larger body surface to the sun's rays and to the warm substratum. When too warm, they may elevate the body by stretching their legs to the fullest extent possible to raise themselves above the warm surface. Certain species have been observed orienting the long axis of the body perpendicular to the sun's rays while warming; later, as their body heat rises, the lizard repositions its body so that its long axis is parallel to the sun's rays. Some lizards sprint over short, hot, sandy areas on hind legs only, with the body elevated. Certain species have the ability, through rapid sideways body movements, to submerge their abdomens a short distance into the slightly cooler area of sand underlying the upper sand surface. Some can dive directly into the sand, "swimming" some distance within it, achieving several purposes—cooling in the lower sand layers, insulative covering, and protection from predators.

The fringe-toed lizard, *Uma notata,* is a prime example of such a lizard. Living only in sandy areas, it is adapted morphologically for that particular habitat. This lizard, with a 2½- to 4½-inch body length plus tail, has toes on the rear feet fringed with projecting pointed scales to provide a "snowshoe" effect on the loose sand. It often runs bipedally at great speed over the sand and literally "dives" into it, rapidly burying itself, moving through the sand some distance, and then remaining still and hidden. To "swim" under the sand, the lizard holds its front legs back against the body, moves its head from side to side, and kicks its hind legs alternately, propelling itself forward. This lizard has overlapping eyelids and ear flaps to prevent the entry of sand into eyes and ears. Its sand-trap nasal passages and nasal valves serve to prevent sand from reaching the lungs as it breathes just under the sand surface. The body form is flattened with a smooth velvety surface, the head is wedge-shaped, and the lower jaw is countersunk into the upper—all features which aid the lizard to enter and move in sand.

FIG. 13.   The fringe-toed lizard, *Uma notata* (2¾ to 4½ inches, snout-vent length), is highly adapted for life in fine sand. Projecting scales on its hind toes provide increased traction on sand. Its flattened body shape, countersunk lower jaw, special nasal valves and ear flaps aid and protect it, permitting it to plunge into and move under the sand in its habitat.

FIG. 14.   The sidewinder, *Crotalus cerastes,* is a fairly small (17 to 31 inches) rattlesnake which moves by means of sidewise locomotion. The track left in soft sand is a series of roughly parallel marks.

Another reptile adapted for sand living is the sidewinder rattlesnake, *Crotalus cerastes*. This seventeen- to thirty-one-inch "horned" rattler, so-called for two hornlike projections over the eyes, is often found in areas of fine windblown sand in the Sonoran and Mohave Deserts. The two "horns" are hinged. When pressure is applied to their tops, they fold down, covering the eyes and fitting neatly into the indentation of scales surrounding them. This protective adaptation is considered valuable for these snakes in hunting rodents in underground burrows where eyesight is of no value and roots, rocks, loose soil, and sand present a danger to the eyes. The sidewinder moves forward with a sidewise locomotion. The snake's body is thrown forward diagonally in a series of loops and the snake appears to be crawling sideways in an S-shaped, flowing curve. The track left in soft sand is a series of unconnected, short, straight lines at a 30-degree angle to the direction in which the snake is progressing. Each line has a J-shaped mark at one end, made by the head and neck. The hooks of the J's indicate the direction of the snake's travel. Sidewinding serves several purposes. The vertical, rather than horizontal, force exerted in this movement is very efficient in moving over a loose surface, minimizing slippage. Sidewinding is a rapid means of locomotion. And it reduces danger of overheating since the amount of contact between the snake's body and the ground is greatly reduced.

For frogs and toads, members of the class Amphibia, the most important means of gaining water is by direct absorption of moisture through the skin. Conversely, moisture can be lost easily by the same means; therefore, to state that numerous species of frogs and toads inhabit the desert seems incongruous although it is true. They are able to live in these areas primarily by avoiding desert conditions. Some live only where permanent water is available. Many others adjust the timing of their life cycle to take rapid advantage of transitory amelioration of desert environmental conditions. Members of this group undergo dormancy underground much of the year, awaiting the arrival of rain during warm periods. Under this stimulus, the adults emerge, gather in the temporary ponds that have formed, and rapidly mate and produce eggs. With like haste, the eggs and tadpoles undergo development, racing to complete these immature stages before their pond waters evaporate.

For example, adult Couch's spadefoot toads (more properly "spadefoots" as these amphibians are not true toads), *Scaphiopus couchi,* a species widespread in the Sonoran and Chihuahuan Deserts, spend ten or more months of the year underground, emerging when the summer rains occur. The males' calls are reminiscent of bleating sheep, and these 2½- to 3-inch toads have loud, far-carrying voices which serve well to bring the individuals together in the temporary ponds. Their calls, one of the pleasant sounds of desert summer evenings, may be heard within an hour or less after the first heavy rain of the season. The eggs of this species have been reported to hatch within nine to seventy-two hours after being deposited in the temporary ponds, and life, from fertilization of the egg to adult form, is completed in as short a time as nine to fourteen days. As the ponds begin to disappear and dryness resumes, the adults retreat underground into old rodent holes or self-made burrows in the moist soil. *Spadefoot* refers to the presence of a sharp-edged "spade," or projection, on each hind foot of these amphibians. Using the spades, the animal burrows, backing into the ground, while rotating the body with the hind feet moving alternately in a circular fashion. These burrows may reach up to 25 inches below the soil surface. If rains of sufficient magnitude fail to arrive the following summer, the spadefoot's long rest may continue for another year. At least in some cases, a semi-impervious covering forms around the spadefoot during this waiting period. It is evidently composed of several layers of skin which have become loosened from the body but not completely sloughed off; it serves to reduce evaporation from the toad's body. It has been found that the spadefoot's tissues can endure even when the animal loses up to 50 percent or more of its body weight.

The desert frogs and toads may display other adaptations. Most are nocturnal. The urinary bladder may be used for water storage; the Great Plains toad, *Bufo congnatus,* is capable of storing up to 30 percent of its gross body weight as

FIG. 15. The spadefoot toad, *Scaphiopus couchi* (2¼ to 3 inches in length), spends most of the year underground awaiting favorable moisture conditions. The "spade" used for burrowing into the ground is shown above as solid black on the hind foot.

water in this manner. Many have a special *seat patch* or *sitting spot,* a ventral region of thin skin through which they can actually absorb water from the ground. Some species are capable of tolerating water with a high level of salinity. The tadpoles of some species are able to endure elevated water temperatures in their often small, solar-heated pools. Certainly one of the most useful capabilities of the desert-dwelling frogs and toads is the enhanced ability to survive a high degree of dehydration. As a group, amphibians are able to tolerate water losses of 7 to 60 percent of their body weight. Additionally, during a moisture shortage, the amphibians are capable of storing large amounts of waste nitrogen in the form of urea within their bodies without ill effect.

Most birds and large mammals do not or cannot use underground escapes to avoid environmental stresses. Additionally, most bird species are diurnally active. These factors do increase the heat-dehydration problem desert birds must face. But birds possess certain positive factors which serve them well in the desert environment—the possession of wings among them. Birds can fly to shade or to resting sites in vegetation in air cooler than that at the ground surface; they may make use of up-flowing air currents to rise hundreds of feet into cooler air where they float with little effort for extended periods. Wings also provide birds with the ability to reach watering sites some distance away, or simply to leave the desert, migrating at certain times of the year to avoid desert extremes.

Many species, however, remain in the desert year-round. Some of these species must live within reach of free water. Others obtain sufficient water from the animal prey they consume; still others are able to survive for at least certain parts of the year on moisture obtained from succulent plant material. Birds can reduce their temperatures through their behavior. They may seek shade, or rest during the hottest part of the day. They may facilitate heat transfer from their bodies by compressing their feathers tightly against their bodies to obtain minimal insulation; they may hold their wings away from the body, exposing the thinly feathered skin in these locations to the air; some species experience increased blood flow to their bare-skinned legs. Birds also reduce their temperature by evaporative cooling, which takes place through the respiratory tract, as they have no sweat glands. For a small animal, however, evaporative cooling is expensive in water terms. *Gular flutter,* or the rapid fluttering of the skin on the ventral

FIG. 16. The roadrunner, *Geococcyx californianus,* is a large member of the cuckoo family, reaching 20 to 24 inches in length. The roadrunner flies short distances but more often walks or runs. It eats insects, lizards, and snakes, including rattlesnakes, which are killed by sharp blows of the bird's strong beak.

surface of the throat, is employed by some birds in what is considered to be an energy-saving means of respiratory evaporative cooling.

As earlier noted, birds excrete uric acid rather than urea with a consequent impressive saving in moisture in comparison to mammals. Experimentally, some species of birds were found to endure high levels of dehydration. The mourning dove, *Zenaida macroura,* survived dehydration until a loss of 30 percent of body weight was reached. Some species are capable of making use of rather saline water. In one study, mourning doves maintained their normal weight when provided with drinking water that was 25 percent seawater.

The most beneficial factor aiding birds in desert living is a general capability shared with nondesert birds. Normal bird temperatures are considerably elevated above those of mammals, being in the 104°–108° F. range. Thus the bird is much delayed in starting to build a heat load under high temperatures. It may, in fact, still be losing body heat to the atmosphere while the mammal's body is gaining heat from the air. Additionally, the bird's body is capable of storing heat gained, to the extent of an elevation in body temperature of four to six Fahrenheit degrees, without ill effect. This stored heat can later be radiated back to the surrounding air as temperatures cool at night. This amount of heat gain is therefore dissipated without loss of costly water. With this tolerance of hyperthermia, some birds can endure body temperatures of 113° F. for several hours. Death occurs when their temperatures reach approximately 116.6° F. Evaporative cooling is thus used by birds to keep their temperatures within limits, but these limits are set at a higher level than those for mammals. (Man's critical body temperature lies between 107.6° and 113° F., dependent upon certain variables.)

Body size is an extremely important factor in heat gain. Small animals have a greater surface relative to their weight than do larger animals; hence the smaller ones gain, percentage-wise, more environmental heat. Heat produced in metabolism is also approximately proportional to the animal's surface area. Obviously, the position of the small mammal in the desert with regard to heat gain and loss is precarious, for

FIG. 17. The white-winged dove, *Zenaida asiatica* (11 to 12½ inches), displays a white wing patch when in flight. Its tail is rounded (unlike that of the mourning dove) and tipped with broad white corners. The harsh cooing of this dove is a familiar sound in mesquite groves and saguaro forests.

water must be used for evaporative cooling to prevent death once body temperatures reach certain levels. The kangaroo rat, a small desert rodent, has been found, if exposed to daytime desert heat, to sustain a water loss amounting to 15 percent of its body weight per hour for evaporative cooling. Obviously such an approach to desert living is highly impracticable for the small desert mammals, most of which display nocturnal habits, retreating underground during the daytime.

Some larger mammals, although they cannot enter underground burrows, do live successfully in the desert. Their large body size relative to surface area provides them a benefit in externally received heat gain, and internal heat production is less intense in large mammals than in small. Large-bodied mammals have an enhanced ability to store heat with only a slight elevation in body temperature. The camel, an outstandingly successful Old World desert inhabitant, has been much studied in regard to its adjustments to desert living. The camel was found to store heat in its body during the hot day, unloading it to the environment in the cooler night temperatures. Dissipation of the same amount of heat through evaporative cooling would cost the camel approximately four to five quarts of water daily. While no camels are found roaming in the

North American desert today, burros introduced by accident and design have prospered there. They too display the ability to store diurnally several degrees of heat to be lost during the night. Heat storage by some large desert mammals thus reduces the need for evaporative cooling, although evaporative cooling remains an important means of heat reduction, particularly when the upper tolerable limits of gain are approached.

The hair of mammals exposed to desert heat acts as a heat shield, preventing an impressive percentage of possible environmental heat gain from reaching the animal's skin. It allows evaporation of moisture from the skin, but slows this process, preventing a too-rapid, wasteful evaporation from taking place. In this regard, it acts in a manner similar to man's clothing, which serves the same useful purpose. Within this "heat shield," certain "windows" occur. These more open areas, largely without fur or only lightly haired, are located on the ventral portions of the animal's body, such as those around the mammary glands, on the scrotum, and in the groin. As the animal is standing, these areas are directed downward toward the shade formed by the animal's body; heat is thus lost by convection from these body sites to the shade.

The mobility of large mammals serves them exceedingly well in the desert. They may be able to travel considerable distances to water sources. They also may seek out cool resting areas in which to spend the hottest hours. And their mobility is helpful in obtaining food. As with the other animals discussed, food habits provide aid in filling moisture needs, carnivores deriving most or all of their water from their prey; the large herbivores derive some moisture from their plant food but also need drinking water periodically.

The desert bighorn sheep is one of the large mammals which inhabit our deserts. This animal is successful in dealing with the desert environment. Living gregariously, the bighorn sheep primarily inhabit rugged mountain ranges where their jumping and climbing abilities are impressively put to use. These heavy-bodied animals may weigh 150 to 200 or more pounds, are approximately three feet tall at the shoulder, may be up to six feet in length, and are a pale tan in color. The males have immense, curling horns; the females' considerably

FIG. 18.  Desert bighorn sheep, *Ovis canadensis* (reaches approximately 4 to 6 feet in body length and up to 200 pounds), survive in the desert by eating a wide variety of the vegetation available and by visiting waterholes as necessary. The desert subspecies is smaller in size and paler in color than its northern subspecies relatives.

smaller horns do not curl as impressively as the males'. The desert bighorns are nonchoosy vegetarians. Living in some of the most desolate and arid of the desert areas, including the stark deserts of Baja California, these animals generally must have access to free water, at least during certain times of the year, but derive a considerable amount of moisture from their diet. Successful as the sheep have been in coping with the desert environment, unfortunately they have not been so successful in their confrontation with man, who has hunted them severely, reduced their access to water sources with agriculture and highways, and released burros, which have pressured the sheep in terms of water and forage availability.

A few small mammals are active above ground diurnally. The tiny antelope ground squirrel, *Ammospermophilus leucurus*, widespread over the southwestern deserts, may often be seen above ground and is active in hot daytime temperatures. The secrets of its success are several. It displays omnivorous eating habits, partaking of water-filled animal materials in addition to plants. Under extreme heat loads, it salivates or drools; the moisture which wets the fur of its chest provides evaporative cooling at a lower metabolic cost than the alternative of panting. It has, for a small animal, an impressive ability to store heat. In keeping with its size, this heat load must be dissipated frequently, rather than on a daily basis as is done by larger mammals. Therefore, the antelope ground squirrel retreats periodically, sometimes as often as every quarter hour, to its underground burrow to spread out to its fullest extent on the cool substratum, thus unloading its heat gain to the burrow floor and walls. Aboveground, too, it often seeks favorable microclimates, resting or foraging in shade, or occasionally climbing up into vegetation.

Jackrabbits (actually hares, rather than rabbits) are surface-dwelling and heat-enduring mammals. Plant eaters, they cannot subsist on dry food alone, but are able to live on vegetation without free drinking water in some desert areas. The black-tailed jackrabbit, *Lepus californicus,* has a wide range in western North America; the antelope jackrabbit, *Lepus alleni,* is found in southwestern New Mexico and south-central Arizona, south into Sonora. The antelope is large—up to ten pounds in weight—and manages to survive in more arid areas than can the black-tailed. The latter is slightly smaller in size than the antelope, at about eight pounds.

FIG. 19. The large, thinly haired, heavily veined ears of various rabbit species serve to radiate body heat to the atmosphere.

Jackrabbits do not retreat underground, but rest in shade during hot days, seeking food nocturnally. The jackrabbit's huge, lightly haired, almost bare-skinned ears serve the animal well in the desert. As the jackrabbit lies resting in his form, a slight hollow in the ground, his ears lie flat, spread along his back. These ears display a high reflectivity to light. The blood vessels in the ears are greatly dilated when conditions are propitious for heat loss from the ears to the environment; they are severely constricted when the animal needs to maintain body warmth.

Of the small retreating mammals, the kangaroo rat, *Dipodomys* spp., is an outstanding desert dweller. These animals, and a few others with a similar pattern, are capable of living for their entire lives on a diet of dry plant food and can survive totally without drinking free water. The kangaroo rat subsists on the very small amounts of water that may be present in its food, consisting of dry seeds, and primarily on water produced by food metabolism. In the bodies of animals, oxidation of 1 gram of starch produces 0.6 gram of metabolic water; one gram of fat yields 1.1 grams of water. The limited water supply thus gained by the kangaroo rat is husbanded and expended in a most frugal, albeit successful, manner. The kangaroo rat is active nocturnally. During the day it plugs the outside opening to its burrow. The temperature in the burrow stays moderate and the relative humidity remains about two to five times higher than that of the outside air. Thus the animal loses little body moisture while in its retreat. Seeds stored in the burrow absorb some of the air's moisture, to be gained by the animal when the food is consumed. The temperature of the kangaroo rat's nasal chambers is lower than that of its body as a whole. As air is inspired, water evaporated from the rat's nasal passages cools the nasal tissues. In expiration, air leaving the lungs has become saturated at the higher body temperature. As this is expired, it is cooled in its movement over the cooler nasal passages and loses some of the moisture carried from the lungs. A near moisture equilibrium thus occurs. The animal's feces are exceedingly dry and firm, containing little moisture. The kangaroo rat consumes little

FIG. 20. The Merriam's kangaroo rat, *Dipodomys merriami,* is one of the most highly adapted desert mammals, able to exist on dry food without need of free water. Several species and subspecies occur in the Southwest deserts; the largest, *D. deserti,* has a body length of 5 to 6 inches and a 7- to 8-inch tail. *D. merriami* is smaller.

protein in its diet; thus the need to eliminate urea is reduced. Its kidneys are capable of producing very concentrated urine, approximately four to five times as concentrated as man's and twice as concentrated as seawater.

Many of the small desert mammals enter a dormant period in response to such factors as cold, heat, drought, or food shortage. We are most familiar with winter dormancy, or *hibernation.* A somewhat similar summer dormancy is termed *estivation.* In both states, the animal's body temperature approaches within a few degrees the ambient temperature; oxygen consumption is greatly reduced; the animal's metabolism slows, thereby conserving energy; and the animal enters a period of torpor. This holding action assists animals to endure unfavorable periods. Some small desert mammals are known to undergo daily torpor cycles. In certain desert-dwelling mice of the genus *Peromyscus,* daily torpor periods of several hours' duration have been found to occur in which the body temperature of the animal drops as much as 50 degrees, with a resultant drop in energy needs.

Adaptations to the desert by the human species will be discussed in later chapters. As one of the desert's large mammals, however, man seldom crawls into burrows; man must wear artificial clothing as a heat shield and to cover exposed, easily burned skin; he requires large amounts of water for elimination of wastes and is incapable of enduring hyperthermia for long; he loses quantities of water in evaporative cooling. His thinking is affected by a water loss equivalent to a 5 percent loss of body weight, and his condition can only be described as critical or dead when this loss reaches 12 to 15 percent. Obviously, man's desert adaptation must be behavioral.

CHAPTER VI

# The Great Basin Desert

IN 1776, when momentous actions were underway on the eastern seaboard, Spanish fathers Garces, Dominguez, and Escalante and their soldier escorts became, in two different expeditions, the first white men to penetrate the great western interior basin of the United States. A quarter-century or so later, fur trappers entered the basin region from the north. Dreams regarding this unknown immense area proliferated in faraway regions. Armchair geographers fantasized, then believed that a river—undiscovered, yet named the Buenaventura—crossed the area and offered a ready route from the great Rockies to the far Pacific. Jedediah Smith, the nineteenth-century American trapper and explorer, traveled the area; the first white women and the first wagons entered it in 1841. In 1844, Lieutenant John C. Fremont made the truth known: No mythical kingdom nor river system to the Pacific existed within the region's interior. The area was in reality a basin—a great desert basin. Fremont was soon followed by highly motivated land and gold seekers who traversed the arid land as they pursued their goals to the west.

The outlines of the Great Basin Desert coincide rather well with the outlines of the floor of the Great Basin itself; extensions of the desert environment also reach into adjacent portions of the Colorado and Columbia plateaus. The Great Basin Desert includes central and southeastern Oregon, southern Idaho, much of Nevada and Utah, and a small part of western Colorado, then projects small extensions into northern Arizona, western California, and southwestern Wyoming. Dr. William G. McGinnies, a desert authority, stated that the Great Basin itself stretches north to south 880 miles, east to west 572 miles, and includes an area of 210,000 square miles. Northernmost of the arid lands, the Great Basin is known as a cold desert. Most of its vast area lies above 4,000 feet in elevation, and its most northern extensions reach to approximately 49 degrees north latitude. Snow is frequent and winter long; freezing temperatures of a week in duration are common. Precipitation in the form of both rain and snow averages four to eleven inches per year, with up to thirteen inches at the higher elevations and more northern latitudes. Approximately 60 percent of the moisture, much of it in the form of snow, is received during the colder months, the majority in the early spring months.

The Great Basin, stretching irregularly from the Sierra Nevada Mountains on the west almost to the Rockies on the east, consists of a series of undrained basins, or bolsons, separated by generally north-south-trending mountain ranges. According to the borders one establishes for the Great Basin Desert, the number of these major bolsons varies, but exceeds 100. Mountain ranges are always in sight in this desert. Most are approximately fifty to seventy-five miles in length and six to fifteen miles in width. Some rise over 10,000 feet in elevation to become islands rising from a sagebrush sea, studded with juniper, piñon, and other conifers. The Great Basin Desert is the classic example of basin and range topography.

*Overleaf:* Fig. 21.    The Great Basin Desert extends the farthest north and is the largest of the four North American deserts. It covers most of Nevada and Utah with extensions into Oregon, Idaho, Wyoming, Colorado, Arizona, and California.

Moisture received by the mountains within this giant inter-mountain basin flows in washes and larger streambeds toward the center of each adjacent basin. Since these basins are without outlet, the water forms *playas* (the floor of a desert basin which receives drainage, becoming a usually ephemeral, shallow lake); occasionally, it is contained within a permanent lake. The water evaporates, leaving its mineral burden in the dry playa, or to accumulate in the remaining lake waters. One of the larger streambeds (by desert standards) contained within this closed system is the Humboldt River in western Nevada. A century and a half ago, it provided for a distance a welcome watered pathway for wagon-tied, California-bound travelers, until its water disappeared into the Humboldt Sink. After that, the pioneers and their animals faced a grueling, waterless desert before beginning their ascent of the Sierras.

The Great Basin has not always been a desert. It was once a land of lakes, and evidence of these yet remains. During the last ice age, glaciers moved far southward, bringing ice melt and wetter weather to the Basin. Water accumulated, forming lakes in many of the basins. Two spectacularly large lakes were created. In the eastern Great Basin, Lake Bonneville covered much of northwestern Utah, with portions of Nevada and Idaho also included under its approximately 20,000-square-mile expanse. In the western Great Basin, the approximately 8,500-square-mile Lake Lahontan was formed. About 12,000 to 15,000 years ago, the glaciers having retreated, the climate of the Great Basin became arid, and the lake waters began their lengthy evaporative shrinking. Today small remnants of these lakes remain. The Great Salt Lake, the remains of Lake Bonneville, is now approximately 2,400 square miles in extent. Pyramid Lake, in western Nevada, approximately 200 square miles in size, is one of several remains of Lake Lahontan.

Accumulation of minerals over thousands of years in these basins has produced today's often highly mineralized lakes. The Great Salt Lake is truly salty—its salt content is approximately eight to ten times greater than that of the ocean; the Great Salt Lake is outranked (barely) in salt content by only one other major body of water, the Dead Sea, itself a desert-locked body of water. The waters of the Great Salt Lake are too highly mineralized for human swimmers to sink; its water burns their eyes and salt crusts on their bodies once they come out. It is too highly saline for survival of fish. Life is present, however, for algae abound within it, and tiny, quarter-inch brine shrimp are often present in fantastic numbers. Nesting birds are attracted to the islands which dot the shallow, briny waters. California gulls, white pelicans, blue herons, cormorants, and other seemingly unlikely species flock to the lake. For the most part, these birds derive their food from the fresh waters and marshes feeding into the lake, or even from waters some distance away. Pyramid Lake, however, is less salty than the Great Salt Lake, and is home of the Lahontan cutthroat, a form of trout, and to other fish species.

Where the ancient lake waters have completely disappeared, leaving vast dry lakes of mineral residues behind, great level salt flats have often been formed. The Bonneville Salt Flats, west of the Great Salt Lake, extends for miles, its salts undotted by plants. Bonneville Salt Flats—baked solid—is often used for car racing.

In environments favorable for plant growth, competition occurs between plant species for room, sunlight, and similar factors. Not so in the desert. There, competition is not so much plant versus plant, but rather more often plant versus environment. Where desert environmental conditions are adverse, relatively fewer plant species survive. The plants of the Great Basin must survive the extremes of both aridity and cold, in addition to other extenuating factors, such as often highly alkaline soils. As a consequence, flora of the Great Basin Desert is limited in comparison to many other desert areas.

Forrest Shreve classified stands of desert vegetation into three general groups, according to the number of dominant species of plants involved in each. In what he called *simple stands,* only two or three species formed 90 to 95 percent of the plant population of the stand, and coverage was a mere 8 to 15 percent. Such stands, unlike the two remaining classifications, tend to display a uniformity of height. Shreve estimated that about 12 percent of the North American desert consists of simple stands. The second classification, that of *mixed stands,* includes areas in which dominance of the vegetation is held by four to twelve large perennials. Approximately 60 percent of the North American desert supports mixed stands; coverage ranges from 15 to 20 percent. The height attained by these species is not uniform; hence the upper vegetational level is irregular. The third classification is that of *rich stands,* with the dominant and subdominant perennial species totaling fifteen to twenty-five. Slightly less than 30 percent of the North American desert supports rich stands. In these stands, coverage may reach 40 to 70 percent, with the "canopy" again broken into different levels.

Large areas of simple stands occur in the Great Basin Desert. Within the limited number of species capable of surviving in that location, certain shrub or semishrub species have been most successful. Best known of these shrubs is the sagebrush, popular trademark of the Great Basin Desert. Trees are not common; cottonwoods and willows grow along some streambeds and, as one leaves the desert to ascend the mountain slopes, piñons and junipers fringe the desert's edge. Ephemerals are limited to a single season—the summer. In some areas, grasses assume seasonal importance. Yuccas occur infrequently. Leafless green plant species are few, represented by *Ephedra*—jointed-stemmed, blue-green, small shrubs commonly called Mormon tea or Mexican tea, which were supposedly once brewed and drunk by these people. Species of cacti are extremely limited; they include small species of prickly pears, such as *Opuntia polyacantha.* This species of prickly pear forms clumps from one to several feet in diameter, but extends to only a limited three to six inches in height. *Echinocereus,* or small hedgehog cacti, also occur.

Cacti are highly susceptible to damage from cold weather. They are injured if the temperature falls below 14° to 23° F. for a short time or below 28° F. for a longer period. Some prickly pear species range far to the north, but they tend to be small in size, and their pads are rather severely depleted of water content before freezing temperatures occur. For germination, cacti seeds require warm soil temperatures—at least 70° F., or preferably a range of about 80° to 90° F.—and the mature cacti need moisture and warmth concurrently for both

FIG. 22.   The big sagebrush, *Artemisia tridentata* (commonly 2 to 4 feet, but up to 7 feet in height), a gray-green shrub of the high desert country, is the popular symbol of the Great Basin. The leaves bear three wedge-shaped teeth at the tips, giving this plant a common name—three-tooth sage. Sagebrush is the dominant plant over extended areas, and many animals are associated with it in a variety of ways.

FIG. 23.   Shadscale, *Atriplex confertifolia,* is particularly prominent in the Great Basin Desert where it often forms almost pure stands on alkaline soils. The plants, compact and rounded, may reach two feet in height and are rigid, spiny, and nearly leafless in winter. Another common name is sheep fat, denoting this plant's usefulness to man.

growth and moisture replenishment. Therefore, with warm summer temperatures limited in duration and more than half the region's moisture being received during the colder months, conditions in the Great Basin Desert are not conducive to the growth of most cacti species. Other succulent or semi-succulent species are only poorly represented.

Shreve summarized the vegetation of the Great Basin Desert as dominated by a small number of species of generally low-statured shrubs, most of them completely or at least partly deciduous, and as displaying a predominance of simple plant communities, with as much as 95 percent of the simple

FIG. 24. The greasewood, *Sarcobatus vermiculatus,* is a salt-tolerant plant often plentiful in the Great Basin Desert. The name greasewood is sometimes incorrectly given to the creosote bush. The greasewood shrub is 3 to 5 feet in height, with numerous branches and somewhat succulent leaves.

stand composed of a single species in some cases. The most common dominants are *Atriplex confertifolia,* shadscale, or sheep fat; *Artemisia tridentata,* the big sagebrush, or three-toothed sage; *Chrysothamnus nauseosus,* or rabbit brush; and *Ceratoides lanata,* mule fat, or winter fat. Soil conditions are of prime importance in determining where an individual species predominates.

Plants vary in their ability to grow in alkaline soil; the halo-phytes are especially adapted for growth in soils with a high salt concentration. These plants often occur in the lower levels of the basins; concentric bands of various species of vegetation ring them, with the species makeup of the various bands dependent upon the plants' tolerances to alkalinity. The highly alkaline soils of the playa centers support no vegetation whatsoever. Circling the playa's edges may occur scattered, hardy, often small-leaved, highly adapted, alkali-resistant plant species such as *Salicornia rubra,* or pickleweed; *Allenrolfea occidentalis,* or iodineweed; and *Sarcobatus vermiculatus,* or true greasewood. Just above this vegetational ring usually occurs *Atriplex confertifolia,* or shadscale. This species tends to dominate lower basin areas, in which it grows in soil too alkaline for sagebrush. That shadscale is also called "salt bush" indicates its growth ability and usual location. Shadscale is a rounded, compact, woody-stemmed bush which seldom grows more than one to two feet in height, often forming nearly pure stands on the alkaline, heavy soils. During the winter the plant becomes rigid, spiny, and nearly leafless. The shrub ranges from the northern Great Basin south into Chihuahua, Mexico, and can be an important browse plant for animals.

One study determined that *Salicornia rubra* and related species were growing in soil with 2.5 percent or more soluble salts. Where the salt content was .8 percent, *Atriplex confertifolia* prospered. With a slight further decrease in salt content and the presence of a coarser soil texture, *Artemisia tridentata*, the big sagebrush, was established. Sagebrush in nearly pure stands or mixed with a limited number of other perennial species blankets vast areas of the Great Basin Desert; it also ranges beyond the Great Basin into the xeric woodlands, pine forests, and into the adjoining Mohave Desert. *Artemisia tridentata* is commonly two to four feet in height, but may reach six or seven feet. Soft gray-green in color, *Artemisia tridentata* bears leaves tipped with three short, wedge-shaped teeth. Actually this sagebrush is not a true sage but is a variety of wormwood. Its popular name is drawn from the sweetish, sage odor its foliage bears. When burned, the sagebrush provides a characteristic, pleasingly odored smoke. Because it has figured in so many romantic/adventure novels, particularly those of Zane Grey, the sagebrush is to many neophytes the universal symbol of desert. In reality, sagebrush is a dominant plant only in the Great Basin Desert; its ubiquitous position is appropriated in the warmer southern deserts by the creosote bush.

Shreve states that nineteen additional species of *Artemisia* are found in rather close association with *A. tridentata* in the Great Basin Desert. Similarly, fourteen additional species of *Atriplex* are associated with the best-known, *Atriplex confertifolia*. He notes additional semishrub species of importance in the Great Basin. One of these, *Chrysothamnus nauseosus*, or rabbit brush, is a compact shrub, usually a foot or less in height, found in the central and northern Great Basin on light or sandy, nonalkaline soils. It blossoms, producing yellow flowers, in late summer. *Atriplex spinosa,* or hop sage, is a stiff-branched shrub from one to three feet in height. It has slightly fleshy leaves, and its fruits are enclosed in purple-red bracts. Growing on alkaline soils in both the creosote and sagebrush desert, it ranges from Washington into southern California. *Ceratoides lanata,* mule fat, or winter fat, derives its common name from its importance as winter forage. The plant reaches 1 to 2½ feet in height and is conspicuous due to gray-white foliage and white hairs about ³⁄₁₆-inch long which grow from the bracts of the fruit. *Coleogyne ramosissima,* or blackbrush, is a small-leaved evergreen shrub found on higher slopes in the southern Great Basin.

The Great Basin's surface appearance presents an overall effect of linear mountain masses separated by immense, lonely intermountain vastnesses which are partially clothed by shrubs of a rather uniform height and repetitious in form. Some who view the land describe the total as monotonous. To the desert lover, however repetitious its plant growth may be, the Great Basin's expansiveness, loneliness, silence, wilderness, and desert essence endow it with a rugged beauty and character not displayed by man-dominated, treed, or planted lands.

As with plant species, some animal species may range through desert and other habitats. Others may be basically desert species and occur in at least portions of all four of the North American deserts; many others are restricted to one or two of the deserts. Some are so restricted in range as to be found only in a portion of a single desert. Literally thousands of species of living things occur in our North American deserts. Though to know them all would be impossible, we can recognize a broad pattern of organization regarding the habitation in and utilization of the desert by many of the animal species. This study or science of the interrelations between living organisms and their environment we know as *ecology.* Before surveying some of the animals to be found in the Great Basin Desert, let us define and clarify certain ecological concepts.

The place where a plant or animal lives or may be found is its *habitat,* or *biotope.* This area may be large, as is the Great

Basin Desert, or even larger, as is the North American desert. Or it may be a small piece of a particular habitat, a microhabitat. A *community* denotes all the populations of living things occupying a given area. A block of nature that includes non-living substances and a community of living organisms which interact to produce an exchange of materials between the nonliving and the living is an *ecosystem*. In this functional unit, the *biotic* (living) and the *abiotic* (nonliving) are inseparably interrelated and interact upon one another. Within this ecosystem, each species of living organisms fills a particular ecological niche. *Niche* denotes the species' position or status within its community and total ecosystem. The niche filled by an organism depends upon the organism's structural adaptation, specific inherited and/or learned behavior, and physiological responses. Simply, niche may be thought of as the "job," or position, the species fills in the ecosystem. Ordinarily no two species occupy an identical niche in a particular ecosystem, although some may occupy very similar niches, differing from one another in only certain fine aspects—they may be active at different times or use slightly different foods, or the like.

The food used by a species is an important factor in the niche it fills. Within the ecosystem exist *food chains,* through which food energy from plants—the basic source—is transferred, through repeated eating and being eaten, from one to the next in a series of organisms. In each transfer, a large proportion of the potential energy is lost. In most chains no more than four or five transfers, and usually fewer, are involved. The chains are of three basic types. In the *saprophytic chain,* food energy moves from dead matter to microorganisms. In the *parasitic chain,* food energy moves from larger to smaller organisms. The most familiar food chain, and the one we will consider, is the *predator chain.* This chain often moves from the plant base through small and finally to larger animals; for example, plant–insect–lizard–roadrunner–coyote. In this chain, the successive members are larger in size but fewer in total number (for example, coyotes are larger and less numerous than roadrunners, which are in turn larger and less numerous than lizards, and so on). In some cases the sequence may be plants, to large herbivore, to carnivore; for example, plants–deer–mountain lion. The term *trophic level* indicates the consumer's distance from the plant source. Plants represent the first trophic level; *herbivores,* or plant-eaters, the second level; primary *carnivores,* which eat the herbivores, represent the third level; and, if present, secondary carnivores and tertiary carnivores represent the fourth and fifth levels. Consumers which are the same number of steps removed from the plant source are said to be on the same trophic level. Food chains in any ecosystem are interconnected with one another, and the pattern formed is known as the *food web.*

Nature abhors a vacuum, states the philosopher-naturalist. And so living things move in, adapt, and exploit to the best of their ability any opportunities for life that may be provided. The usual end result is that species fill every possible niche in each ecosystem. Some species—for example, the coyote—fill a particular niche in several ecosystems. In some cases, the same species may fill approximately the same niche in similar but separated habitats, with the species population in one habitat genetically differentiated to some degree, as revealed by appearance or adaptation. Such a genetic variant within a species, adapted to a particular environment yet remaining interfertile with all other members of the species, is known as an *ecotype.* Similar or related but not identical species may fill essentially the same niche in similar ecosystems. For example, a particular species of ground squirrel in one desert may not be present in a nearby desert, but a very similar species fills essentially the same niche; the white-tailed antelope ground squirrel, *Ammospermophilus leucurus,* of the Great Basin and Mohave Deserts is replaced in southern Arizona and Sonora by the Harris antelope ground squirrel, *Ammospermophilus harrisii.* Finally, some organisms, often phylogenetically distant from one another, undergo parallel evolution, adapting to similar environmental conditions to fill similar niches in habitats distant from one another. The American sidewinder rattlesnake has adapted to a sandy habitat with sidewinding locomotion. The horned viper of Africa has evolved the same solution to similar environmental conditions. The American kangaroo rat's adaptations to life in an arid environment have been achieved through remarkably similar means by the jerboa of the African deserts. The big-eared American kit fox, especially adapted for a rodent-catching way of life in the North American deserts, is matched similarly by the big-eared, rodent-catching fennec fox of Africa. Organisms which occupy the same ecological niche in similar habitats of different biogeographical regions are termed *ecological equivalents*.

Some generalizations (to which exceptions do arise) may be applied to desert animals. Desert mammals tend to have fur of a lighter color than do members of their species or closely related species inhabiting more humid, cooler climates. The cause of this coloration has not been precisely determined. Ecologists postulate that lighter colors may provide protective coloration against the desert's light, often-faded colors, or that heat and humidity may be involved in the change in hair pigmentation, or both. Desert mammals and birds display a high surface-to-body weight ratio. Under identical conditions, *homiothermal* animals (those having a relatively uniform body temperature maintained nearly independent of the environmental temperature) give off equal amounts of heat per unit of surface area. "Bergmann's Rule" postulates that as temperatures decrease from the equator toward the poles, the body shape of birds and mammals tends to display a lower ratio of body surface to body weight. "Allen's Rule" postulates that over this same temperature gradient, the body extremities tend to become shorter in proportion to trunk size. The end result is a reduction in the surface area from which heat is lost to the atmosphere from the stocky bodies of Arctic animals, and a proportionate increase of heat-radiating body surface in the desert animals. The foregoing rule applies only to birds and mammals. The opposite is true of poikilothermic animals, which generally attain larger body sizes in warm climates than they do in cold climates.

A species population, particularly plant, which exerts a major controlling effect on the nature of a community is termed an *ecological dominant,* or indicator. In the Great Basin Desert, two major communities are easily recognized: In the first, the halophytic species, particularly shadscale, *Atriplex confertifolia,* are the dominants; in the second,

*Artemisia tridentata,* the big sagebrush, is the ecological dominant. Around these dominants and accompanying species, ecosystems are developed. The common names of some species exemplify their presence in and about, and their ties to, the dominant species. For example, inhabitants in the sagebrush community include the least or sagebrush chipmunk, *Eutamias minimus;* sage sparrow, *Amphispiza belli;* sage thrasher, *Oreoscoptes montanus;* sage grouse, *Centrocercus urophasianus;* and sagebrush lizard, *Sceloporus graciosus.*

The sagebrush lizard is small—2 to 2½ inches in length, plus tail. Gray or brown above, it usually displays blotches or crossbars. It often has a black bar on the shoulder with a rust color on the sides of the neck and body, and blue belly patches. This ground dweller is found in the vicinity of brush heaps, rocks, logs, or bushes. It retreats to these areas or occasionally climbs up into vegetation when frightened. The sagebrush lizard prefers open ground with scattered low bushes, requirements met by the sagebrush habitat, although it also ranges into manzanita brushland, pine and fir forests, and piñon-juniper woodland. Its food consists of insects, ticks, scorpions, spiders, snails, and similar animal life.

The sagebrush, or least, chipmunk is a roughly rat-sized rodent with short grayish fur marked by contrasting stripes on the head and the length of the body. Its tail is narrow, round,

FIG. 25. The sage sparrow, *Amphispiza belli* (5 to 6 inches in length), is a ground feeder in dry brushy habitat, such as the sagebrush plains or open chaparral.

lemon-yellow or grayish-yellow on the underside, and long—equaling approximately 80 to 90 percent of the head-and-body length. In addition to living in the sagebrush habitat, this chipmunk ranges into juniper woodland. Chipmunks can be differentiated from some similar-looking ground squirrels by the presence of stripes on the sides of their heads. The sagebrush chipmunk hibernates through the cold winter months. It carries food in internal cheek pouches and stores caches of food in its underground burrow for early spring months or for periods during the winter when it may awaken. Chipmunks in general eat seeds and fruits, although the sagebrush chipmunk consumes insects, especially the larvae of Lepidoptera (butterflies and moths) in the spring, becoming more of a seed-eater later in the summer.

Both the sage thrasher and sage sparrow breed in the sagebrush habitat, building their nests in the sagebrush itself and often using fine shreds of the bark as nesting material. The thrasher is almost robin size, and is similar to the robin in shape. Its back is gray, its tail is short with white corners, its breast is heavily striped; it has a straight and slender bill and pale yellow eyes. It often sits atop the sagebrush, voicing its pleasant song and nervously jerking its tail. The sage thrasher is an insect eater and has a habit of often running rapidly from one protective bush to another. This thrasher ranges from Washington and Montana south to southern California, southern Arizona, and New Mexico; it winters in the more southern areas.

The sage sparrow is a small gray bird with a single dark spot on the lighter breast and dark marks on the side of the throat. Its breeding range is throughout most of the Great Basin, reaching into central California. This sparrow winters from the southern edge of the breeding range to the deserts of California, Arizona, New Mexico, and western Texas.

The sage grouse, or sage hen, is one of the very interesting, distinctive inhabitants of the sagebrush community. Individuals of this species are approximately the size of a small turkey; the males average twenty-eight inches in body length, the females twenty-two inches. These birds are gray-brown with a contrasting black belly and spike-like tail feathers. The range of the sage grouse is close to that of the sagebrush, from southeastern Washington and Montana to eastern California, Nevada, Utah, and northern Colorado. The sage grouse are strong runners; they dash through the intervening open areas between sagebrush and the other plants under which they find protection from raptors. Their mottled black, brown, and gray coloration serves as camouflage in their habitat.

The sage grouse is best known for its courtship displays. Early in the spring, the males assemble in special clearings among the sagebrush, called *strutting grounds.* Displays by the males usually take place in the very early morning or late afternoon. Each male chooses a territory, often with a small hillock included. He displays his plumage, erecting a spectacular white ruff about his neck, and spreads, erects, and fans his tail. He begins to beat his wings; he struts stiff-legged and gulps air, filling his lungs and the two air sacs on his breast. The bird arches his wings, contracting the muscles around the air sacs. With his head withdrawn into the white ruff, the balloonlike air sacs protruding from the breast feathers and framed by the wings, and the whole backed by the spiked, spread tail, the male sage grouse is a most unusual apparition, apparently very attractive to the observing females. The finale of each display is provided when the air is released from the air sacs with loud plops which can be heard as much as a half mile away. These displays are repeated many times on different occasions and are accompanied by fighting; eventually, one male becomes dominant and may mate with three-fourths or more of the hens in a particular group. In the winter, the sage grouse live in flocks that may include several hundred individuals. During that period, they feed primarily on the leaves of sagebrush. After mating in the spring, the males break into smaller groups. In the fall the males, females, and young join into the larger flocks.

Another interesting inhabitant of the sagebrush is the pygmy rabbit, *Brachylagus idahoensis,* the smallest of all rabbits, measuring approximately eleven inches in length. This rabbit is confined to the Great Basin, occurring from eastern California, Oregon, and Washington into southern Idaho, northern Nevada, and western Utah. Even within this limited range, the pygmy rabbit is local in distribution. The young of this species, as are all rabbits (not hares), are born naked with eyes closed, in contrast to the precocial young of the hares of the genus *Lepus,* which includes the jackrabbits. The young of *Lepus* species are born with full fur and functioning eyes and ears; they are able to hop about within a few hours after birth. The pygmy brush rabbits occur in patches of dense sagebrush where they live in burrows at the bases of the plants; their food is thought to consist almost entirely of sagebrush.

The black-tailed hare, commonly called the black-tailed jackrabbit, *Lepus californicus,* is widespread in western North America. This large hare, with an average body length of twenty-two inches, sports huge black-tipped ears. Dorsally it is grayish, and nearly white ventrally. The upper side of its tail is black, with the color running up onto the rump; below, the tail is buffy-gray. Food of this often-numerous hare is grass and shrubs. These animals are often seen bounding across roads in the Great Basin Desert, and in years of bounty many are seen road-killed.

The few inhabitants of the sagebrush ecosystem we have

FIG. 26. The sage grouse, *Centrocercus urophasianus* (males 26 to 30 inches, females 22 to 23 inches), is a resident of the sagebrush habitat, eating the plant's leaves and nesting under it.

just surveyed serve as less than a mere beginning in knowing the totality of the literally hundreds of animal species of the Great Basin Desert. In looking at the species inhabiting that desert as a whole, we see certain patterns. Many animals, such as the pygmy rabbit and sage grouse, consume vegetation, as do many insects and other animals. These plant-eating animals may be consumed by predators. Some animals, such as the sagebrush chipmunk, cross lines and eat both plant and animal material. Any community must necessarily include more animals to be eaten than eaters. In this regard, the Great Basin Desert, like the other three North American deserts, has a large insect population, at least seasonally, which provides food for many animals. It also has a huge rodent population, which supplies a large food bulk for many predators. As a group, rodents have become well adapted to life in the desert, as exemplified by the kangaroo rat.

Two kangaroo rat species found in the Great Basin are *Dipodomys microps* and *D. ordii. D. ordii,* known as the Ord kangaroo rat, has an extensive range from southern Canada south to central Mexico and from eastern Oregon to the Gulf coast of Texas. Pack rats or wood rats occur, including the desert pack rat, *Neotoma lepida,* which builds its home within stacks of debris which it collects. A multitude of mice occur, including white-footed, *Peromyscus* spp.; harvest mice, *Reithrodontomys* spp.; and grasshopper mice, *Onychomys leutogaster,* which are unusual in that they have departed from the vegetarian diet, with which mice are ordinarily associated, to become carnivores. Up to approximately 90 percent of their food may consist of grasshoppers and other insects. Kangaroo mice, too, are present; they resemble the kangaroo rats in some ways, but are much smaller. *Microdipodops pallidus,* a kangaroo mouse found in the Great Basin Desert, has a tail larger in the middle than at the base, due to an accumulation of fat. This stored fat serves as a reserve energy source and also helps to maintain the animal's balance when jumping.

Meadow mice, or voles, usually inhabitants of moister habitats, are represented in the Great Basin by the sagebrush vole, *Lagurus curtatus.* This species is often found in arid sagebrush habitat far from surface water. These animals feed on sagebrush and other vegetation, are active both diurnally and nocturnally, and do not hibernate. The females breed a few hours after giving birth, and the gestation period is a mere twenty-one days, providing a good example of the productive capacity of the smaller mammals to produce food for the larger.

Pocket gophers, also usually associated with more moist areas, occur, with *Thomomys bottae* found in the Great Basin Desert. Ground squirrels form a large part of the staff of life for other creatures. These squirrels include members of the genera *Ammospermophilus*.

Carnivorous amphibians of the Great Basin Desert include the Great Basin spadefoot toad, *Scaphiopus intermontanus*, and leopard frog, *Rana pipiens*. Lizards, primarily carnivorous, which occur in the Great Basin include the longnosed leopard lizard, *Gambelia wislizenii*; black-collared lizard, *Crotaphytus insularis*; side-blotched lizard, *Uta stansburiana*; northern desert horned lizard, *Phrynosoma platyrhinos*; the western whiptail lizard, *Cnemidophorus tigris*; desert spiny lizard, *Sceloporus magister*; and zebratail lizard, *Callisaurus draconoides*. Among the snakes represented are striped whipsnake, *Masticophis taeniatus*; red racer, *Masticophis flagellum*; gopher snake, *Pituophis melanoleucus*; western long-nosed snake, *Rhinocheilus lecontei*; night snake, *Hypsiglena torquata*; and the Great Basin rattlesnake, *Crotalus viridis lutosus*. All of the snakes are carnivorous, preying on a wide variety of animals.

Birds of the Great Basin Desert are extremely varied. Some breed there in the desert habitat. Others breed along the lake shores or on islands in the lakes, such as those of the Great Salt Lake. Still other species are transitory, simply pausing in their migration. In their food habits, as a group, these birds vary from eaters of plant products to insect- and larger-animal eaters to carrion feeders, such as ravens, *Corvus corax*, and turkey vultures, *Cathartes aura*. Birds of prey include red-tailed hawks, *Buteo jamaicensis*; Swainson's hawks, *Buteo swainsoni*; American kestrel, *Falco sparverius*; Cooper's hawks, *Accipiter cooperii*; rough-legged hawks, *Buteo lagopus*; and great horned owls, *Bubo virginianus*. Several species of sparrows occur, as do the mourning dove, *Zenaida macroura;* nighthawk, *Chordeiles minor;* poorwill, *Phalaenoptilus nuttallii;* black-chinned hummingbird, *Archilochus alexandri;* gray flycatcher, *Empidonox wrightii;* northern flicker, *Colaptes auratus;* horned lark, *Eremophila alpestris;* and chukar, *Alectoris chukar.*

Larger mammals found in the Great Basin Desert include the coyote, *Canis latrans;* badger, *Taxidea taxus;* bobcat, *Felis rufus;* bighorn sheep, *Ovis canadensis;* mountain lion, *Felis concolor;* and mule deer, *Odocoileus hemionus.*

FIG. 27. The pronghorn, *Antilocapra americana* (body length approximately 4 feet; weight 90 to 125 pounds), are grazing and browsing animals once abundant in the sagebrush country and the grasslands. They were practically eliminated from most of their range by explorers and settlers. With protection, the species is increasing.

THE DESERTS OF THE SOUTHWEST

Among the interesting large herbivorous mammals of the Great Basin Desert are the wild horses, which were introduced, and the native pronghorn. The wild horses, despite persecution by man, prospered for a period in the sagebrush habitat. These small, extremely alert horses roam in bands controlled by the stallion leader. Although some ranchers heartily dislike the horses, many other people admire their spirit and see them as symbols of freedom, independence, and the will to survive under adverse circumstances.

The pronghorn, *Antilocapra americana,* is the only living species of its family. Pronghorns were once abundant from southern Canada to the plateaus of Mexico, and from California to the Mississippi Valley. So pressured by hunting did they become that they were virtually eliminated from most of their area. Protected by law for many years, they are now more numerous, although still limited in numbers. Once again, in some states, they are hunted in season. These relatively small herbivores are sometimes incorrectly called antelope. Bucks average approximately 115 pounds; does, approximately 90. The upper portions of the animal are deep tan, and the rump, underportions, and two bands across the neck are white. Both sexes have unique horns. The outer sheath has a forward-projecting prong approximately halfway between base and tip. The sheath is shed each fall; its replacement starts developing from the end of the remaining bony core and extends downward to the base of the core. The pronghorn are well equipped for the temperature extremes of their desert environment, with thick, tubular hair containing large air cells. With their heavy hair layer lying close to the skin in winter, they are well insulated. Each hair, however, can be elevated or depressed as needed. In warm temperatures, the hair can be held somewhat erect, allowing air circulation to the skin.

Pronghorns graze and browse, eating grass and shrubs, such as rabbit brush and sagebrush. They band into large groups in winter and roam about in summer in smaller bands. Animals of the open grassland and sagebrush, they are extremely alert, have an excellent sense of sight, are constantly on guard against enemies, and yet display great curiosity—a

FIG. 28. The Mohave Desert, smallest of the North American deserts, covers southwestern Nevada, a portion of southeastern California, and barely extends into western Arizona. Included within its boundaries is arid Death Valley, credited with the second highest world's official temperature record, 134.6° F.

trait which contributed to their rapid reduction by hunters. The pronghorns, if alarmed, erect the white hair of the rump patch. The distinctive flash of this white fur serves as an alarm for other herd members. These animals are among the fastest in the world. They have been clocked at 70 mph for three to four minutes at a time, and 30 mph appears to be an easy speed for them. They can make twenty-foot bounds and reportedly can detect movement four miles distant. The sight of pronghorns flashing their white signals, bounding across the terrain at speeds up to 50 miles per hour, is one of the many pleasures to be experienced by the fortunate human observer in the Great Basin Desert.


CHAPTER VII

# The Mohave Desert


THE MOHAVE is the smallest of the four North American deserts. It lies primarily in California but also includes the approximate southern quarter of Nevada and projects two small extensions into west-central and northwestern Arizona. Basically it extends eastward from the southern end of the Sierra Nevada Mountains in southern California to the Colorado River on its eastern border, and northward and eastward from the San Bernardino Mountains to the point where creosote bush largely disappears and the Mohave blends into the Great Basin Desert. The western and southern sections of the Mohave, flanked on their borders by mountains, lie at the desert's highest elevations—approximately 5,000 feet; from these high sections, the desert gradually slopes toward the Colorado River at near sea level. The elevation of three-fourths of the Mohave Desert is between 2,000 and 4,000 feet.

For the most part, this desert's topography is of the basin-and-range type; the area contains numerous north-south-trending mountain ranges. A higher percentage of area is covered by mountains in the Mohave than in the adjoining Great Basin. The Colorado River lies along or briefly enters portions of the Mohave's eastern border. Two occasional waterways cut the desert. The Mohave River rises in the adjoining San Bernardino Mountains, flows north-northwest more than 100 miles, and dies in the desert in an alkaline flat. The Amargosa River (Amargosa means "bitter") originates in the desert itself and terminates in Death Valley. Limited amounts of drainage do flow to the Colorado River but, for the most part, the Mohave Desert is a land of undrained basins. This desert, like its Great Basin neighbor, was once, at the end of the last ice age, a wetter, lake-dotted area. At that time, major rivers drained into a series of lakes. One of these lakes, located in Death Valley, received the water from both the Mohave and Amargosa. Even today, populations of tiny pupfish remain in isolated small bodies of water in the Mohave Desert as remnants of the populations that once resided in the plentiful waters.

Precipitation decreases in the Mohave Desert from west to east. The western portions receive approximately five inches annual precipitation; the eastern portions approximately two inches. In some areas, however, rainfall is extremely irregular. Bagdad, California, in the southeastern Mohave Desert, is credited with the United States' record for the longest period without measurable rainfall—767 days. Rainfall is received primarily in the winter months, although in the Mohave's eastern portions, in particular, occasional summer thunderstorms occur in scattered locations. Severe frosts occur only in the western sections; snow may fall in the more elevated portions but seldom lasts for any length of time.

The Mohave Desert is subject to certain generalizations. It is, like the Great Basin, a shrub-dominated desert but is more arid than its northern neighbor. Ephemerals in the Mohave appear primarily in the spring—late March, April, and May—although summer storms may bring the later blossoming of some species. Cacti species are limited, although more are found in the Mohave than in the Great Basin; the cacti species are primarily prickly pear and cholla. Tree species are limited, although the Mohave's most distinguished plant is the Joshua tree, *Yucca brevifolia*. Forrest Shreve described the Mohave Desert as characterized by a limited display of life forms and a simple composition of most communities, and as exhibiting a very strong control of the distribution of its vegetation by the texture and salt content of the soil. Approximately one-fourth of the Mohave's plant species are endemic, restricted to this particular desert.

The averages and generalizations for the Mohave Desert as a whole must be modified to fit its most infamous portion, Death Valley, which is described geologically as a graben. As defined by Webster's, a *graben* is "a depressed segment of the earth's crust bounded on at least two sides by faults and generally of considerable length as compared with its width." Death Valley fits the definition well. It is approximately 190 miles long, from five to twenty miles wide, and banked by mountain ranges on both the east (the Grapevine and Funeral ranges) and the west (the Panamints). The mountains rise rapidly from the valley with practically no foothills, only alluvial fans at their bases. In the Panamints the tallest peak reaches 11,045 feet, yet only fifteen miles away, in the trough of Death Valley, the lowest point in the Western Hemisphere—282 feet below sea level—is surrounded by 550 square miles which lie below sea level. In this trough pit, the world's second highest official temperature, 134° F., has been recorded, as has the United States' lowest annual average precipitation, 1.6 inches. Ralph and Florence Welles, collaborators with the National Park Service in an eight-year study of bighorn sheep in Death Valley, found that for the month of July 1959, the average daily maximum air temperature was 120.1° F. Ground-surface temperatures of as high as 190° F. were recorded in 1958. During the Welleses' study, the lowest humidity level recorded was 3 percent. Little wonder that on charts showing expected survival time for man without water, resting in shade and exerting himself not at all, Death Valley

FIG. 29. The cholla cacti, *Opuntia* spp., are composed of a main trunk which supports branches of numerous cylindrical joints. The joints are readily knocked loose from the plant and, because they are heavily spined, easily become attached to the unwary animal or human passing by.

ranks as the most extreme area in the United States. Under these conditions, man could expect to survive no more and perhaps less than two days during the month of July.

From its known conditions of heat and aridity, its stark, sere, but geologically fascinating terrain, and its folkloric reputation as the devil's domain, Death Valley is an obvious candidate for the classification of a lifeless desert land. It comes as somewhat of a surprise then to learn that Death Valley National Monument, covering approximately 3,000 square miles, has a total of more than 600 species of native plants, including some, such as the Death Valley sage, *Salvia funerea*, which are found nowhere else. Several hundred major animal species are reported to be present in the Death Valley area. The casual visitor may not see even a small fraction of this number. Some bird species, for example, may be transients or may be present only part of the year; other species may retreat limited distances up the mountainsides during the periods of greatest heat and aridity; and those desert-wise species who brave the desert floor will do so only when optimum conditions for their well-being prevail, as at night or during the winter months.

Sagebrush ranges down from the Great Basin into the Death Valley area. Creosote bush, *Larrea tridentata,* in concert with white bursage, *Ambrosia dumosa,* is present. In many areas where the soil is alkaline, salt-tolerant plants such as the familiar shadscale grow. The Welleses' bighorn sheep study revealed that the sheep, ranging along the lower mountainsides, alluvial fans, and into the valley, fed on at least forty-three different plants. Among those plants grazed or browsed were: galleta grass, *Hilaria jamesii;* evening primrose, *Oenothera* spp.; alkali sacaton, *Sporobolus airoides;* Mohave aster, *Machaeranthera tortifolia;* white brittlebush, *Encelia farinosa;* Mormon tea, *Ephedra nevadensis;* and mallow, *Sphaeralcea* spp. Occasionally the mesquite, *Prosopis juliflora,* was eaten. The sheep's most dependable food, year-round, was desert holly, *Atriplex hymenelytra.* Desert holly, as a member of the genus *Atriplex,* is one of the so-called salt bushes. Its silvery leaves and large, light green, disk-shaped, succulent fruiting bracts make this plant attractive; obviously, it is of great importance to the bighorn.

The bighorn is among the most interesting inhabitants of Death Valley. It is approximately the size of a small deer, or about four feet in head-and-body length; the relatively small desert subspecies weighs 100 to 200 pounds. The horns of the mature males are gigantic, forming massive spirals—arched backward, then curved forward. The females' horns are smaller, rarely forming a half circle. The horns are never shed. The animal's color is a grayish-brown with a lighter abdomen. The bighorn is thought to have ranged much more widely prior to modern man's takeover of the countryside. Today these animals occupy the remote mountain slopes and peaks where they have less competition for food and a measure of protection from enemies—primarily man.

The Welleses' study determined that the Death Valley Desert bighorn need water the year round, drinking every three to five days in hot, dry weather and every ten to fourteen days in cold weather. They move about in small bands, usually in a family group, often made up of three to five individuals. Infant mortality was high, but of those surviving the first year of life, most lived about ten years. On the basis of their study,

FIG. 30.   White bursage, or burro weed, *Ambrosia dumosa* (approximately 1 to 1½ feet in height), is a low, bushy shrub associated with creosote bush over vast arid portions of the Sonoran Desert. The plants are low and rounded with numerous branches, the leaves and branchlets whitened by a cover of short hairs.

FIG. 31.   The screwbean mesquite, *Prosopis pubescens,* is characterized by tightly coiled seed pods, as compared to the straight pods of the other mesquites. The plant may assume shrub size or that of a small tree, to 30 feet in height. It ranges along desert streams from California to southern Nevada and Utah, into New Mexico and Texas, then south in both mainland and peninsular Mexico.

the Welleses listed some traits of the bighorn sheep which aid in their success in the desert environment: (1) They eat very little of any one plant at a time; since they travel constantly while feeding, they seldom destroy vegetation. (2) They are dispersed widely in small bands, and thus do not exert population pressure on their environment. (3) They are able to subsist for long periods on completely dormant or dead plant material. (4) Green forage is used, when available, to supply at least a part of the sheep's water needs, allowing them to range some distance from surface water sources in their search for food.

The Welleses reached the conclusion that predation by

wild animals plays very little part in bighorn mortality, at least in the Death Valley area, although possible predators were noted to be present: mountain lions, coyotes, bobcats, and golden eagles. They concluded that the world's supreme predator—man—is the bighorn sheep's greatest danger. Hunting, mining, expropriation of water and range, introduction of disease through livestock, introduction of burros, encroachment of housing, and building of highways across the ranges of these extremely timid, retiring animals—all have taken and continue to take a toll of the bighorn populations. Highways are a major menace, often isolating one mountain range from another, blocking the travels of the sheep which will not approach or attempt to cross the busy roadways.

Feral burros, offspring of individuals escaped or released by prospectors, miners, and other desert dwellers in the past, are present not only in Death Valley but in many parts of the North American desert. These alert, tough little animals are extremely well suited to desert life. They are capable of covering long distances in the heat, enduring rather extreme dehydration, and then hydrating rapidly once waterholes have been reached. Additionally they will deign to eat almost any plant available. The end result at times is pressure on the native wildlife.

Burros are charged with monopolizing and fouling waterholes, discouraging the shy, quiet-loving bighorns from coming to water as often as needed; consuming water and forage needed by the bighorns; and trampling and killing vegetation around waterholes where it is most needed by the sheep—also thereby destroying habitat normally used by smaller, less obvious, but nonetheless important animal species.

The list of Death Valley's pressured animals extends from bighorn to small fish. The approximately two-inch-long pupfish of Death Valley National Monument are a relict population from a moister past. The pupfish, *Cyprinodon* spp., live in small, often very saline bodies of water in which temperatures fluctuate greatly on an annual basis, reaching high levels during summer months. Five species of pupfish occur in the Monument. Irrigation and consequent drops in water levels,

FIG. 32. Approximately 22 species of wood rats, or pack rats, *Neotoma,* are found from northwestern Canada to Central America. These rats vary from about 12 to 16 inches, including tail, and build large nest-homes of piles of debris. Desert species readily incorporate cactus pieces into their nests; they also consume a great deal of cactus, which supplies moisture.

plus the introduction of other fish species into desert fish habitats, severely threaten native species such as those in Death Valley.

Death Valley's five species of pupfish, plus four other species of small fish found there, unlikely as their presence may seem in the United States' hottest, driest area, are joined by other species of another unlikely type—the amphibians: red-spotted toad, *Bufo punctatus,* and bullfrog, *Rana catesbeiana.* Thirty-six reptiles, seventeen of them snake species, occur in the Monument, including the Mohave Desert sidewinder, *Crotalus cerastes cerastes;* Panamint rattler, *Crotalus mitchelli stephensi;* western black-headed snake, *Tantilla planiceps utahensis;* desert rosy boa, *Lichanura trivirgata gracia;* and western blind snake, *Leptotyphlops humilis.* Over 300 species of birds have been recorded in the Monument, and fifty-three mammal species occur. These include several species of bats; a variety of species of mice; pocket gopher, *Thomomys bottae;* four species of kangaroo rats; pack rats; blacktail jackrabbit; desert cottontail rabbit, *Sylvilagus audubonii;* ringtail cat,

THE DESERTS OF THE SOUTHWEST

*Bassariscus astutus;* antelope ground squirrel; kit fox, *Vulpes macrotis;* gray fox, *Urocyon cinereoargenteus;* coyote; bobcat; mountain lion; mule deer; and wild horses. Despite its name, this valley and its surrounding area appear to hold more life than death.

The Joshua tree, popular symbol of the Mohave Desert, is the object of varying emotions. An early traveler through the Mohave called them "dagger trees," the Mormons christened them "Joshua trees," and Captain John C. Frémont described them as "the most repulsive tree in the vegetable kingdom." Certainly this tree yucca is the distinctive ecological dominant in the area in which it occurs, yet its pattern of occurrence is disjunct. For although the range of the Joshua tree follows rather closely the boundaries set for the Mohave Desert, this plant occurs typically only along the higher edges of the desert. As one moves outward from the mountains to lower elevations, the Joshua trees become smaller and fewer. Eventually, stands of creosote bush, with associated species, become the dominant vegetation. Communities of creosote and bursage, *Ambrosia deltoidea,* reminiscent of large portions of the Sonoran Desert's landscape, actually cover approximately 70 percent of the surface of the Mohave Desert. In the ecosystems dominated by Joshua trees, however, the finest, most interesting development of the Mohave Desert's flora and fauna occurs.

Some of the prime stands of the Joshua tree occur in Joshua Tree National Monument. In this area, the trees, their accompanying plant species, and interrelated animal species have been protected and well studied. The Monument is located in southeastern California, well south of Death Valley, and just east of the San Bernardino Mountains, which form a portion of the edge of the Mohave Desert. The Monument, 872 square miles in area, lies along the junction of the Mohave Desert to the north (of which it is a part) and the Colorado section of the Sonoran Desert to the south. Rainfall averages approximately 4 to 4¼ inches per year over much of the lower area, most received during December and January, with occasional scattered storms occurring from July to October. The Joshua trees require more moisture than this limited amount.

They grow at higher elevations where increased precipitation is received and where runoff from adjoining, even higher elevations, reaches them. The range of the Joshua trees was once greater, when moisture in the area of the Mohave was more plentiful.

Although the Joshua tree habitat is of primary interest in this desert area, other dominant plants exist in portions of the Monument and the surrounding desert. Creosote bush belts occur at lower elevations, up to approximately 3,000 feet; yuccas dominate from 3,000 to approximately 4,200 feet; above that lies a piñon belt. A study of the vertebrate animals of the Monument by Alden H. Miller and Robert C. Stebbins of the University of California at Berkeley listed species members of some of these habitats. For the Monument as a whole, including the piñon belt, they recorded a total of 5 species of amphibians, 36 reptiles, 167 birds, and 42 mammals.

The creosote-bush habitat covers expanses of the valleys and alluvial fans of the Monument; regularly occurring animals include the Merriam kangaroo rat, *Dipodomys merriami;* desert tortoise, *Gopherus agassizii;* antelope ground squirrel; and the black-throated sparrow, *Amphispiza bilineata.* Some communities are dominated by Bigelow cholla cactus, *Opuntia bigelovii.* Among the animals Miller and Stebbins listed as occurring in these cactus communities are black-throated sparrows; house finches, *Carpodacus mexicanus;* and particularly wood or pack rats, which often incorporate quantities of cholla joints in the exterior of their house-mounds. Along the washes, other communities occur. Smoke trees, *Dalea spinosa;* desert willows, *Chilopsis linearis;* catclaw, *Acacia greggii;* and mesquite, *Prosopis* spp., all grow in this more moisture-favorable environment. Birds are attracted to the tree habitat, including verdins, *Auriparus flaviceps;* phainopepla, *Phainopepla nitens;* roadrunner, *Geococcyx californianus;* Costa's hummingbirds, *Calypte costae;* and mockingbird, *Mimus polyglottos.* Occasional oases occur, allowing a growth of cottonwood trees, *Populus fremontii;* mesquites; willows; and California fan palms, *Washingtonia filifera.* Many species of animals are drawn to the oases for water, plant food, and prey. Among these species are the

FIG. 33. The Gambel's, or desert, quail, *Callipepla gambelii* (10 to 11½ inches) is a plump, chickenlike bird. The body is gray with markings of buff, chestnut, and white; the male has a black throat and belly. A particularly striking slender topknot of dark feathers curves forward from the top of the head. These birds come to water when it is available, but derive much of the moisture they need from green plant foods.

hooded oriole, *Icterus cucullatus*; brown towhee, *Pipilo fuscus*; mourning dove; Gambel's quail, *Callipepla gambelii*; house finch; coyote; mule deer; mountain sheep; and several species of bats.

Despite Frémont's opinion, many people do not find the Joshua tree ugly, though it does differ greatly from the more familiar trees of Frémont's moister home territory. The Joshua tree is a tree-sized yucca. All yuccas are members of the lily family, though their grizzled exterior would seem to belie the family relationship. Yuccas are shrubs or trees which develop from a *caudex*, or stem base, and are sometimes branched. They have clusters of sharp-pointed, long, narrow, stiff, bayonetlike leaves, which, when dead, may form a *shag*, or "skirt," about the trunk or branch. The Joshua tree normally has a single trunk which often branches a short distance above the ground. The end of each terminal branch is encircled by a mass of leaves. Eventually, a flower cluster is produced at the branch terminus. Following blossoming, the branch forks. Other factors, such as insect damage to the tip,

FIG. 34. The Joshua tree, *Yucca brevifolia,* is the largest yucca in the United States. This species' range is confined to the Mohave Desert. Clusters of leaves grow near the end of each branch, where the plant's clustered flowers are also produced. Following flowering on each individual branch, the branch then forks. These trees attain an average height of 20 to 30 feet but occasionally grow taller.

may also cause a branching. In time, the many-limbed yucca assumes tree form.

The Joshua tree may reach thirty feet, or occasionally even forty feet, in height; one has been recorded as having a diameter of four feet. The bark resembles a corky rind, rough and broken by fissures. The trunk interior contains no solid cylinder of wood, hence no growth rings; rather, it is composed of pith, which may eventually disintegrate to some degree, leaving a partially hollow cylinder. Large, branched clusters of blossoms appear in the spring; each individual flower is 1½ to 2¾ inches in length. These blossoms are dull-green to cream in color; they open for a single night, and bear an odor likened

THE DESERTS OF THE SOUTHWEST

FIG. 35. The desert night lizard, *Xantusia vigilis* (1½ to 1¾ inches, snout-vent length), is gray, olive, to dark brown, speckled with black. This small secretive lizard is often found under Joshua tree debris, but is also associated with other species of yuccas, agaves, cardon cacti, and occasionally ranges into the piñon-juniper belt.

to mushrooms. The fruit is a large six-celled pod with compressed, thin, black seeds. The roots extend both vertically (although not to any great depth) and horizontally; new trees often grow from underground runners.

Joshua trees form "forests" in which they are joined by such other plants as sagebrush; creosote bush; goldenhead, *Acamptopappus schockleyi;* and others. Also occurring in the Mohave Desert is another important species of yucca, smaller than the Joshua tree—the Mohave yucca, *Yucca schidigera.* The Joshua trees, as the dominant and tallest species in their habitat, serve in varying ways as bases for animal life. One animal species exceedingly dependent upon these and other yuccas is the yucca moth.

The fertilization of flowers by insects inadvertently carrying pollen from one to another is a familiar story, but the yucca's relationship with small white moths of the genera *Tegeticula* and *Parategiticula* is deeper. The moth larvae develop within the yucca fruit, devouring a portion of the developing yucca seeds. Through her actions, the female moth instinctively assures that seeds will develop for these young. When yucca flowers blossom, they are visited by the female yucca moth. Moving from one flower to another, the female moth gathers pollen which gradually forms into a large ball carried under her head. Moving to yet another flower, the moth climbs part way up the pistil, or female portion of the plant, inserts her ovipositor into the plant's ovary, and lays her eggs. Then she climbs to the top of the pistil and with her head rubs some of the pollen she carries into the flower's stigma. In so doing, she has achieved fertilization of the flower and insured seed production for her young. The larvae eat only part of the seeds, bore their way through the capsule wall, fall to the ground, enter it, and remain there until the following year, when they emerge as adults to repeat the process. This behavior is indeed remarkable, for the moth collects a material for which she has no direct need and uses this material to bring about a result she cannot perceive. The material gathered and the action undertaken are of no direct benefit to her, yet they benefit the species as a whole. Certainly her action benefits the yuccas also, which appear to be dependent on the yucca moths for fertilization. This symbiotic relationship is so close that as different species of yuccas have evolved, so also have different associated species of moths.

Another animal species very closely affiliated with the Joshua tree is the small desert night lizard, *Xantusia vigilis*, often referred to as the yucca night lizard. Only 1½ to 1¾ inches in snout-to-vent length plus tail, this lizard superficially resembles the geckos, the night-active lizards also having a rather velvety-appearing skin. Night lizards are yellow, gray to brown, with black speckling. They occur in desert areas from southern California, Nevada, and Utah to Sonora and southern Baja California. The night lizard has achieved success in its desert environment by using the microhabitat provided by the Joshua tree. The lizard lives in the spiny branches and in and under the plants' litter or fallen branches. Shade, with attendant reduced temperatures; protection from desiccation;

FIG. 36.   The Scott's oriole, *Icterus parisorum* (7¼ to 8¼ inches), is a handsome bird. The male is lemon-yellow with a black head, wings, and tail; the female is a duller, greenish yellow. This oriole is often found in the Joshua tree forests, where its pouched nest hangs from these yuccas, although it also ranges into oak and piñon country.

protective cover from predators; food—all are provided for the night lizard in its tiny world by the tree, its debris, or the other creatures attracted to these. The lizard feeds on spiders, caterpillars, ants, beetles, crickets, termites, flies, and other moisture-filled food. *Xantusia vigilis* is also found associated with some other species of yuccas and occasionally with other plants, such as sagebrush, but the optimum conditions for this lizard are provided by the bulk of the Joshua tree and its debris. Most often night active, as indicated by its name, *X. vigilis* is also sometimes active diurnally when conditions are favorable to it.

An interesting Joshua tree–animal association of times past was that of the plant with the extinct giant ground sloth. Fossilized sloth dung found in Gypsum Cave in 1930 near Las Vegas, Nevada, revealed that approximately 80 percent of the diet of those animals consisted of Joshua tree leaves.

Birds are among the great appreciators of the Joshua trees. The author Edmund C. Jaeger reported that at least twenty-

FIG. 37. The ladder-backed woodpecker, *Picoides scalaris*, is small (6 to 7½ inches), cross-barred with black and white on the back, wings, and sides of the tail. The crown of the male's head is marked with red. It is the only woodpecker in the desert with a black-and-white-striped face. This bird drills holes in trees, agaves, and yuccas, including the Joshua trees.

five species of desert birds use the Joshua tree as nesting sites. Among these species is the Scott's oriole, *Icterus parisorum.* These beautiful birds breed from southeastern California, southern Nevada, north-central New Mexico, and western Texas far south into Mexico. They live and breed in the Joshua tree country in summer, hanging nests constructed of yucca fibers from the Joshua trees. They feed from the flowers of this yucca, eat portions of the fruiting pods, and consume insects—all of which are moisture-rich.

The red-shafted flicker, *Colaptes auratus,* and the ladder-backed woodpecker, *Picoides scalaris,* are among the birds excavating holes in the branches of the Joshua trees. Later, their abandoned holes are occupied by a good many other bird species, including the ash-throated flycatcher, *Myiarchus cinerascens;* western bluebird, *Sialia mexicana;* and Bewick's wren, *Thryomanes bewickii.* Other bird species use the Joshua trees as vantage points from which to search for prey.

Fig. 38. The sparrow hawk, or American kestrel, *Falco sparverius* (9 to 12 inches) is a small falcon, about the size of a jay. The species is found over most of North and South America. This beautiful bird is brownish, with a black-and-white face pattern; the males have blue-gray wings. Among its nesting sites are cavities in saguaro cacti.

The screech owl perches there by night, and the American kestrel, *Falco sparverius*, by day. The loggerhead shrike, *Lanius ludovicianus*, is one of the many species which may seek shade under the Joshua's spiny leaves.

Pack rats sometimes climb the Joshua trees and cut leaves from the plant. These they incorporate into their nests, which are sometimes constructed around the bases of the Joshua trees. Debris under these trees is also used as cover by other creatures—insect, reptile, and mammal.

The animal life in the Joshua tree habitat is, in fact, high in species. Miller and Stebbins reported four amphibian species, twenty-five reptiles, fifty birds, and twenty-eight mammals, all occurring in the Joshua tree community within the Monument.

Amphibians include the western toad, red-spotted toad, California treefrog, and Pacific treefrog. In the reptile group the desert tortoise occurs, as do ten species of lizards: the

39

40

FIG. 39. Cicadas (approximately 1 to 2 inches in length) "sing" loudly and shrilly by vibrating membranes stretched over a pair of sound chambers situated one on each side, near the base of the abdomen. This noise is often heard midday even on very hot days. Eggs are laid in twigs; the newly hatched young drop to the ground and burrow into it. Underground, the insect feeds on juices of plant roots. Later it emerges, hangs from a plant or object, the skin splits down the back, and the adult emerges.

FIG. 40. Unlike most lizards, the western banded gecko, *Coleonyx variegatus,* is active at night, feeding on insects, spiders, and other arthropods. It is occasionally mistaken as the young of a Gila monster. Adult size is 4 to 6 inches.

banded gecko, collared, leopard, chuckwalla, zebra-tailed, desert spiny, side-blotched, desert horned lizard, and whiptail lizards. Snakes represented are the rosy boa, red racer, western patch-nosed, spotted leaf-nose, glossy, gopher, kingsnake, long-nosed, western shovel nose, night, California lyre, Mojave rattlesnake, speckled rattlesnake, and sidewinder.

The bird list is particularly long: the turkey vulture, red-tailed hawk, golden eagle, prairie falcon, sparrow hawk, Gambel's quail, mountain quail, white-winged dove, mourning dove, roadrunner, barn owl, screech owl, great horned owl, elf owl, poor-will, lesser nighthawk, white-throated swift, red-shafted flicker, ladder-backed woodpecker, western kingbird, Cassin kingbird, ash-throated flycatcher, black phoebe, Say

FIG. 41. The great horned owl, *Bubo virginianus* (18 to 25 inches with a four-foot wingspread), is the only "horned" large North American owl and ranges from the tree limit in the Arctic to the Straits of Magellan in South America. Extremely adaptable, feeding largely on rabbits and rodents, the species lives in habitats as diverse as forests and deserts.

FIG. 42. The poor-will, *Phalaenoptilus nuttallii* (7 to 8½ inches) is a crepuscular bird (active at dawn and dusk) which catches insects while in flight. Its familiar song is heard at dusk in the desert. The bird's brownish coloring with delicate black markings affords it camouflage as it rests during the day on the ground or horizontally on limbs. Near Joshua Tree National Monument, this bird was first discovered to enter a state of winter torpor, its body temperature and oxygen usage greatly reduced during the period when its insect food supply is greatly reduced.

FIG. 43. The Le Conte's thrasher, *Toxostoma lecontei* (10 to 11 inches), is a pale grayish-brown bird with a darker tail and a slender, curved beak. These birds are often found in flat, open desert, and spend much of their time foraging on the ground for insects.

phoebe, horned lark, cliff swallow, raven, verdin, Bewick's wren, cactus wren, canyon wren, rock wren, mockingbird, Bendire thrasher, Le Conte thrasher, blue-gray gnatcatcher, black-tailed gnatcatcher, phainopepla, loggerhead shrike, western meadowlark, hooded oriole, Scott's oriole, Bullock

FIG. 44. The verdin, *Auriparus flaviceps*, is a very small (4 to 4½ inches) gray bird with a yellowish head, resident from southeastern California, southern Nevada and Utah, into New Mexico, Texas, and Mexico. Its enclosed nest consists of thorny twigs and is located in bushes or low trees. Entrance is gained through a vertical passage opening in the side of the nest.

FIG. 45. The western pipistrelle, *Pipistrellus hesperus*, is the smallest bat in the United States and one of the smallest in the world. It has a forearm length of 1 to 1⅙ inches; body length of approximately 3 inches. This true desert bat is in some cases the only bat species found over vast creosote-bush areas. It varies in color from pale yellow to gray to reddish brown

oriole, brown-headed cowbird, house finch, lesser gold-finch, Laurence goldfinch, brown towhee, black-throated sparrow, and the song sparrow are all found among the Joshua trees.

The mammal species represented include: four bats—the California myotis, western pipistrelle, big brown, and pallid; two rabbits—the Audubon cottontail and the black-tailed jackrabbit; the antelope ground squirrel; the Beechey ground squirrel; the pocket gopher; three species of pocket mice; the Merriam kangaroo rat; the western harvest mouse; the cactus mouse; deer mouse; grasshopper mouse; two species of wood or pack rat—the desert and the dusky-footed; the California vole; coyote; kit fox; gray fox; raccoon; badger; bobcat; and mountain sheep.

The list of species is impressively long. Consider, though, its potential length if invertebrate species also present in the Joshua tree habitat were included. Consider also the complexity of the habitat's food web and of other relationships between its living and nonliving components! Obviously, only the human species interprets the Mohave Desert as the home of both the devil and Joshua. Several hundred other species interpret it simply as home—and a very satisfactory one at that!

# CHAPTER VIII

# The Chihuahuan Desert

MAPS PROVIDE interesting reading, particularly maps of the Chihuahuan Desert where place names in English and Spanish give clues to the type of country and something of its history. Dog Canyon, Grave Pit, Elephant Tusk, Backbone Ridge, Cow Heaven Mountain, and Sotol Vista Overlook appear in English, as do Mule Ears Overlook, Dogie Mountain, Maverick Mountain, Adobe Walls Mountain, and Fossil Knob. Across the border appear euphonious Spanish names, such as Laguna Grande and Bolsón de los Muertos (Bolson of the Dead). In Spanish, the word *sierra* often appears, as do the words "mountain" and "peak" in English. Other names indicate the numerous scattered points of higher elevation: Juniper Canyon, Pine Canyon, Lost Mine Peak, Panther Peak. Obviously the Chihuahuan Desert was not tame, flat, green land when it was given these names. Nor is it today. Most of this desert lies in Mexico, is difficult of access, and is less familiar and less thoroughly studied than the desert lands of the United States. In this very isolation lies a good deal of the fascination of the Chihuahuan Desert.

The Rockies and associated ranges divide the North American continent, sweeping from Canada through Mexico. The lowest point of this ridge is located in southeastern Arizona and southwestern New Mexico. No majestic peaks loom over this area of high plain, dotted with small mountains. Desert grassland covers it; to the east lies the northern portion of the Chihuahuan Desert. To the west is the Sonoran. This elevated plain is of sufficient altitude to prevent the two deserts from being contiguous, but is low enough to allow certain plant species to make the crossing from one to the other; hence, small areas in southeastern Arizona resemble the Chihuahuan and are indeed often referred to by some authorities as Chihuahuan Desert.

Limited portions of southern New Mexico and southwestern Texas are Chihuahuan Desert. Over 90 percent of this desert, however, is in Mexico, south of Texas and New Mexico. In Mexico, Chihuahuan Desert covers portions of the states of Chihuahua, Coahuila, Zacatecas, Durango, Nuevo León, and San Luis Potosí. The Mexican portion of this desert primarily occupies a vast intermountain plateau. The Continental Divide regains altitude and grandeur south of the United States–Mexico border, forming the great Sierra Madre Occidental range, which extends north to south in western Mexico. A similar range, the Sierra Madre Oriental, flows north to south in eastern Mexico. These immense mountain ranges, each approximately 800 miles in length and more than 100 miles in breadth, have peaks up to 12,000 feet in elevation. Between these two ranges lies the Chihuahuan Desert plateau.

The Chihuahuan Desert is second in size only to the Great Basin Desert and is the most southern of the four North American deserts, extending even farther south than the Sonoran Desert's southerly Baja California portions. Due to its plateau location, elevations within the Chihuahuan Desert lie primarily above 3,500 feet. Forrest Shreve outlined the physical conditions of this desert. He states that a small percentage of the desert along the Rio Grande lies below 3,000 feet; nearly half of the desert is above 4,000 feet; some of it extends to over 6,000 feet. Precipitation ranges from three to twenty inches, 70 to 80 percent of this occurring between mid-June and mid-September. Summer temperatures average ten to twenty degrees lower than those of the Sonoran Desert. Winter temperatures may reach low levels, with periods of up to seventy-two hours of freezing temperatures. Therefore, although the Chihuahuan Desert lies at rather low southern latitudes, it is of sufficient elevation and receives sufficient of its moisture during the hottest months when it is most needed to have the "desert condition" somewhat ameliorated.

In addition to the two main mountain masses which outline the eastern and western borders of this desert, numerous lesser mountain ranges with a general north-south orientation

FIG. 46. The Chihuahuan Desert is second in size and extends to the lowest southern latitudes of the four North American deserts. This desert is located primarily in Mexico with small portions extending into New Mexico and Texas.

THE DESERTS OF THE SOUTHWEST

jut from the plateau-desert. Notable areas of limestone are found in this desert, and the Sierra Madre Oriental range is composed largely of limestone. Both the limestone and significant deposits of gypsum greatly influence the species of vegetation growing in these locations. The Rio Grande cuts through the northern reaches of the Chihuahuan Desert, providing the most spectacular piece of United States' Chihuahuan Desert in the western Texas Big Bend area—so-called for the lengthy loop in the Rio Grande at that point. This river receives drainage from a portion of the northeastern Chihuahuan Desert; thus water from this desert, unlike that from the other three North American deserts, flows eastward toward the Gulf of Mexico. However, much of the Chihuahuan, like the other three deserts, lacks outlet to the sea and a great deal of the runoff is directed into vast undrained basins, or bolsons.

Summer rain and cold winter temperatures result in a single growing-blossoming season; in this desert, summer-blooming ephemerals, rather than those which bloom in late winter or early spring, assume prime importance. The creosote bush is a familiar dominant in many areas of this shrubby desert. Cacti are more prominent than in the Great Basin and Mohave deserts, but do not assume the importance they do in the Sonoran Desert. *Opuntia* species are well represented, some barrel cacti are present, and smaller cacti species—such as the hedgehogs and mammillarias—are numerous. Large columnar cacti are found only in the extreme southern portions. Trees are relatively few and small, confined largely to waterways or rocky hills. The mesquites, *Prosopis* spp., are one of the main species represented. The Chihuahuan Desert abounds in the leaf-succulent plants, such as agaves, and the semi-succulents, such as yuccas.

As the Great Basin has its sagebrush, the Mohave its Joshua tree, and the Sonoran its saguaro as popular symbols, the Chihuahuan is most noted for the agave known as lechuguilla, *Agave lecheguilla*. This agave grows in great masses or mats over the arid mesas and limestone hills; where it occurs in crowded profusion, it constitutes in a good many human minds a pest and one of the "afflictions" of the desert,

FIG. 47. The lechuguilla, *Agave lecheguilla,* is the symbol of the Chihuahuan Desert where it is exceedingly abundant on arid mesas and limestone cliffs. The individual leaves are approximately 8 to 16 inches in length, each with a terminal spine. The flower stalk reaches 6 to 13 feet in height.

FIG. 48. *Yucca elata* is a handsome plant with a trunk from 6 to 15 feet high, which may have two or three branches. The leaves are ten to twenty-six inches long, narrow, and thin. When dead, they bend downward to lie along the branch. A panicle of white flowers is produced from a naked flowering stalk.

jabbing legs and ankles of man and beast, causing a sharp, lingering pain, and capable of severely injuring horses' legs and hooves. This character would seem to belie the generic name of these plants, *Agave,* from the Greek word meaning "noble" or "admirable." Common names for various species of agaves include maguey, amole, mescal, century plant (erroneously thought to blossom only after 100 years of growth), and lechuguilla (diminutive of *lechuga,* or little lettuce).

The agaves are succulent-leaved to varying degrees. The leaves are arranged in a basal rosette on the ground around a very short stem, are evergreen, tough, narrow, long, and thick. Each leaf ends in a short, sharp, terminal spine; often lesser spines, prickles, or threads grow along their margins. After a lifespan of several years, each agave blooms a single time, then dies. At blossoming, a naked, tall flower stalk is quickly produced, which bears numerous succulent flowers in its upper portions. Occasionally agaves are confused with yuccas. Yuccas usually have trunks, whereas the agaves in most species grow at ground level; agave leaves are larger and succulent; and the agaves die after their single blossoming, whereas the yuccas do not. Agaves produce seeds in three-celled capsules, but also grow by means of underground sprouts; hence, where favorable conditions prevail, the agaves may grow in vast colonies, as in the case of the Chihuahua's lechuguilla.

Agaves as a group have long been important to man. The leaves are a source of fiber. Industrial alcohol, as well as such alcoholic drinks as mescal, tequilla, and pulque, are derived from them. Soap is made from the stems of some species. Indians of Mexico and the United States prized the central stem, crown, or head of the plant as a food. They buried the crown in a stone-lined, previously heated pit where it baked for many hours before being eaten.

Agaves are prominent plants wherever they occur. The lechuguilla is prominent, not so much because of its size, which is relatively small by agave standards, but because of its numbers. *Agave lecheguilla* has ten to thirty leaves, each approximately eight to sixteen inches in length and 1 to 1½ inches in width. These leaves are armed with spines along the margins and with a terminal spine. The flower stalk, when produced, is six to thirteen feet in height; flowers are greenish- or yellowish-white and may sometimes be tinged with purple. The plant occurs up to elevations of approximately 5,000 feet, and ranges from southeastern New Mexico and southwestern Texas south into Mexico, in an area fairly coincident with the borders of the Chihuahuan Desert.

Yuccas, too, form an important element in the vegetation

of portions of the Chihuahuan Desert. Among others these include *Yucca baccata,* *Y. torreyi,* and *Y. elata. Yucca elata* is a fairly large yucca reaching to fifteen feet in height, usually with two or three branches. Its leaves are ten to twenty-six inches in length, only ⅛ to ⁵⁄₁₆ inch wide, thin, and flexible, with the dead ones reflexing and forming a shag along the branches. This species is found in the Sonoran Desert also, and in the desert grasslands. It is notable for its ability to grow in White Sands—the area of immense drifting dunes of gypsum in southeastern New Mexico. *Yucca elata* is a pioneer plant in these areas, which are composed of up to 94 percent granular gypsum. Its roots grow deep, and its upper portions often strive to keep head above drifting dune; thus these plants manage to grow in this location; by their eventual death and decay they help pave the way for other plant species, which use the decayed organic material of the yuccas. Gypsum holds moisture well, retaining much that it receives; hence *Y. elata* finds moisture but very little else to promote its well-being in these spectacular dunes, located near Alamogordo, New Mexico, and now protected as White Sands National Monument.

Agaves are members of the amaryllis family, while yuccas belong to the lily family. The lily family also includes a plant similar in appearance to the yuccas, the sotol, *Dasylirion wheeleri,* sometimes commonly referred to as desert spoon because the base of its leaf resembles a spatula-spoon in shape. Sotol are large plants with a subterranean stem, or one which extends above the ground for only a short distance. The leaves are linear, elongated, ribbonlike, are not spine-tipped, but have prickled edges, and are often numerous, numbering into the hundreds. The flowers are small, whitish, numerous, and produced in an elongate plume atop the flower stalk. This stalk emerges from the center of the leaf cluster and may reach seven to eight feet in height. As with its near relatives, the plant was used by Indians for fibers, and the flower stalks were roasted and eaten, as was, occasionally, the pulp of the trunk.

Yet another member of the lily family represented in the Chihuahuan Desert is the genus *Nolina,* in some areas re-

ferred to as "bear's grass." These plants, too, bear a similarity
to the yuccas, although they usually appear more grasslike.

One of the interesting Chihuahuan plants is candelilla, *Euphorbia antisyphilitica*. This plant is made up of numerous,
pencil-thin, pale-green, waxy stems, which contain a milky sap.
The stems are practically leafless and closely bunched; the
plant reaches one to three feet in height. The wax may be removed from the stems by boiling them in water to which sulfuric acid has been added. The wax, skimmed off the top, can
be sold for use in floor waxes and chewing gum; collecting this
wax is a part-time occupation of some Mexican citizens.

The guayule, *Parthenium argentatum*, like the candelilla, is
a plant of the limestone areas and is yet another distinctive
plant of the Chihuahuan Desert. This low-branching shrub
with narrow, silvery leaves has stems which yield a high percentage of rubber when processed; the plant was, for a time,
cultivated in the United States for that purpose.

FIG. 49.   Sotol, *Dasylirion* spp., is a large plant resembling yuccas
and species of *Nolina*. Flowers of the sotol are produced in dense
panicles.

FIG. 50.   The candelilla, *Euphorbia antisyphilitica*, is a plant of
the Chihuahuan Desert. The numerous stems from 1 to 3 feet in
height are clustered and appear almost leafless. The stems are wax-covered; hence another common name is waxplant.

Certainly two of the very characteristic plants of the Chihuahuan Desert, also found in other North American deserts, are the creosote bush and the ocotillo, *Fouquieria splendens.* Creosote is the ubiquitous, drought-resistant, enduring plant widespread throughout the three southern deserts; the northern line along which it disappears is, in general, the southern boundary of the Great Basin Desert. In Mexico, creosote bush is given the common name *hediondilla,* or literally "little stinker." The name refers to the plant's odor. Particularly when dampened by a shower or when its leaves are crushed, the plant gives off an odor somewhat reminiscent of creosote. Actually, a good many desert-oriented individuals find the odor quite pleasing, often associating it with the arrival of moisture in the desert. Yet another common Mexican name is *gobernador,* or governor, referring to its dominance over vast areas.

The creosote bush has no main trunk, but rather several or many main branches, which arise from a root crown. The many branches and their lateral twigs bear numerous small, evergreen, resin-coated, moisture-conserving leaves. Under moisture stress many, but not all, of the leaves are lost. Following rains, the bush produces many small yellow flowers which become white, hairy seed capsules. The plant may reach twelve feet in height under favorable conditions. More often it is three to six feet tall. The bushes are widely spaced, each sucking up moisture for some distance around itself. The intervening spaces are often dotted by one or two smaller plant species. The creosote sparsely covers areas where nothing or little else will grow. When moisture is occasionally available, the plant uses it liberally, but has a remarkably well-developed ability to cut back and simply endure when conditions are not propitious. Under such conditions, its color is a pronounced olive-gray and its normal, ethereal, nonsubstantial appearance becomes increasingly less substantial. Its shade is thin, but nonetheless shade for small creatures; its foliage is relished by only a relatively few animals, but feeds some; its roots help hold the desert earth in place and provide neat, reinforced areas under which small animals may dig their burrows; its flimsy branches provide perches for birds; ground squirrels

FIG. 51. The white-footed mice, *Peromyscus* spp. (approximately 7 to 10 inches in total length), are the most widespread rodents in North America, occurring in forests, woodlands, grasslands, and deserts; they live below sea level in Death Valley. They are small to medium-sized mice with soft fur, long whiskers, and a tail not less than one-third the length of the mouse.

FIG. 52. The desert pocket mouse, *Perognathus penicillatus* (approximately 7 inches in length), is one of several species of pocket mice found in the desert. These nocturnal burrow-dwellers store and eat seeds.

and lizards climb into it on occasion; small things can hide from birds of prey under it; and, for humans, the desert would be a much duller, more stark habitat without it.

The ocotillos are among the most distinctive plants of the Sonoran and Chihuahuan deserts. The plant consists of numerous stems, often approximately twenty-five to thirty or more. These straight, normally unbranched stems arise from a short crown, and are approximately ten to twelve feet in length, or occasionally longer. The result is a stiff-looking, fanned-out, stick arrangement, the total group forming an inverted cone shape. The stems are dull gray-green and armed with spines their entire length, each spine having developed from the petiole of a shed leaf. Much of the year, the branches remain leafless. However, within a few days following a shower, the plant produces a new crop of small, green leaves; these are borne up and down the length of each stem. When moisture once again becomes scarce, the leaves are quickly shed. Several crops of leaves thus may be produced each year.

The ocotillos' orange-red flowers are borne on the upper portion of each stem and are often produced when no leaves are present on the plant. The individual stems have long been used in wattle-and-daub construction in the Southwest and Mexico and are sometimes closely planted to form a living fence. The individual stems root and produce leaves following showers, but never branch to form complete plants.

Two smaller, but widespread plants of the Chihuahuan Desert are the varnish leaf acacia, *Acacia vernicosa,* a spiny, low shrub often found on the Chihuahuan Desert plains; and the tar bush, black brush, or hojase, *Flourensia cernua,* a

FIG. 53. Catclaw, *Acacia greggii,* is a shrub or small tree to 23 feet in height and 8 inches in trunk diameter. It is much branched with a broad crown. Fragrant yellow flowers are produced in dense clusters. The spines, which are treacherous and will tear clothing or flesh when they are inadvertently snagged, give the plant its common name.

FIG. 54. The salt bush *Atriplex canescens* is a shrub 3 to 6 feet high which grows on moderately alkaline slopes in both the sagebrush and creosote bush deserts in addition to desert grassland and oak woodland. Its range from eastern Oregon to North Dakota and south into Mexico makes it the most widely distributed species of its genus in the United States.

FIG. 55. Mormon tea, *Ephedra* spp. (often averaging 3 to 4 feet in height), is a low plant with slender, bunched, jointed stems which appear to be leafless; actually, the leaves have been reduced to scales. This primitive-type plant has conelike flowers; female and male flowers grow on different individual plants.

shrub three to six feet high, common on limestone soils in the Chihuahuan Desert.

The area covered by the Chihuahuan Desert is vast. It is bordered by high mountains on two sides and contains more mountains of considerable height within it. Animals that normally live some distance up the mountains thus often enter the desert to some extent. It is dotted by vast bolsons. Some contain dry alkaline lake beds. Others have water fed by springs; for example, Cuatro Cienegas contains a marsh supplied with gypsum-rich water from thermal springs. Water, or lack of it, or the quality of it, affects the biota greatly. The Rio Grande, a major river (although now much emasculated by irrigation use) enters the desert, influencing the animal life in that area. The plant life, too, is varied. The habitat possibilities in this desert are therefore exceedingly numerous, and the animal species and possible interrelationships between the individual animals, the species, and their environments are staggering to imagine.

One area of the Chihuahuan Desert which has been studied and reported upon is that of Big Bend National Park, among the largest of the national parks in the United States, covering 1,106 square miles. Its southern border is the Rio Grande where the river bends first to the southeast, then to the northeast. The confines of the park stretching to the north includes typical Chihuahuan Desert country, as well as mountains rising out of the desert to a maximum elevation of approximately 7,800 feet. Officials have compiled checklists of the animal species which occur in the park. Admittedly, some of these are found in the higher elevations, yet inasmuch as desert terrain is the primary type in the park, these numbers give a good indication of the richness of the desert life. Ten amphibian species have been recorded in the park, 55 reptile species, 382 bird species, and 75 mammal species. Included among the reptile species are four rattlesnakes: Mohave, *Crotalus scutulatus;* western diamondback, *Crotalus atrox;* rock rattlesnake, *Crotalus lepidus;* and the black-tailed, *Crotalus molossus.* Only in this one of the four North American deserts does the secretive copperhead, *Agkistrodon contortrix pictigaster,* dwell. The latter is known to reach as far west as the Davis Mountains and the Big Bend area. It may occur in desert shrublands but is more often found near permanent water.

FIG. 56. The kit fox, *Vulpes macrotis* (approximately 30 inches in total body length), is well adapted for life in the hot, arid desert. Chiefly nocturnal, it sleeps in shade or underground dens during hot periods. Its yellowish-buff hair blends into the desert background at night; the large ears aid it in locating rodent prey, which provides it not only with food but with much of the moisture it needs; and the bottoms of its feet are covered with long fur as an adaptation to the sandy soil.

FIG. 57. The Mexican free-tailed bats, Brazilian free-tailed, or guano bats, *Tadarida brasiliensis* (forearm length of 1½ to 1¾ inches; body length approximately 4 inches), live in immense colonies in caves of the southwestern United States. This species is the famous inhabitant of Carlsbad Caverns. Dark brown to dark gray in color, this bat is rather small with long, narrow wings. Its name derives from the fact that the lower half of the tail is free from the interfemoral membrane.

Among the larger mammals represented are those found ranging over at least some of the other deserts and often other habitats as well: coyote, peccary, mule deer, black-tailed jackrabbit, Audubon cottontail, kit fox, gray fox, badger, ring-tailed cat, bobcat, bats of several species, and an occasional mountain lion. Bighorn sheep are occasionally reported, and pronghorn, once plentiful in the Chihuahuan, are represented in limited number.

The Chihuahuan is a challenging, interesting, beckoning desert to the admirer of dry lands. Some of us who include ourselves in that group, however, regret that we did not experience it earlier. In the last 200 years in the Chihuahuan Desert, modern man has greatly reduced the pronghorn and bighorn and tamed the Rio Grande. One wonders—what will he be able to achieve for the Chihuahuan and its three related North American deserts in the next century and a half?

# CHAPTER IX

# The Sonoran Desert

REPRESENTED WITHIN the Sonoran Desert are more plant life forms, more types of cacti, and more species of plants and animals than in any of the other three North American deserts. The Great Basin, Mohave, and Chihuahuan deserts have cold winters, whereas the Sonoran has mild winters. In the Sonoran, when freezing temperatures occur, they are of short duration. The Sonoran Desert is a subtropical desert, and tropical and subtropical locations tend to have, in general, more plant and animal species than do temperate climates. The biseasonal rainfall pattern of the Sonoran Desert promotes the establishment and growth of more plant species than does a primarily single season rainfall pattern. Also the topography of the Sonoran Desert is extremely varied, ranging from sand dunes, volcanic fields, foothills, mountains, to valleys and plains, as well as large portions of it being bordered by the waters of the Pacific Ocean and the Gulf of California. Thus many types of habitats and microhabitats exist to promote a variety of plant and animal species.

In *A Natural History of the Sonoran Desert,* Dr. Mark Dimmitt states that the Sonoran Desert supports "a rich spectrum of 2000 species of plants, 550 species of vertebrates, and unknown thousands of invertebrate species." The Sonoran Desert represents the "cream" of North American deserts.

Lying like a horseshoe around the head of the Gulf of California, this desert is an elongated area spanning twelve degrees of latitude, reaching as far south as 3 degrees north latitude. The Sonoran is a large desert covering 100,000 square miles. In terms of political boundaries, it covers extreme southeastern California, most of the southern half of Arizona, much of Sonora, most of the Baja California peninsula, and the islands in the Gulf of California. Elevations increase as one moves from west to east across it. Those within the desert are chiefly below 2,000 feet, but range from 235 feet below sea level to 3,500 feet above. Latitude and elevation in varying combinations produce a range of climatic conditions. Forrest Shreve reports that, not uncommonly, parts of the Sonoran have ninety consecutive days with a maximum temperature of 100° F. Located not far south of Death Valley in the Mohave Desert, portions of the Sonoran Desert share similar extremely high temperatures.

High mountains delineate portions of the desert's borders. Others rise above the desert surface, some to elevations great enough to sustain a mountain-related biota. Such mountains are tall enough to produce orographic lifting, causing rain to fall on their flanks and peaks, a great deal of which eventually drains to varying distances into the desert below. One of the primary factors in producing the range of plant species represented in the Sonoran Desert is the biseasonal rainfall pattern, with both winter and summer precipitation. The proportion of summer to winter rainfall increases from west to east, with the eastern desert portions receiving approximately half their allotment in the summer and half in winter. Average annual precipitation varies from Bataques' record 1.2 inches to twelve to fourteen inches on the eastern border.

Much of the Sonoran Desert is within the basin-and-range province; however, this desert, more than the others, has developed a dendritic drainage pattern. The Colorado River bisects it, and several major rivers seasonally flow through it from the western flanks of the Sierra Madres to the Gulf. The Salton Sink, or Basin, is one of the few major undrained basins of the desert. In 1905, due to human error, water from the Colorado River managed to breach its bounds, and before it could be controlled, flooded into the Salton Sink, turning it into today's Salton Sea. The desert encircles the Gulf of California, and the Pacific Ocean forms part of the desert's western border in Baja California. Both bodies of water influence the adjoining dry land and its biota. The boundaries of the Sonoran Desert adjoin or grade into a variety of types of vegetation, ranging from semidesert grassland, Chihuahuan desert scrub, Sonoran desert scrub, Sinaloan thornscrub, to chaparral, and the vegetation of the Mohave Desert. Thus this

FIG. 58. The Sonoran Desert, third in size of the four North American deserts, covers much of southern Arizona, southeastern California, the Baja California peninsula, and the Mexican state of Sonora.

THE DESERTS OF THE SOUTHWEST

FIG. 59. The Sonoran Desert can be divided into six distinct subdivisions on the basis of vegetation.

desert presents plant and animal species possibility of access at its edges; raw material for evolutionary adaptation to this particular desert's conditions has been abundant.

The total result of these many factors has been the development of an arboreal desert—seemingly, but not actually, a contradiction in terms. The Sonoran Desert differs from the other North American deserts in having two distinctive, very visible, life forms—large columnar cacti, such as the saguaro, which often serves as a trademark for this desert, and legume trees, such as palo verdes, mesquites, and ironwoods. These two forms result in a higher visual "profile" for portions of this desert, as compared to the other three deserts, which bear a lower-statured, shrub cover. The Sonoran Desert is sometimes described as a "lush" desert—another contradiction in terms. On the basis of vegetation, this desert is often broken into either six or seven subdivisions. This classification is the work of Forrest Shreve. Much of the information we are presenting is available due to Shreve's exhaustive desert work. Shreve first divided the Sonoran Desert, giving each subdivision both a geographic and a vegetative-classificatory name according to the indicator vegetation in each: (See maps) (1) Lower Colorado Valley or *Larrea-Franseria* (now *Ambrosia*) region; (2) Arizona Upland or *Cercidium-Opuntia* region; (3) Plains of Sonora or *Olneya-Encelia* region; (4) Foothills of Sonora or *Acacia-Prosopis* region; (5) Central Gulf Coast or *Bursera-Jatropha* region; (6) Vizcaino or *Agave-Franseria* (now *Ambrosia*) region; and (7) Magdalena or *Lysiloma-Machaerocereus* (now *Stenocereus*) region. Shreve's Foothills of Sonora subdivision has been reclassified and is no longer considered desert by most ecologists.

The Lower Colorado Valley is the largest, lowest, hottest, and driest of the subdivisions. It lies around the head of the Gulf, extends northward to Needles, California, westward to approximately Indio, California, and eastward to Gila Bend, Arizona. On the Mexican mainland, one leg extends south along the Gulf coast for a long distance, then juts inland. A long narrow strip flows southward along the Baja Gulf coast to Bahia de los Angeles. The Gila River flows east to west across southern Arizona, terminating in the lower Colorado River, which when it carries water that far empties into the head of the Gulf. The Lower Colorado Valley subdivision includes the valleys of the lower Gila and Colorado rivers.

Vast areas of this region consist of gently sloping bajadas, or plains, covered by *Larrea tridentata,* the creosote bush, and *Ambrosia dumosa* or white bur sage. Due to heat and aridity, these two drought-enduring standbys may form up to 95 percent of the plant cover present over these areas. *Ambrosia dumosa* is a small, hemispherical shrub approximately one foot in height with a maze of slender stems. The leaves are silvery green, giving rise to one common name, white bursage. Another name is burro weed, or burro bush—burros are said to be fond of the plant. Often appearing dead, yet alive, white bursage is the commonest plant—even more common than the creosote bush—in the driest, hottest areas of this part of the Sonoran Desert. Certainly whatever it lacks in appearance is more than compensated for by its tenacity and endurance.

Along dry washes in this region grow small trees. Primary species are western honey mesquites, *Prosopis glandulosa;* blue palo verdes, *Cercidium floridum;* ironwood, *Olneya tesota;* and smoke trees, *Dalea spinosa.* Mesquite trees are widespread, significant shrubs or trees of the southwestern deserts and semiarid areas. These hardy trees produce long, straight, nonsplitting seed pods relished by animals and historically collected as a basic food source by many Indians. Their wood has brightened many a desert campfire, provided the posts for innumerable fences, and long served for construction in a wood-scarce land. Passed through the intestinal tracts of cattle, the seeds emerge digested only sufficiently to promote immediate germination. Mesquites have thus been ready-planted in often overgrazed rangeland, further deteriorating it and arousing ranchers' ire. To animals, however, the mesquite is a blessing.

The ironwood is a leguminous tree that occurs almost entirely in the Sonoran Desert, but only in the warmer sections. The gray, rough bark and gray-green foliage make it a handsome, rugged-looking tree. Its blossoms are purple, produced in the late spring. The heart wood is dark and extremely hard—hence the name. It constitutes long-burning desert firewood without equal.

Palo verde (green stick) trees are named for their chlorophyll-bearing, yellow-green trunk and branches. Leaves, when produced during favorable moisture conditions, are exceedingly small and numerous; they are rapidly shed under moisture stress. Photosynthesis is conducted primarily by the trunk and branches. The so-called Mexican palo verde, *Parkinsonia aculeata,* bears long "streamers," portions of the primary leaflets. This species ranges southward to South America and is often planted as an ornamental around homes in desert country. The blue palo verde, *Cercidium floridum,* displays a blue-green color in the branches and leaves. This palo verde grows along the washes, where some underground water is available. In the spring, the tree is covered by masses of yellow flowers, which provide spectacular desert scenery. A third palo verde is the foothill palo verde, *C. microphyllum,* found in much of the Sonoran Desert, except in the more western portions. Its branches are more yellow-green than those of the blue palo verde. The foothill palo verde grows above the washes on the bajada slopes. It, too, becomes a

FIG. 60.   The handsome ironwood tree, *Olneya tesota,* attains a height of 10 to 30 feet. Its bark is gray, the leaves blue-green, and the peatype flowers are purple. The ironwood is a tree of lower, warmer elevations and occurs in southern California and Arizona, then south in Baja California and Sonora.

THE DESERTS OF THE SOUTHWEST

FIG. 61. Palo verde (green stick) trees have trunks and branches, green with chlorophyll, which carry on most of the photosynthesis for the plant. The small leaves are produced only when moisture conditions are favorable. The Mexican palo verde, *Parkinsonia aculeata* (left), is distinguished by its long narrow "streamers." The blue palo verde, *Cercidium floridum* (center), is a tree of the washes in the Sonoran Desert. The foothill palo verde, *Cercidium microphyllum* (right), is the species found on the bajadas and foothills in the same desert. *Parkinsonia* grows to approximately 45 to 50 feet; *Cercidium floridum* to about 30 feet; *Cercidium microphyllum* to about 26 feet.

mass of bright yellow in the spring. The beans of the *Cercidium* were a food source for desert Indians.

Smoke trees grow only in frost-free areas of the Sonoran Desert. So adapted to the desert is this shrub or tree as to have practically dispensed with leaves. Much of the year, the plant stands bare of leaves, and its mass of sharp spine-tipped branches, ashy gray in color, gives rise to its similarity to a puff of smoke over a desert wash, and gives it its common name. The seeds of these trees, like those of some other desert-wash species, are extremely tough and must be abraded before germination is initiated. Germination occurs when moisture conditions are propitious for the plant's growth, as the seeds are tumbled about among the rocks and gravel of the wash during floods. The smoke tree blossoms with deep purple flowers in late May and June.

In the desert, as one ascends rocky slopes or bajadas away from the more level intermountain plains, the vegetational cover often reveals a change in character. The upper elevations, with more rock, provide better anchorage for plants and better opportunity for water penetration. In the Lower Colorado Valley, as one leaves the *Larrea-Ambrosia* plains, palo verdes, ironwoods, ocotillos, barrel cacti, and other cacti species are found. Another plant which often occurs is *Encelia farinosa,* or brittlebush. This handsome plant is a hemispherical shrub usually one or two, occasionally three, feet in height. Its light green, oval leaves are produced twice a year following the two rainy seasons. The large yellow flowers, too, are borne twice a year on long, bare, projecting stems which display the flowers at their tips some distance above the outer limits of the remainder of the plant's vegetation. The green foliage, bright flowers, and composition of the plant as a whole make it most attractive, particularly against the dark lava rocks where it frequently grows.

An outstanding plant found in particular locations in this area is the fan palm, *Washingtonia filifera.* These palms grow in colonies of a few trees in isolated desert canyons in southern California, Baja California, and Mexico. A single colony exists in western Arizona in the Kofa Mountains. Palm trees must have quantities of water for survival, but can tolerate alkaline water well. They are found growing near springs in desert oases. The fan palms are large trees, attaining a height up to fifty feet, or occasionally more, with a trunk-base diameter up to 3½ feet. In the fan palms, the leaf blades are nearly circular in outline, and the divisions or splits in the blade extend half or two-thirds of the way to the base. The result is a palmate arrangement (unlike that of the date palm, a plant introduced and cultivated in southern California, whose leaf blade is elongated and pinnately arranged, divided all the way to the midrib). Old leaves of the fan palm hang downward along the trunk forming a heavy thatch. The tree produces small white male and/or female flowers in June which develop into a hard, blackish fruit. The leaves have long been useful to man, who has used them for thatched roofs and walls; the fruit is edible. Certainly these trees and the accompanying springs

FIG. 62. The California fan palm, *Washingtonia filifera*, may reach 50 or more feet in height. The leaves are fan-shaped; once dead, they hang in a thick thatch against the trunk below the green, living leaves. Palms grow only where water is available to them, but are tolerant of alkaline water.

or seeps serve as important gathering points for birds and other animal life which visit them.

In the Colorado Valley, vast carpets of ephemerals occur in favorable years. These displays primarily follow winter rains and are often outstanding, particularly in the sandy areas.

The Lower Colorado Valley subdivision of the Sonoran Desert is particularly noted for its areas of sand dunes and its volcanic fields. The dunes occur near the head of the Gulf and in the area a short distance to the north, near Yuma, Arizona. Those near Yuma are known as Algodones (Cotton) Dunes; they extend approximately fifty miles in length and are about five miles wide. The other major group of dunes lies just to the east of the upper Gulf in Sonora. They bear the fitting and descriptive name El Gran Desierto. Most outstanding of the little eroded or degraded volcanic areas is the one surrounding Pinacate Peak, just east of El Gran Desierto. Both the dune and volcanic areas are extremely isolated, stark, beautiful desert.

The Arizona Upland is one of the very interesting subdivisions of the Sonoran Desert and one of the best studied. It includes the eastern half of Arizona's portion of the Sonoran Desert and extends well into northern Sonora. To the west and south, it abuts the Lower Colorado Valley subdivision. To its north and east lie mountains. With higher elevations, increased precipitation, and a more favoring biseasonal distribution of rainfall, plant growth is more diversified and plentiful in the Arizona Upland than in the Lower Colorado Valley region. The two genera with which this area is designated are *Cercidium*, the palo verdes, and *Opuntia*, genus of the prickly

FIG. 63. The saguaro cactus, *Carnegiea gigantea*, is the largest cactus found in the United States, reaching up to 50 feet in height, weighing as much as 8 to 10 tons, and living 150 to 200 years.

THE DESERTS OF THE SOUTHWEST

pear and cholla cacti. It is also referred to as a stem-succulent desert, acknowledging the important presence of these plants, particularly the saguaro cactus.

Saguaros, *Carnegiea gigantea*, are the symbol of the Sonoran Desert, although they do not occur throughout this desert. The range of the saguaro is primarily the confines of the Sonoran Desert east of the Colorado River and south into northern mainland Mexico. Only a few specimens occur in California, just across the Colorado River. This massive columnar cactus may reach forty feet or exceptionally more in height. It consists of a single, pleated, cylindrical trunk, which throughout its length is spine-adorned along the ridges. When the plant reaches a height of approximately fifteen to twenty-five feet, it branches, often producing five or more "arms." These arms grow outward from the trunk briefly, then turn upward. A mature plant may weigh seven or eight tons, with three-fourths or more of its weight being water content. Flowers with white petals and yellow centers ring the tips of the individual arms and trunk in the spring. Each flower is pollinated by birds, bats, and insects on the single night and following day that it is open. A fruit is formed, which splits open to reveal a bright red pulp with one or two thousand tiny black seeds. Saguaros may survive for 150 to perhaps 200 years. Certainly each saguaro represents an important focal point around which the lives of many animal species revolve. So important did the Tohono O'odham Indians find its fruit that their annual calendar started the new year with the Month of the Saguaro Fruit Ripening. The fruit was eaten fresh, cooked into a jam, or dried for later use; the seeds were ground for flour; the juice was fermented for an alcoholic beverage used in the dances and celebrations held partially as a measure to bring the summer rains. Today the Tohono O'od-hams continue to collect the saguaro fruit, although they arrive in the saguaro forests in automobiles or pickups rather than by horse or afoot. The best stands of these giant cacti are the forests protected by national monument status just outside Tucson, Arizona.

The Arizona Upland section of the Sonoran Desert contains numerous low mountain ranges and vast bajadas. Be-

FIG. 64. The numerous straight, usually unforked branches of the ocotillo, *Fouquieria splendens,* arise from a short crown and resemble a stick bouquet reaching 8 to 12 or more feet in height. This plant rapidly produces leaves following a moderately heavy rain. Despite the spines, these plants are not cacti.

tween these, on the flatter, gently sloping, lower plains, creosote bush and *Ambrosia* spp. dominate. But as one ascends the bajadas and hills, a richer mixture of vegetation prevails. Saguaros predominate due to their size. But the ocotillos, barrel cacti, prickly pear and cholla cacti, mesquites, palo verdes, and brittlebush are also present. In one small northwestern section where the Arizona Upland plant species meet and briefly mix with those of the Mohave Desert, saguaros and palo verdes grow beside Joshua trees, junipers, and oaks.

The Plains of Sonora subdivision joins the Central Gulf Coast and Lower Colorado Valley subdivisions on its western border, the Arizona Upland to the north, and the former Foothills of Sonora subdivision to the east and south. Its species designation is *Olneya-Encelia,* or ironwood-brittlebush. This subdivision is dominated by trees and shrubs. In addition to ironwood, foothill palo verde and mesquite are important. Here additional species of palo verde are also found, including the Sonoran palo verde, *C. sonorae,* as is another species of ocotillo known as the tree ocotillo, *F. macdougalii.* Organ pipe cactus, *Stenocereus thurberi,* occurs. This large cactus has no main trunk; it branches with five to thirty-five branches at ground level. The plant may reach ten feet in height. The fruit is red, spine-adorned, about the size of a small tennis ball, and tastes a little like watermelon—it is eaten by man and animal. A second common name for this cactus is *pitahaya dulce* (sweet pitahaya). Also present is a similar-appearing cactus, *Lophocereus schottii,* known as old man cactus, or senita. This plant, too, branches at the ground and has several erect arms, but the arms are thicker-ribbed than those of the organ pipe; additionally, many coarse, hairlike spines around the tips of the stems give the old man a bearded look. The plant grows to twelve feet and produces bright red, practically spineless fruit.

The Central Gulf Coast is a subdivision located on opposing portions of the Gulf coast, one on the mainland, the other on the peninsula. Both elongated strips share common vegetational characteristics. This subdivision is noted for its trees with trunks of large diameter and is designated by Shreve as the *Bursera-Jatropha* region.

Fig. 65. The organ pipe cactus, *Stenocereus thurberi,* is a large plant composed of numerous columnar branches 9 to 20 feet in height. This species barely enters the United States in southwestern Arizona. It ranges south in Baja California and Sonora.

*Bursera microphylla* is the distinctive elephant tree, or torote. These trees have disproportionately thick trunks and main branches in relationship to their height, which is often six to ten feet and occasionally greater. The outer layer of the trunk's bark exfoliates in very large, curling pieces, exposing fresh yellow bark beneath. The foliage is dark green and evergreen. Another species of *Bursera* is also present and important in the vegetation—*Bursera hindsiana*, or torchwood, a shrub or small tree to ten feet in height.

*Jatropha cinerea*, or lomboy, is an abundant shrub or tree which may reach twenty feet in height. A member of the Euphorbiaceae, or spurge, family, lomboy has limber, smooth-barked branches. Its leaves are grayish green and are quickly produced following rain, then shed when dryness prevails.

The most distinctive plant of this subdivision is the boojum tree, or cirio, *Fouquieria columnaris*. Cirio refers to the plant's similarity in appearance to a candle. The term "boojum" comes from Lewis Carroll's reference to a strange mythical creature on faraway shores. The boojum is a member of the family Fouquieriaceae, as is the ocotillo, and in many ways it closely resembles a single gigantic ocotillo branch. The boojum is a polelike tree, most often unbranched, which tapers in diameter toward the upper tip and may reach a height of seventy feet. Along the entire length of the trunk are many pencil like, tiny, short branches which bear the small leaves. As with the ocotillos, the boojum's leaves are produced following rains, and several crops a year may be grown. Occasionally some individual plants may branch, often near the top, serving only to increase the plant's bizarre appearance; occasionally, the tip of one bends back down to the ground to form an outlandish arch. Small tassels of tiny white flowers grow at the tip of the trunk or the branches. Great forests of these plants provide the strangest of desert landscapes. The boojums' range is exceedingly restricted; they are found only in Baja California; on Isla Angel de la Guarda, an island in the Gulf; and in one small location on the mainland across the Gulf from the main stands.

A good many of the species widespread over the Sonoran

Desert, including creosote bush, ironwood, ocotillo, mesquite, palo verde, and brittlebush, are also present in the Central Gulf Coast region. Various species of cholla cacti are abundant. The most distinctive cactus of this region, however, is the cardón, *Pachycereus pringlei*. This huge cactus is similar in form to the saguaro, but more massive. The cardón may reach sixty feet in height and weigh ten tons. Its many arms, from five to thirty, branch from the trunk at a point closer to the ground and are directed upward at a sharper angle than those of the saguaro. Cardóns are thought to live occasionally to be 200 years of age. Like the saguaro, the cardóns are often

FIG. 66. The boojum, *Fouquieria columnaris*, is one of the most unusual plants of the desert. Related to the ocotillo, this plant consists of a single, stout column which occasionally forks near the top. Along its trunk or main branches occur many very short, pencil-like branches. The plant may reach a height of 70 feet. It occurs only on the Baja California peninsula, on Isla Angel de la Guarda, and in a single small location on mainland Mexico.

*The Sonoran Desert*

present in large numbers and are the focal point in terms of food, lodging, and even narrow bands of shade for innumerable animals.

Between the mainland and peninsular Gulf Coast sections are numerous Gulf islands. Most lack fresh water. They are covered by vegetation typical of the Gulf Coast subdivision. The animal life on them is varied; the species present on these isolated islands vary from one island to another and are influenced by evolutionary forces working in isolation. The islands are host to many species of sea birds which nest or rest in the extreme desert habitat but live off the Gulf's exceptional bounty. Biologically these islands provide some of the most intriguing, although not exactly typical, areas of the Sonoran Desert. Some hold great forests of cardón and bats, which live among the rocks and fish for their food with their feet in the Gulf water while in flight. Rattlesnakes on one or more islands have dispensed with their rattles, or are in the evolutionary process of doing so.

The Vizcaino region occupies the central third of the Baja California Pacific coast. This portion is extremely arid, receiving strong winds from the Pacific Ocean. Though the winds have a high humidity level, they contribute little moisture to the desert. Although much of this region is stark desert, several distinctive plant species occur within its boundaries. Shreve defined it as an area of leaf-succulent plants, and he applied the designation *Agave-Franseria* (*Ambrosia*).

*Franseria* or *Ambrosia* in this case applies particularly to *A. chenopodifolia,* or bursage. Several species of agaves are represented, including, *A. shawii,* the maguey and *A. cerulata,* the blue agave. The root crowns of these plants formed a very basic and important food source for the Indians of the peninsula. *Yucca valida,* or datilillo, is a plant somewhat resembling the Joshua tree; it may grow to a height of twenty feet. The boojum tree is an important plant of this region, as are the cardón and ocotillo, *Fouquieria diguetii.* Another plant commonly called elephant tree is found in this region. *Pachycormus discolor,* or copalquin, is a squat, very heavy-trunked tree, found only in Baja California. It too displays curling sheets of exfoliating bark. Copalquin, as well as other plants, is sometimes seen covered with dodder—a parasitic, orange plant. Also found growing on cacti, shrubs, and trees is ball moss, or *Tillandsia recurvata,* which resembles a mass of straw or twigs and grows high above the ground attached to another plant. This plant is not a moss, but rather an *epiphyte*—that is, a nonparasitic plant that grows upon another plant or object and derives its moisture and nutrients from the air, rain, and debris that may accumulate about it. *Tillandsia recurvata* is found growing in areas which receive coastal fog; it is similar to the Spanish moss found in the southern United States.

The Magdalena region is composed of the southern portion of the peninsular desert bordering the Pacific coast and extending into the central and east-central portions of the southern peninsula. To the north, it adjoins the Vizcaino and Central Gulf Coast regions; to the south and east, it abuts nondesert regions. Shreve designated the Magdalena as a tree and stem-succulent desert, or the *Lysiloma-Machaerocereus* (now *Stenocereus*) region.

*Lysiloma candidum,* or the palo blanco, is a lovely straight-trunked tree. It has a spreading crown of branches and bright green leaves which contrast with the silvery-white, smooth bark. This light, airy-appearing tree may reach thirty feet in height.

*Stenocereus gummosus,* pitaya agria, or galloping cactus, forms vast thickets of its sprawling and/or erect branches. The plant, its ridged branches armed with long spines, may reach a height of three to ten feet. Its famous but far less abundant relative is *S. eruca,* or creeping devil. This cactus is composed of thick, spined, ridged stems which grow across the ground surface, the growing tip often slightly elevated above the ground. The stem roots as it grows, and eventually the older portions die. The end result is a cactus that does "creep" or advance across the landscape. The stems, up to fifteen feet in length, growing at various angles to one another, their "heads" elevated, resemble gigantic, alert worms advancing across a science fiction landscape. The cardón grows in this region, and cholla, mesquite, peninsular palo verde, peninsular ocotillo, lomboy, and organ pipe cacti also play an important part in the vegetation of this region.

For the most part, animals—particularly birds and larger mammals—are less closely tied to specific type habitats than are plants. Thus a good many of the animal species in any one of the vegetational subdivisions of the Sonoran Desert is likely to be found in one or more of the others. Again, we find the same pyramid of vast numbers of insects and rodents supporting larger and less numerous species, which are themselves often prey to yet larger and even less numerous ones. As the Joshua tree is a dominant species in one habitat, supportive of many animal species ranging from insect to reptile, bird, and mammal, so the dominants in other habitats serve as a focal point for animals. Outstanding examples are the saguaros, cardóns, chollas, and others. The variety of habitats and microhabitats available to animal species in the Sonoran Desert is particularly great, and animal life is rich in numbers and varied in species.

For example, in Saguaro National Monument near Tucson, Arizona, a checklist of species reported from the desert and foothill areas, in which the saguaros and related desert vegetation occur, lists 8 amphibian species, 4 of turtles, 19 lizard, 29 snake, 124 bird, and 69 mammal species.

By no means is the following list of the species of animals in the Sonoran Desert complete, but it provides an indication of some of the important species occurring in that desert, or in certain portions of it.

FIG. 67. Stink beetle, or Pinacate beetle, are two common names for these large (about 1 inch long), black, shiny beetles of the genus *Eleodes*. When disturbed, these insects often elevate the rear portion of the body and as a defensive measure release a foul-smelling, oily fluid from glands located at the tip of the abdomen.

THE DESERTS OF THE SOUTHWEST

FIG. 68. The zebra-tailed lizard, *Callisaurus draconoides* (snout to vent length 2½ to 3½ inches), is a slim-bodied, long-tailed, long-legged lizard adept at running at high speed. The undersurface of the tail is white with black crossbars. When running the lizard curls the tail up over the back displaying the "zebra" tail. This lizard is found in the Sonoran, Mohave, and portions of the Great Basin deserts.

Of the amphibians found in the Sonoran Desert, three examples include: Couch's spadefoot, *Scaphiopus couchi;* red-spotted toad, *Bufo punctatus;* and the Colorado River toad, *Bufo alvarius.*

Reptile species include the desert tortoise, *Gopherus agassizii,* and many lizards: Gila monster, *Heloderma suspectum;* chuckwalla, *Sauromalus obesus;* banded gecko, *Coleonyx variegatus;* desert iguana, *Dipsosaurus dorsalis;* zebra-tailed lizard, *Callisaurus draconoides;* Colorado Desert fringe-toed

FIG. 69. The side-blotched lizard, *Uta stansburiana* (1½ to 2⅓ inches, snout-vent length) is brownish with a blue or black spot on the side of the chest behind the axilla; hence its common name. This lizard is one of the most widespread and abundant of the arid areas, being found in all four North American deserts.

lizard, *Uma notata;* leopard lizard, *Gambelia wislizenii;* collared lizard, *Crotaphytus collaris;* desert spiny lizard, *Sceloporus magister;* long-tailed brush lizard, *Urosaurus graciosus;* side-blotched lizard, *Uta stansburiana;* desert horned lizard, *Phrynosoma platyrhinos;* and flat-tailed horned lizard, *Phrynosoma m'calli.*

The snake species represented are exceedingly numerous. Some of them are: western blind snake, *Leptotyphlops humilis;* rosy boa, *Lichanura trivirgata;* spotted leaf-nosed snake, *Phyllorhynchus decurtatus;* coachwhip, *Masticophis flagellum;* western patch-nosed snake, *Salvadora hexalepis;* gopher snake, *Pituophis melanoleucus;* glossy snake, *Arizona elegans;* kingsnake, *Lampropeltis getulus;* long-nosed snake, *Rhinocheilus lecontei;* western ground snake, *Sonora semiannulata;* western shovel-nosed snake, *Chionactis occipitalis;* banded sand snake, *Chilomeniscus cinctus;* night snake, *Hypsiglena torquata;* Arizona coral snake, *Micruroides euryxanthus;* Sonora lyre snake, *Trimorphodon biscutatus;* black-tailed rattlesnake, *Crotalus molossus;* tiger rattlesnake, *Crotalus tigris;* western diamondback, *Crotalus atrox;* sidewinder, *Crotalus cerastes;* speckled rattlesnake, *Crotalus mitchelli;* and the Mojave rattlesnake, *Crotalus scutulatus.*

FIG. 70. The cactus wren, *Campylorhynchus brunneicapillus,* is a large (7 to 8¾ inches), light brown bird with a heavily spotted breast and a white stripe over the eye. This bird builds numerous large enclosed nests and is adept at constructing and entering these nests from a side entrance even when they are placed in the extremely spiny cholla cactus.

71          72

FIG. 71. The elf owl, *Micrathene whitneyi,* is sparrow-sized (5 to 6 inches) and the smallest owl in the world. It is often associated with the saguaro cacti, living in holes hollowed in these or other trees by woodpeckers. Where the owl occurs, its call is a familiar one at night-fall in the early summer.

FIG. 72. The Gila woodpecker, *Melanerpes uropygialis,* 8 to 10 inches in length, is fawn colored with a black-and-white barred back, wings, and tail. The male sports a round red cap. These birds are prime excavators of holes in the saguaros, which are later used by other bird species.

A very few of the very many bird species include: the road-runner, *Geococcyx californianus;* phainopepla, *Phainopepla nitens;* verdin, *Auriparus flaviceps;* cactus wren, *Campy-lorhynchus brunneicapillus;* elf owl, *Micrathene whitneyi;* brown-crested flycatcher, *Myiarchus tyrannulus;* caracara, *Caracara plancus;* turkey vulture, *Cathartes aura;* Gambel's quail, *Lophortyx gambelii;* Gila woodpecker, *Melanerpes uropygialis;* gilded flicker, *Colaptes chrysoides;* white-necked

FIG. 73. The Harris ground squirrel, *Ammospermophilus harrisii*, is very similar to its California relative, the antelope ground squirrel, *Ammospermophilus leucurus*. Both are approximately 6 inches in length, with a fluffy tail 2 to 4 inches long, which is usually carried curled over the back. The underside of the tail of *A. leucurus* is white; that of *A. harrisii* is gray. These animals are active even on hot days and occasionally climb into vegetation to obtain seeds or foliage.

FIG. 74. The round-tailed ground squirrel, *Spermophilus tereticaudus*, is 5 to 6 inches in body length with a 2- to 4-inch tail. It is readily identified by its pencil like, nonbushy tail. Its color is a pinkish-cinnamon, slightly lighter on the belly. This ground squirrel lives in burrows in the Mohave and Sonoran deserts. The animal is diurnal when active and hibernates during the colder months.

FIG. 75. The blacktail jackrabbit, *Lepus californicus,* occurs in all four North American deserts. Body length of this hare is approximately 18 to 25 inches; ears measure 6 to 7 inches. Vegetation-consuming and largely nocturnal, this rabbit often rests during the day in slight hollows in the soil called forms. This species is marked by black ear tips and a black streak on the top of the tail.

FIG. 76. The ringtail, or cacomistle, *Bassariscus astutus,* is approximately 15 inches in body length with an additional 15 inches of tail. This shy animal inhabits rocky canyons and foothills. It is nocturnal and carnivorous and ranges in favorable habitats from southeastern Oregon to southern Mexico. Pale brown in body color, the ringtail has a bushy tail ringed with alternating black-and-white rings.

*The Sonoran Desert*                                                     145

FIG. 77. The coatimundi, coati, or chulla, *Nasua nasua* (body length of 16 to 24 inches, with a tail approximately the same length), lives basically in Mexico but is extending its range northward in Arizona and New Mexico. Primarily, these animals live in wooded areas and are seen most often in the desert mountains. They travel over the ground or through trees in troupes. The long tail serves for balance and to some extent for grasping.

FIG. 78. The badger, *Taxidea taxus* (body length of 20 to 24 inches), ranges from southern Canada to central Mexico. Flatbodied, a grizzled gray to brown in color with a white abdomen, black-and-white face markings, and a white stripe extending from the nose to approximately the shoulders or further along the back, these animals weigh approximately twenty to thirty pounds. They are powerful diggers, devouring rodents and reptiles, which they often dig out of the earth.

FIG. 79.    The bobcat, *Felis rufus,* is approximately 25 to 30 inches in body length. It is reddish brown, marked with darker spots, and has lighter underparts. The tail is short, approximately 5 inches, and black-tipped; the backs of the ears are black with a white stripe. Throughout their range from western Canada south through Mexico and Central and South America, bobcats are important predators.

FIG. 80.    The collared peccary, javelina, or *Tayassu tajacu* (3 feet in length; 20 to 24 inches high) ranges from southern Arizona, New Mexico, and Texas to South America. It is covered with coarse, grizzled gray hair. These animals travel in bands and prefer brushy areas. They are legally hunted in some areas.

raven, *Corvus corax;* LeConte's thrasher, *Toxostoma lecontei;* white-winged dove, *Zenaida asiatica;* mourning dove, *Zenaida macroura;* curve-billed thrasher, *Toxostoma curvirostre;* western red-tailed hawk, *Buteo jamaicensis;* common poor-will, *Phalaenoptilus nuttallii.*

Mammals of this desert are for the most part represented by others of their own or related species in the other deserts. These include the pocket gopher; deer; pocket, cactus, and grasshopper mice; desert shrew; pack rats; kangaroo rats; various ground squirrels, such as the Harris, antelope, and round-tailed; rabbits, including the desert cottontail, blacktail jackrabbit, and antelope jackrabbit; skunks of various species; gray fox; kit fox; coyote; ringtail cat; coatimundi; badger; bobcat; peccary; mule deer; mountain lion; bighorn sheep; and pronghorn.

Webster's gives one definition of desert as "desolate, sparsely occupied, or unoccupied." Obviously Webster never visited the desert known as the Sonoran.

CHAPTER X

# Planning Desert Exploration and Enjoyment

INTELLIGENT PREPARATION and common-sense execution often provide the difference between an enjoyable and a miserable desert exploration. They may occasionally provide the difference between life and death. Many books have been written on camping, hiking, and backpacking equipment and techniques, and others are constantly being added to the list. In this book, we are concerned primarily with factors of particular significance to desert exploration and enjoyment. We concentrate on the two most problematic factors associated with the desert environment: heat and aridity. Cold weather can also occasionally provide the desert outdoor enthusiast with difficult problems—including snow and freezing temperatures—particularly in the higher desert regions such as those in the Great Basin Desert. Numerous publications present information on how to cope with cold weather stress, and thus this problem will not be our primary concern.

All degrees of desert exploratory activity are possible. They range from simple sightseeing in the family vehicle along desert highways and in parks and monuments to back-trail reconnoitering with four-wheel drive to backpacking, where the hiker must depend upon two feet and the equipment and water he or she carries. Equipment suggestions vary with the type of activity. Remember, however, that by means of a wrong turn and mechanical problems even a simple summer sightseeing trip may conceivably become, rather rapidly, a serious survival problem.

## Clothing

Clothing is a matter of personal choice, but remember:

1. Although daytime temperatures may be high, the desert cools rapidly after the sun sets. A sweater, sweatshirt, or the like sometimes, but not always, feels comfortable in the late evening, even in the summer. In winter and during periods of moderate temperatures, coats or jackets will be needed at night and during some days. A very cold wind may whip across the desert in winter; when it does, some sort of head covering—a stocking cap, sweatshirt hood, or the like—will feel extremely comfortable.

2. Many hikers prefer to wear shorts. However, in some cases long pants are advisable for the hiker, even in summer. They provide a degree of protection against cactus spines, dehydration, sunburn, scrapes and scratches from brush and rocks, and rattlesnake bite (a loose pants leg may help foil or

lessen the force of a rattlesnake strike). One compromise is to wear pants that are now available which have long legs attached by zippers. The transition from long to short, or short to long, is easily made.

3. You may prefer short-sleeved shirts or blouses during warm temperatures, but remember that long sleeves can be valuable, particularly in preventing sunburn or where possible dehydration is a problem.

4. A hat which provides shade for the head and allows some air circulation is a valuable asset. For summer hiking, it should be considered a necessity. One of us, caught in an emergency situation, exposed to 100° F.–plus temperatures in desert sun from dawn to dark without any head protection, now attests that the giddiness, fuzzy thinking, and other problems which develop from partial dehydration with hot sun beating on one's head and neck all day underscore the need for a hat, or at least for an emergency substitute.

## Footwear

Whether you are out for a half-day hike or a two-week backpack into one of the remote desert regions, proper footwear is one of the most important pieces of your equipment. Remember that a hiker with painful feet is more than an unhappy hiking companion; he or she is a liability to self and group. Such individuals have been the downfall of many an outing, for no group is much better than its poorest member—or the feet of its poorest member. Wear sandals in the desert only if you plan to stay inside, on city sidewalks and well-maintained paths, or are prepared to face the circumstances from venturing away from these. In many regions, tennis shoes and similar footwear may be fine for hiking; however, in the desert where one encounters cactus spines, shrubs, sand, and sharp rocks, tennis shoes are not entirely practical for hiking. In addition, these shoes readily conduct heat from the ground surface to the feet. (Remember the temperature of that surface may register 160° F. or more on a hot day.)

Boots—*well chosen, well broken in*—can be of great value to the desert hiker. Among their advantages are: (1) support for the foot and ankle in rugged, often rocky, ankle-twisting terrain, (2) insulation from desert heat through the boots themselves and the fairly heavy socks worn with them, (3) protection against sand, gravel, and the like entering the footwear and rubbing against the skin, and (4) protection from cactus spines and rattlesnake bite (a high percentage of rattlesnake bites occur on the ankle and lower leg).

In choosing desert wear, consider boots which: (1) reach at least to your ankle bone, or preferably higher, (2) are of fairly tough leather to withstand spines and sharp rocks, (3) have soles of tough design which will provide good traction, and (4) are as lightweight and cool as possible while fulfilling the foregoing criteria.

## Socks

Personal preference plays a role in choice, but a good many hikers prefer the two-pair method; they wear a light- or medium-weight cotton or nylon inner sock and an outer, thicker, wool sock—yes, even in the desert! Carry extra socks to provide a change when yours become wet or compacted. Also, remember that your feet will perspire heavily during hot weather hiking.

## Sleeping Bag

For many years a bedroll, consisting primarily of a good wool blanket, was considered standard for the hunter, camper, cowboy, or other individual sleeping outside. Sunset seldom signaled an enjoyable, beautiful, star-filled night, but often marked the start of a dreaded time of chill and shivering. Following World War II, a wide portion of the outdoor public was introduced for the first time to lightweight, warm bags at reasonable weight and price levels. Since then, the sleeping bag industry has displayed a rapid series of modifications in design and materials. Today, a wide choice of sleeping bag types is available over a varying price range. You tend to get what you pay for. In purchasing a bag, consider how you will be using it and the criteria to be met to fill your particular needs; then buy accordingly.

To stress the need for warmth in a sleeping bag may appear incongruous in a discussion of desert camping, but it is not. Over much of the North American desert country, nighttime temperatures often drop below freezing, snow falls, and strong cold winter winds are common during part of the winter. In warmer weather, nighttime temperature lows usually drop far below daytime highs, and even following the very hottest summer days, an outdoor sleeper usually wants at least a lightweight covering during the predawn hours.

## Shelter

One of the most beautiful experiences the desert can offer is the view of its fantastically clear evening sky with infinite numbers of stars bright against the blackness. Lying back and integrating oneself into the desert at such times is an experience that will long be remembered. For this reason, many desert campers feel that sleeping in a tent on such a night is a waste akin to sleeping in a cheap hotel when far better accommodations are available. Beautiful desert nights should be enjoyed; however, at times the desert can be a harsh place in which to camp. It rains in the desert occasionally and blows rather frequently. The person without protection gets just as wet, cold, and windblown in the desert as he or she does in many other environments. Therefore a tent or shelter of some sort is often an asset. Personal considerations, such as price, size, anticipated uses, transportability, ease of use, weight, and the like, must all be evaluated when purchasing a tent.

Some people prefer to sleep in a tent in the desert for a reason other than weather. Summer nights are the most active period for much of the desert fauna. Snakes and scorpions represent probably only a relatively small risk to the person sleeping on the desert's surface but, in spite of the old horse-hair rope trick—which certainly does not work—nothing can guarantee that these small creatures will not inadvertently make their way into your camp. (Consider the more likely possibility that you are in *their* camp, and that they are even less enthusiastic about your presence than you are about theirs.) If the camper worries about the presence of these guests (and admittedly, at times, one should), this concern detracts from the trip. Some modification can be made. A small, zippered, floored tent is one possibility. (Make sure it provides for plenty of air circulation for warm summer evenings.) Small, lightweight tents are now available that have a mesh top, which allows one to view the night sky above from within the tent. A rain flap can be pulled over the mesh if sun, cold, or rain makes it advisable to do so. Another possibility is the use of a small, compact, lightweight cot to elevate the sleeper a few inches above the "intruders." Hammocks may occasionally be useful in some areas, such as along washes where larger trees grow. During the winter months, cold temperatures generally keep snakes and scorpions inactive at night and reduce the need for vigilance.

## Packs

Once you have done some hiking in the desert environment, you may decide to go farther and stay longer. For these journeys, the hiker must be able to carry a quantity of food, water, and various equipment. A backpack is the answer.

The backpack is your home when you are in the wilderness. When you are ready to buy one, research your purchase carefully:

Consider the type of design you want and need in the bag.

Consider the size needed.

Consider the pack construction and the conditions to which you will be subjecting it.

Consider the fit. *Make sure the pack is comfortable.*

# Additional Items

Where you go, how you get there, what you plan to do, how long you will stay, how fully you plan for the unforeseen, your preferred style of desert exploration—all play a part in what you take with you in your desert exploration. Make your own checklist, and add to it as experience dictates. Don't lose it between trips. Refer to it before you leave home. You can easily grow confident and careless, with subsequent regrets in the field. The following items are of significance to you:

1. **Water.** Even if you are simply auto-exploring on established roads, you should carry some water with you. You may well need it for passengers or vehicle. Simply driving in hot weather, one consumes liquids far beyond normal, and one should be prepared for this change, plus an overheated radiator, plus the possibility of a mechanical breakdown or wrong turn, which would prolong one's stay in the desert environment.

In camping carry plenty of water. In hot weather, consider *a gallon and a half per person minimum for drinking,* per day, adding what will be used for washing, cooking, dishes, and so on. This minimum is for a resting or only moderately active person. The truly active individual will require considerably more. In backpacking *consider very carefully the water that will be needed.* (See Figures 81–84 and Tables 1 and 2 in Chapter XI.) Backpacking is strenuous physical exercise, and the backpacker's body requires a great deal of water even when temperatures are moderate; certainly very large amounts are needed for exertion in heat. *Do not depend for your water on waterholes, wells, tanks, and other sites marked on your maps* unless you positively know they have water— and then doubt them. Remember that a gallon of water weighs approximately 8.3 pounds. The amount of water you can carry is definitely limited. *Plan your water supplies for desert backpacking very carefully.* Nothing else is so important.

In all degrees of desert exploration, from car to backpack, the wisest course is to determine the amount of water you think you will need, then take considerably more. You may never need the extra, but the one time you do, you may need it desperately.

2. **Water containers.** The explorer who travels by vehicle has a choice of various types of water containers. Campers often prefer five-gallon metal or plastic cans. However, even if your base in desert exploration is a vehicle, remember you will probably take hikes away from it. Be prepared when leaving your water supply to carry water with you in canteens or other containers. (Plastic and aluminum containers are available.) When choosing containers for hiking, and particularly for backpacking, choose durable, sturdy, tough ones; those of polyethylene plastic are not only durable but lightweight and semitransparent, allowing quantity determination. Bladder-type water containers are convenient. Some are designed to be carried on a hiker's back and have a drinking tube attached. A bladder container carried in a pack has an advantage in that the container collapses in size as the water is taken from it.

Never use glass bottles for water transport; before the advent of plastic bottles, occasional desert travelers died when their last glass bottle of water shattered. For backpacking, smaller containers should additionally allow for efficient packing and be versatile so that punches or the like can be mixed in them.

The hiker engaged in summer backpacking in areas where water is scarce and separated by long distances (an activity to be recommended only for the experienced, well-conditioned desert backpacker, and only after intensive planning) may find it necessary to carry several gallons of water (remember that three gallons of water will weigh approximately twenty-five pounds). To transport large amounts of water while backpacking, collapsible polyethylene jugs are most appropriate; they will shrink in bulk as the water supply diminishes.

3. **First aid kit.** A first aid kit should always be available. Its contents will be discussed in Chapter XIII.

4. **Compass and maps.** Both compass and maps are extremely important and should be carried. Buy a compass of some degree of quality—if you need one, you'll need one that works. An oil-filled rather than an air-filled compass is recommended. Check to see that the base has an edge long enough

to make drawing a line easy (for taking a bearing on a map). The United States Geological Survey topographical map series is excellent; these maps may be based on 15-minute quadrangles (covering 15 minutes of both latitude and longitude, or roughly 1 inch to a mile); or on 7½-minute quadrangles. These maps are carried by map stores and by many outing stores. Also available in many outing stores are maps of local hiking trails, which may prove valuable. Maps are interesting reading. Buy them, study and enjoy them, and take care of them—no doubt you'll use them over and over.

5. **Communication aids.** You may wish to consider three optional items: a citizens band radio, a cellular telephone, and a global positioning system (GPS). The last can advise you of your position by map coordinates (obviously you need the maps for this to be of assistance). GPS units, once very expensive, are now much more affordable, and they can serve multiple functions in desert exploration.

Cell phones may be of great importance in a survival or medical emergency situation. But a word of warning in regard to their use. Search and rescue organizations are being stretched to their limits in some areas for, increasingly, individuals who have gotten themselves into trouble in the out-of-doors due to their ignorance, poor preparation, or foolhardiness, are relying on cell phones to summon help and rescue. When truly needed, a cell phone can be a lifesaver, but do not depend on one as a substitute for personal responsibility.

6. **Signaling mirror.** A lightweight, metal signaling mirror should be carried. It is an invaluable, powerful aid in signaling. Its use will be discussed in Chapter XIV.

7. **Knife.** One of the handiest items to be carried is a knife, which need not be fancy; a useful style is one fashioned after a Boy Scout model. The knife should have a good strong main blade for general cutting and a smaller very sharp blade which may be used for removing spines and splinters and for delicate cutting.

8. **Flashlight.** A flashlight may prove to be a more important piece of equipment than one might judge. It is often used for searching in one's pack at night; it may prove to be helpful in signaling at night; and it serves a very important purpose in

summer nighttime camping. You should use a flashlight when walking in the desert on warm nights—on your bedtime bathroom retreat, for example. The light may prove a valuable aid in preventing you from stepping on or unduly upsetting a prowling rattlesnake. Be sure to take sufficient batteries on your trip. Beware of the light switch being inadvertently pushed to the "on" position while the flashlight is in a pack, thereby wasting batteries. The batteries may be reversed in the light after use to prevent this accident, or a piece of adhesive tape may be placed over the switch when the light is not in use.

9. **Whistle.** A whistle is useful for signaling; its use is particularly advisable on longer hikes and backpacks, especially for children. A whistle can be worn around a child's (or adult's) neck for use in case he or she becomes lost, hurt, or frightened. Its sound carries farther than the human voice, and blowing a whistle is much easier and less costly physiologically than continued shouting.

10. **Matches.** Always carry waterproof matches, or matches in a waterproof container. If you become lost, you have a means of signaling and keeping warm.

11. **Rope.** Rope has numerous uses, ranging from pitching a tent to making a clothesline to emergency and first aid requirements. Parachute cord which is about 550-pound test is the best. The weight of a little extra cord is well worth the uses you will find for it.

12. **Plastic sheet and tube.** A six-foot square of clear or almost clear plastic and a four-to-six-foot length of plastic tubing can be used for construction of a solar still under emergency situations. The still and its use are described in Chapter XIV.

13. **Sunglasses.** Some people feel that sunglasses detract from the desert's scenery and its total effect. However, for many people, dark glasses provide relief and protection for the eyes. Certainly the daytime desert environment offers a great deal of bright sunlight and glare. Excessive exposure to this glare without the protection afforded by colored glasses tends to impair distant vision and retard adjustment of the eyes to nighttime conditions.

14. **Toilet articles.** Toilet items will be those of personal preference. Don't forget toilet paper. Other items that are particularly helpful in the sunny, dry desert are sunburn lotion, a tube of lip salve, and drops for dry eyes.

15. **Pocket comb.** You may want to comb your hair, but primarily a comb can be an invaluable aid for removing cactus joints from body and clothes. See Chapter XIII.

16. **Repair kit for equipment and clothing.** When the outdoorsman takes off a pack and drops it only to see one of the joints separate, or is sleeping by the campfire when the wood pops and sends an ember through the outer covering of a sleeping bag so that the heretofore contained filling starts flying, he or she will be thankful for a repair kit. Recommendations include a few ounces of such specific repair equipment as ripstop nylon repair tape for repairing bags and coats; needles and safety pins of various sizes; thread—a few lengths of assorted weights; clevis pins and steel wires for repairing pack frames; and other items suitable for your specific equipment.

## Before You Leave Home

1. *Always notify someone as to your destination and the date you expect to return from a desert trip.* Give yourself a little leeway as you set the time for your return. Let it be understood that someone should come to your aid if you have not returned at that time. Notify your contact when you do return home. If you change your plans as to destination or return, notify your contact. If you are in an area where you do not have personal contacts to fill this role, notify the local sheriff's office of your plans. If you are flying, the same rules apply; you must also *file a flight plan and stick to it or change it officially.* One of us, involved in a plane crash in Baja California on a flight which did not follow the flight plan, can testify to the vital importance of this rule. The other, waiting at home for the plane's return, can testify to the anguish caused to the person responsible for the search and the waiting. Breaking these

rules can be deadly for the hiker, flyer, or backpacker who has developed a problem. It can also prove time-consuming, expensive, and even dangerous to other people—the searchers—when search and rescue services, including vehicles, airplanes, and helicopters, must be employed. When such services are needed, they are invaluable, and no price tag can be placed on them. But when a hiker, flyer, or the like has changed plans, failed to notify contacts, and been delayed beyond a deadline, the mistake can be costly, both in money and emotional upset, as well as in terms of survival.

2. Obtain maps of the area where you will be hiking. Study these maps ahead of time to learn something about the country.

3. Prepare yourself to be a good outdoorsman. A course in first aid may prove invaluable. Learn some basic survival skills and practice them. Learn to use a signaling mirror. Learn about the plants and animals of the area you will be visiting. Learn to use a compass and to read topographic maps before you get into the field. Learn to camp effectively, efficiently, and enjoyably, not only by doing it but also by reading some manuals which provide you with ideas. Learn some of the simple mechanics of your vehicle, if you are not already knowledgeable in that regard.

## Camping Sites

If you are choosing a camping site away from established campgrounds, remember:

1. Do not camp in a dry wash. A sandy-bottomed, tree-lined wash is an inviting location for a camp. Such a site is, however, subject to a flash flood. Flash floods are infrequent but can be exceedingly powerful when they do occur. Remember that such floods may occur in your area under clear skies; the rain that caused them may have fallen some distance away. Enjoy the washes by camping above them and hiking down into them or building your campfire in the wash bottom.

2. Avoid camping directly next to piles of debris, abandoned buildings, pack rat nests, masses of rocks, or the like, as these are potential rattlesnake areas. To sleep away from such areas is certainly wise.

## Camping Manners

The desert is a particularly delicate ecosystem. Any scars on its surface will remain for exceedingly long periods; garbage consigned to it will endure, and endure, and endure. *Leave no sign of your desert sojourn behind upon your departure.*

1. Take all of your garbage that cannot be *completely* burned—*all of it*—home with you. If you do burn paper, be sure it is completely burned and the ashes buried. Carry out all cans, aluminum foil, pop-top lids, and every other nonburnable item. Do not bury such materials. The desert is dry; breakdown of such materials may never occur. Besides, animals almost invariably dig up any buried garbage. Remember the rule: If you can carry it in full, you can certainly carry it out empty.

2. If you are camping away from areas with toilet facilities, bury human wastes deeply. If no camp toilet has been set up, keep a regular shovel or hand shovel available in camp, and establish and enforce the rule that anyone leaving camp for bathroom purposes is to take and use the shovel.

3. *Do not:* molest animals or their homes; damage plants; deface rocks or ruins; roll boulders down hillsides; leave rocks overturned, thereby destroying the habitats of living things; collect or remove from their sites Indian artifacts (these artifacts are protected by law, and stringent penalties are given for infractions; additionally, you may be destroying archaeological evidence of importance); target practice.

4. *Do:* close gates after opening them; respect waterholes, the land in general, and the living things who make their homes there; look, explore, enjoy, and leave things as you found them, or better. No law prohibits picking up and carry-

ing out garbage left by a slob camper who preceded you—and you may gain considerable righteous pleasure in doing so.

## Special Considerations for Exploring Desert Country in Mexico

Some of the most interesting and isolated of the North American desert lies in Mexico. Visitors from the United States are generally welcomed; however, certain additional considerations should be kept in mind when traveling in Mexico.

1. Good manners are imperative. When in Mexico, you are a guest in a foreign country. Do not forget that you are a guest; do not abuse the privilege of visiting. Respect the culture of the area, and do not demand that conditions and services be identical to those in the United States.

2. American citizens must fulfill certain Mexican government regulations in order to enter Mexico. These include obtaining individual personal permits, as well as vehicle permits, both available at the border. Proof of U.S. citizenship and vehicle registration are among the documents needed. Regulations and fees change from time to time and may differ depending upon the Mexican state in which you plan to travel. Contact the nearest Mexican Ministry of Tourism office, Mexican consulate, or check www.embassyofmexico.org for current regulations when you plan to travel.

3. You will need to purchase special vehicle insurance through your insurance agent or from an office at the border. Your regular insurance does not cover your vehicle in Mexico.

4. **NEVER** have illegal drugs in your possession. **NEVER** have firearms or ammunition in your possession unless you have obtained a permit to do so. (Such permits may be granted to hunters upon application, but the process of obtaining one is lengthy and complex.) Possession of a single weapon or bullet can carry a penalty of up to five years in prison. (Hunters, before entering Mexico, check for any stray ammunition inadvertently left in your vehicle.) A tourist cited

for firearms possession can be incarcerated in a Mexican prison at least until the trial date, which can be up to one year from the date of the offense. *Drug and firearm violators are prosecuted, and Mexican jails and prisons are definitely not to be recommended as places to spend your vacation.*

5. In many respects, Mexican law differs from that of the United States. In practice, burden of proof of innocence may be yours, rather than the prosecution bearing the burden of proof of guilt.

6. Established camping facilities are relatively few in Mexico, although their number is increasing.

7. Take precautions with food and water obtained in Mexico. If you have doubts about the water, purify it. Just because water comes out of a hydrant or faucet does not necessarily mean it is pure. Ice, too, may be contaminated. If possible, purchase purified water. "Montezuma's Revenge," or intestinal upset, can be a problem for American tourists; avoid foodstuffs that may be contaminated.

8. Driving is more difficult in Mexico than in the United States. Highways are often narrower. Bridges are sometimes narrower than the highway on which they occur. Directional signs are often few or lacking, requiring inquiries as to the route. Avoid night driving. Highways are usually not fenced, and many traverse open rangeland. Watch for cattle and horses on the road, particularly if you must drive at night when they are very difficult to see. Also, particularly in rural areas, some Mexican vehicles are in need of repair—beware of those being driven at night without taillights. In some cases, road shoulders are narrow or lacking; beware of disabled vehicles stopped on the road itself.

## Desert Driving

*Do not drive off established roads or trails in the desert.* The desert possesses one unique quality—its accessibility. This accessibility is contributing to rapid deterioration of portions of the desert, for with the popular onslaught of cycles, four-wheel-drive vehicles, dune buggies, and similar sport vehicles, the deserts are becoming crisscrossed with myriad trails and off-road tracks. Where this occurs the desert's surface is being irreparably scarred.

This is especially true where the surface is covered by desert pavement or cryptobiotic soil. Desert pavement is found on areas of low slope or flat plains and consists of underlying soil surfaced with small stones which have become closely packed together to form a stony surface. Usually only very limited vegetation or none is present on it. Driving over desert pavement disturbs the smooth placement of the stones, thereby exposing the underlying soil and resulting in erosion and clear-cut vehicle tracks. In some areas a spongelike, cryptobiotic ("hidden life") crust is formed on the desert's surface. This layer is formed by physical processes and microorganisms. When walked or driven on, this cryptobiotic crust is disturbed and erosion results.

On most of the desert's surface, vehicle tracks are, for all intents and purposes, permanent. A single set of tracks may conceivably endure twenty-five years; well-worn tracks last much longer. Permanent or even semipermanent tracks carved on the desert's surface by vehicles are an unneeded and unwanted legacy for future generations.

Certainly all degrees of desert vehicular travel exist, ranging from interstate freeways to back roads. The vehicle and equipment needed will depend on the type of travel you plan. Rules for all types of desert travel include the following:

1. Have your vehicle maintained in good condition for desert travel. If your car is in mediocre or poor condition for city travel, it certainly is not ready for the desert.

2. Service stations are often long distances apart in the desert—even on major highways. Fill up on gas and water when opportunities are presented.

3. Carry a tool kit and extra vehicle parts (see checklist at the end of this chapter for suggestions).

4. Use common sense when preparing for a trip and when driving in the desert. Be sure the radiator is in good working order. If your car becomes overheated, check the radiator (carefully! avoid being burned). If the water is at the proper level, drive in a lower gear in order that the motor's rotations

per minute will be higher, and the water pump will move the water through the radiator at a higher rate. If you continue to have problems, avoid driving in the heat of the day, and drive at night or during the cooler parts of the day. Remember, too, that your tires are rapidly rotating on the desert's surface, which may be superheated. This heat certainly provides added stress on tires and possible attendant difficulties.

5. In certain areas, particularly in southern California, sandstorms may be severe. On major highways, electrical signs advise travelers if blowing sand is extreme, and travel should be delayed until the storm abates. Not only may driving be dangerous at such times, but wind-blown sand is highly damaging to vehicles' paint and glass, efficiently sandblasting them—very often to the extent that a new paint job and replacement of windshield and windows are needed.

6. In parts of the open desert, strong winds may occur with or without accompanying sand and dust. These winds may pose a hazard for taller, lighter vehicles, such as campers. At such times, warnings may be issued, via electric signs and/or local radio, to high-profile vehicles, advising them to delay travel until the wind lessens.

7. Dust storms and vehicular traffic on highways can be lethal. Along some highways, fields have replaced desert growth. When these lie bare at certain times of the year, a strong wind may pick up the soil in such quantities as to completely obscure the vision of highway drivers. Some roads, such as the one between Phoenix and Tucson, Arizona, have a system of electrical signs which are activated at the scene, or remotely, to warn drivers of impending danger. Cautions, particularly for high-profile vehicles, may be given first. If the storm intensifies and the dust problem becomes serious, drivers are warned that travel is no longer safe, and the highway is closed. Severe dust clouds vary in density and will, at times, limit a driver's vision to only the interior of the vehicle. This may cause drivers to panic and stop their vehicle in the traffic lane, which often results in rear-end collisions. If you are engulfed by a dust storm, immediately reduce the speed of your vehicle and drive carefully off the traveled portion of the

highway. Stop your vehicle as near the right-of-way fence as possible. Turn your vehicle's lights off and wait until the dust storm has passed. Two points are very important: *Get as far off the road as possible; turn off all lights, including flashers.* It is important that lights be turned off immediately for if you do not, following vehicles may think you are still moving, may attempt to follow your taillights, leave the road, and in the dense dust hit your car before realizing it is stationary. *Never stop your car on the highway. Get off the roadway before your ability to do so is blocked by increasing impairment of vision. Always obey warning signs and radio announcements regarding dust and sandstorms.*

8. Beware of flash floods and of crossing flooded washes in your vehicle. The depth and force of water in these washes can be very deceptive. Each year in the deserts, a number of people drown as a result of such accidents. Remember that flood water may move rapidly from the area where it was received into areas where no rain or only small amounts have fallen. A wall of water may hit a car crossing a wash. More often, a driver misjudges the water's depth and attempts to cross. The vehicle may be swept away by the force of the flowing water, or the motor get wet, causing the car to stall, whereupon rapidly rising water then tumbles the vehicle downstream. Passengers and driver may drown in the vehicle, or if they are able to escape from it, often may still drown in the turbulent waters, which carry smashing boulders, logs, and other debris. Floods in washes, like sand and dust storms, usually dissipate within hours. *Wait them out,* rather than risk lives for the sake of a few hours' time.

As one leaves the highways and main desert roads, additional considerations are necessary with regard to road conditions and driving techniques.

1. It is always safest to travel with a second vehicle when entering remote areas.

2. Your vehicle should be capable of the type of travel you are planning. People who do a great deal of back-country desert driving usually have pickups and/or four-wheel-drive

vehicles, which provide the necessary power and high ground clearance.

3. Tires should be sturdy and chosen for the type of traveling to be done—that is, heavy-duty, wide-track tires are needed for rugged trail or sand driving. Sharp rocks, cactus spines and other thorns, and sharp vegetation are tire hazards.

4. Carry a rather extensive array of tools and spare parts. (See the checklist at the end of this chapter.) Know how to use them.

5. In turning your vehicle around on desert roads, remember that the road shoulder is often soft. Maneuver your car back and forth on the roadway itself, cutting your wheels sharply and reversing their angle each time you reverse the gear. This back-and-forth method may be time-consuming, but not nearly so time-consuming as getting yourself free if you become stuck.

6. Washboard roads are common in the desert. Driving on these roads can be frustrating and jarring. One method used to smooth the ride on this type of road is to increase speed. A vehicle traveling at about 45 miles per hour rides smoother than a vehicle traveling at 15–20 miles per hour. However, this increased speed sacrifices some control over the vehicle. You may easily lose control on such a road before you realize what is happening; slamming on the brakes tends to cause a further loss of control.

7. Rocky roads are very hard on a vehicle, particularly on the tires. Take it easy, drive slowly and carefully, watch the road, and attempt to miss as many rocks as possible, particularly those with sharp points and edges.

8. Move slowly; if in doubt about the road ahead, stop, get out, check the road on foot. Check clearances, for high centers may rupture oil pans. Gas tanks can be punctured on some vehicles. Overhangs may cause driving wheels to become suspended above the ground.

9. Soft sand is probably the most common barrier found in the desert. If you encounter sand, look for an alternate route. If none is available, get out and check the sand; determine if it is somewhat solid and coarse or is soft and fine. If you de-

cide to attempt a crossing, remember that standard, narrow tires are swallowed in sand faster than oversized tires—larger tires have a broader "footprint," hence increased flotation. You can increase these footprints by deflating your tires to some extent. Do not deflate them, however, unless you have at your disposal the means to pump them back up again. When determining whether to go across the sand, determine how far you must go to solid ground, and logically determine whether you can make it if you use a burst of speed. If you decide on this course of action, don't change your mind in the middle of the operation. Slowing down at that point is likely to slow you to a full stop and a state of being stuck.

10. Regardless of how much driving experience you have had, you will undoubtedly find yourself stuck at some time, if driving desert back roads. Getting unstuck is not a serious problem if you have come prepared. First determine where the nearest solid ground is. Do not try to power yourself out, because you will only power yourself into your own ditch. (Remember that a stuck four-wheel-drive vehicle is stuck twice as badly as a two-wheel-drive vehicle.) The minute you feel you have lost traction, stop. If you are with another vehicle, its driver will probably be able to pull you out with a tow chain.

If yours is the only vehicle and some simple shovel work combined with pushing by the vehicle's occupants is insufficient to free you, more complete measures will have to be undertaken. First jack up the buried wheel or wheels. Watch that the jack does not slip off the pad. Be sure to block the unjacked tires with rocks so the vehicle does not roll. Dig the wheel out, and make a gradual ramp for the wheel to climb up. When these steps are accomplished, lay the sand mats (pieces of heavy wire mesh, boards, or sturdy carpet about four feet or longer by twelve inches wide) down under the wheel, and extend one end in the direction in which you will drive. If you do not have sand mats, you may improvise; use bushes, sticks, stones, even floor mats or cool cushions from your vehicle's seats. Let your vehicle down. Release some air from the tires, both front and rear (only if you have a pump with which to reinflate them). Ideal tire pressures vary but, as an average figure, nine to twelve pounds is about right. Check to make sure the undercarriage is clear and will not high-center. You are now ready to ease out—with emphasis on the *ease.* This method of jacking up one or two tires, if necessary, should get you out. If it does not, try again with your vehicle unloaded.

11. In general, desert driving requires experience and good judgment. Do not abuse your vehicle. Concentrate on your driving, and avoid placing unnecessary stresses upon your vehicle when covering difficult terrain.

In no way is this chapter meant to discourage or frighten the novice desert enthusiast. Most of the precautions extended are simply common sense reduced to print. In any habitat (including cities)—and the desert no more than any other—one is advised to follow certain survival rules which apply to meeting the conditions presented there. If one follows basic rules and uses common sense in desert exploration, one has provided a degree of insurance for a pleasant, safe trip. The benefits to be reaped from successful, hassle-free desert exploration are very great. Enjoy the desert. Respect it. Share responsibility for it. Consider the motto, "take nothing but pictures; leave nothing but tracks, and place these very carefully."

## Checklist: Suggested Items for Vehicular Maintenance and Repair

**GENERAL DESERT TRAVEL**

> spare tire (mounted and inflated)
> tire iron and lug wrench
> jack
> jumper cables
> fan belt
> radiator hoses
> heater hose

tool kit (including crescent wrench, set open-end wrenches, pliers, and both regular and Phillips screwdrivers)
oil
water
emergency flares
shovel

All of the above items, except that two spare tires, two jacks, and two tire irons should be included
two platforms for the jacks (twelve-inch squares of heavy plywood)
two sand mats
tire repair kit
12-volt tire pump
spark plug wrench
fuel pump
radiator stop leak
transmission fluid
hydraulic fluid
power steering fluid
gasket sealer
siphon hose
baling wire
box assorted screws, nuts, bolts
socket set
electrical equipment (including fuses, set of points and condenser, spark plugs, roll electrical tape, electrical wire)
fire extinguisher
tow chain, or at least fifty feet of ¾-inch nylon rope
gas can, at least five-gallon, full
water can, at least five-gallon, full
gloves
axe

# CHAPTER XI

# Man, Heat, and Dehydration

THE DESERT'S most serious environmental conditions are ordinarily those produced by heat and aridity. These two factors are of vital concern to those people whose survival in the desert is in question, as too many individuals learn each summer in our southwestern deserts. For just as the plants and animals of the desert must adapt their bodies and/or lifestyles—either morphologically, physiologically, instinctively, or cogitatively—to survive in heat and aridity, so must the animal called man. Of these four means, only the last—use of intelligence—is applicable for *Homo sapiens*. When faced with a desert survival problem, man, so long removed from coping with life on a mere survival basis, often fails to recognize physical limitations in regard to heat tolerance and moisture need. Today, due to the increased frequency with which man lives in, works in, or visits the desert, deaths and accidents in which heat and dehydration play a role are increasingly frequent; yet most such incidents could be avoided through proper preparation, knowledge of the human body's limitations, and intelligent use of survival techniques.

Not until World War II were complete and extensive physiological studies done on man in the desert. The American Armed Forces were fighting in some of the most extreme desert areas of the world, requiring the determination of how much water a fighting or working man required and what limitations heat placed upon him. Through exhaustive, basic research conducted at that time by Dr. E. F. Adolph, Professor Emeritus of Physiology at the University of Rochester, and his associates, we now know rather precisely what happens to man as he becomes dehydrated and how best to prevent this condition.

The human body gains heat through four major means: (1) direct radiation from the sun and reflected radiation from the

FIG. 81. Man's total heat gain balanced by his evaporative heat loss.[*]

[*] Reprinted from *Physiology of Man in the Desert*, courtesy of E. F. Adolph.

ground and sky; (2) convection in which the air molecules carry heat to the skin; (3) conduction through body contact with surface areas, such as the ground; and (4) the production of metabolic heat by the body itself. The body picks up heat in any environment in which the ambient temperature exceeds that of the surface of the body, or at approximately 92° F. and above. The body's heat gain must be reduced when it reaches a certain level, or fever ensues, leading ultimately to death if it is not dissipated. Man's tissues and organs function properly over only a narrow range of temperature, with approximately 107° F. the maximum limit. Evaporative cooling of the skin and adjacent areas by evaporation of sweat produced by the more than two million sweat glands distributed over the human body is the body's primary heat-reducing means. The inner core of the body is cooled when its heat is transferred to the blood, which is then directed to the cooler peripheral body areas adjacent to the skin.

This evaporative cooling is efficient but costly in terms of water loss; it is particularly costly where heat is intense and water supplies are limited. Water lost from the body through

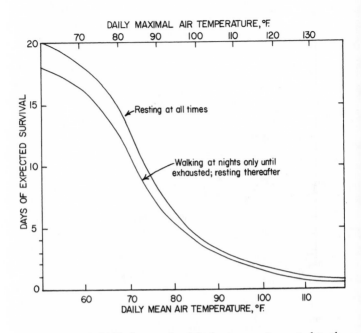

FIG. 82. Probable limits of a dehydrating man's survival in the desert when he has no water to drink.°

° Reprinted from *Physiology of Man in the Desert,* courtesy of E. F. Adolph.

sweating must be replaced; if it is not, dehydration and attendant complications ensue. Approximately two-thirds of the human body is composed of water, and the body needs it all, state Adolph and his associates. As one becomes dehydrated, the blood becomes more concentrated, and the blood flow becomes inadequate, partially because the blood volume has been reduced. In turn, this retarded blood flow causes the body's inner core temperature to continue to rise. Adolph and associates report that as dehydration occurs, pulse rates and rectal temperatures increase; breathing is faster; some numbness and tingling are apparent; and low morale and sleepiness may occur. As dehydration progresses, breathing is difficult; nausea and gastrointestinal upsets occur; loss of appetite and difficulty in muscular movements are apparent; the individual

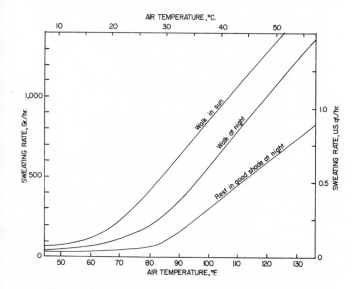

FIG. 83. Relation between average sweating rates and prevailing air temperatures in the desert.°

° Reprinted from *Physiology of Man in the Desert,* courtesy of E. F. Adolph.

becomes emotionally unstable. By the time a person has lost water equivalent to 5 to 6 percent of body weight, he or she often shows signs of exhaustion and may become unable to walk and carry on ordinary activities. At an 8 percent deficit, the flow of saliva has nearly ceased. At 10 percent, people cannot be expected to cooperate among themselves. If the water loss reaches 12 percent of body weight, circulation is so impaired that an explosive, deep body heat rise is likely to occur, leading to death. In cooler environments, man may endure greater water deficits; he will become gradually weaker, dying at a deficit of 20 to 25 percent.

Man in the heat of the desert is usually partially dehydrated much of the time. This condition, known as voluntary dehydration, is especially prevalent between meals. Voluntary dehydration occurs because the sensation of thirst is not always present, even under partial dehydration. The deficits tend to be replaced during meals and over leisure hours. Because voluntary dehydration does occur, one who is subjected to desert heat should, to a certain extent, force himself to drink if water is available even though he is not thirsty. Any water which is not needed will eventually simply be excreted. The body can go into debt for water to a slight extent—about 1 to 3 percent of the body weight—without too drastic an effect. Any greater dehydration, however, tends to produce low morale and other early symptoms of dehydration.

Since desert air is ordinarily very dry, sweating rates can be deceptive. The skin may appear dry when actually the sweating rate is high; perspiration is being rapidly evaporated without remaining for any length of time on the skin's surface. By holding one's hand over one's arm for a few minutes and then removing it, one can see that a quantity of sweat is pouring out at all times when the body is undergoing heat stress. The body produces approximately eighty calories of heat per hour through its metabolic activity. Dissipation through sweating of this heat gain alone requires five ounces of water each hour. In high desert temperatures, man accumulates heat from other sources also. Adolph and associates measured sweating rates of man in various activities in the desert. They found that a man walking at the rate of approximately 3.5 miles per hour in the sun with an air temperature of 100° F. lost an average of one quart of water in perspiration each hour! Under identical environmental conditions, the same man driving a vehicle lost ¾ quart, while the man resting in the shade lost a mere ¼ quart, or one cup. In other experiments, the researchers determined the daily water needs for men undertaking various activities in the desert on days with a daily mean temperature of 90° F. Those men who were inactive and remained in the shade required approximately five to six quarts of water; those moderately active in the sun required approximately seven to eight quarts; and those working strenuously in the sun required approximately nine to ten quarts. Men on maneuvers in vehicles in the desert when the maximal air temperature was 102° F. were reported to drink an average of six quarts of water per twenty-four hours; men working in the sun at the same temperature drank a maximum of twelve quarts in

THE DESERTS OF THE SOUTHWEST

twenty-four hours—and the researchers called attention to the fact that desert temperatures are often much higher than 102° F., with a consequent greater water need. The studies also determined that a man *resting in shade* during the hottest month, July, in a part of our most extreme southwestern desert country, Death Valley, would require nine quarts of water per day for maintenance alone. They projected survival statistics for a man *resting in the shade, doing no walking, and having no water* under various shade temperature conditions. Days of expected survival at shade temperature of 120° F. was two; at 110° F., three days; at 100° F., five days; and at 90° F.,

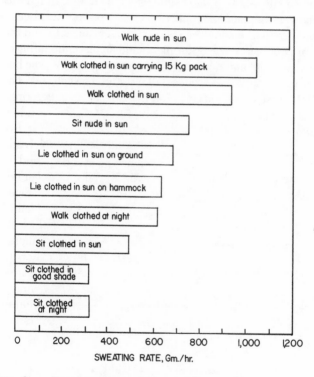

FIG. 84. Sweating rates under ten conditions of exposure to the desert at air temperature of 100° F. (dry-bulb).°

° Reprinted from *Physiology of Man in the Desert,* courtesy of E. F. Adolph.

*Man, Heat, and Dehydration*

seven days. These and similar findings obviously have profound implications for the desert hiker.

Dehydration prevention measures are simple: (1) Imbibe amounts of water sufficient to equal those amounts lost through sweating, and/or (2) reduce sweating to a minimum. The individual facing an emergency survival situation in the desert may often find the first alternative impossible due to lack of water; the second may be difficult to practice, although not impossible. If some water is available, use of the two means in intelligent conjunction is advised. Adolph and his associates established certain general guidelines for survival under conditions of water shortage in the desert, with the primary maxim that each ounce of sweat a person can cheat the body from expending is an ounce of water gained for the body. For people as much as for plants and animals, the difference between life and death may at times hang on the precarious balance of a mere few ounces of moisture. Adolph and associates advise that if some water is available in an emergency sit-

TABLE 1.

Days of expected survival in the desert under two conditions*

| Condition | Max. daily shade temps., °F. | Available water per man, U.S. quarts | | | | | |
|---|---|---|---|---|---|---|---|
| | | 0 | 1 | 2 | 4 | 10 | 20 |
| | 120 | 2 | 2 | 2 | 2.5 | 3 | 4.5 |
| | 110 | 3 | 3 | 3.5 | 4 | 5 | 7 |
| | 100 | 5 | 5.5 | 6 | 7 | 9.5 | 13.5 |
| No walking | 90 | 7 | 8 | 9 | 10.5 | 15 | 23 |
| at all | 80 | 9 | 10 | 11 | 13 | 19 | 29 |
| | 70 | 10 | 11 | 12 | 14 | 20.5 | 32 |
| | 60 | 10 | 11 | 12 | 14 | 21 | 32 |
| | 50 | 10 | 11 | 12 | 14.5 | 21 | 32 |
| | 120 | 1 | 2 | 2 | 2.5 | 3 | |
| | 110 | 2 | 2 | 2.5 | 3 | 3.5 | |
| Walking at night | 100 | 3 | 3.5 | 3.5 | 4.5 | 5.5 | |
| until exhausted | 90 | 5 | 5.5 | 5.5 | 6.5 | 8 | |
| and resting | 80 | 7 | 7.5 | 8 | 9.5 | 11.5 | |
| thereafter | 70 | 7.5 | 8 | 9 | 10.5 | 13.5 | |
| | 60 | 8 | 8.5 | 9 | 11 | 14 | |
| | 50 | 8 | 8.5 | 9 | 11 | 14 | |

*Reprinted from *Physiology of Man in the Desert*, courtesy of E. F. Adolph.

THE DESERTS OF THE SOUTHWEST

uation, a fully hydrated man who decides to walk during the daytime should carry two gallons of water for every twenty miles he expects to cover. If he walks at night, he should carry one gallon for every twenty miles. A healthy, hydrated man can walk ten miles in three to four hours during a summer day in the desert without water supplies before he dehydrates to the point of exhaustion. However, if the distance to be covered is more, the basic rule of the desert should be obeyed: Walk only at night. Without water and walking only at night, a man can expect to cover no more than twenty to twenty-five miles in average summer weather before dehydration collapse—that is, however, obviously more than twice the distance he could expect to walk during daylight hours. Night walking should be started about nine or ten in the evening and continued until sunup to make use of the coolest hours.

The individual who does not walk or otherwise exert himself but stays in one location and follows general rules for reducing sweating expends approximately half or less the amount of water in sweat as does the man walking during the day. As do many animals, man should utilize the microenvironment most beneficial to him. A resting man should make use of the most complete shade available. If possible, while

TABLE 2.

Attainable distance before occurrence of limiting water deficit[*]

| Daily mean temp., °F[**] | Number of miles, if the transportable water supply per man, in U.S. quarts, is: | | | | |
|---|---|---|---|---|---|
| | 0 | 1 | 4 | 10 | 20 |
| 40 | 170 | 190 | 260 | 400 | 640 |
| 50 | 170 | 190 | 260 | 400 | 640 |
| 60 | 130 | 150 | 200 | 310 | 490 |
| 70 | 90 | 100 | 140 | 210 | 340 |
| 80 | 45 | 50 | 70 | 110 | 170 |
| 90 | 20 | 25 | 35 | 50 | 80 |
| 100 | 15 | 18 | 20 | 30 | 50 |
| 110 | 9 | 10 | 15 | 20 | 30 |
| 120 | 7 | 8 | 10 | 15 | 25 |

[*]Reprinted from *Physiology of Man in the Desert,* courtesy of E. F. Adolph.
[**]About fifteen degrees below maximal.

resting he should be elevated from the ground. Ground-surface temperatures may reach 160° F. or higher, and the first few inches of air above that surface are also superheated. Removing oneself to a level just above this may place the body in air having a temperature thirty or more degrees lower. Insofar as possible, one should also stay shielded from winds, which increase evaporation of sweat and contribute to body heat gain through convection.

To remain clothed is exceedingly important. Contrary to much popular belief, the retention of clothing has been proved to help slow down the sweating process, by preventing perspiration from evaporating so fast that only a part of its cooling effect is used by the body. In addition, clothing insulates the body against heat gain by radiation and convection by reflecting much of this incumbent energy. For reflective purposes, white clothing is ideal. Under no circumstances should the clothing be so tight as to interfere with the evaporative cooling of the body. Thus the optimal clothing would be made of thin, loosely woven white cloth to allow air circulation. A hat is very important in the desert. Through the use of a simple, lightweight hat, the heat gain and attendant loss of water from the head and neck area are greatly reduced. The ideal hat is one, such as a man's straw hat, that projects well up off the head and allows air circulation. Clothing and a hat are also important in protecting the body from the direct rays of the sun, which can burn even a darkly tanned skin quite easily and quite severely. In the desert sunlight, the person who removes his trousers, shirt, and hat subjects the body to a heat gain equivalent to a rise in air temperature of ten Fahrenheit degrees—certainly a convincing reason for remaining fully clothed under conditions of stress. Research determined that a person walking nude in the sun at a temperature of 100° F. had a sweating rate approximately *four times* that of a person sitting clothed in good shade.

When faced with a water emergency problem, keep your mouth closed; to prevent unnecessary evaporation of moisture from the mouth, refrain as much as possible from talking, and do not smoke. If water is not available or is very limited, eat little or nothing, as digestion of food requires water; also refrain from ingesting salt, which increases water need. Do not drink urine, blood, or saltwater, all of which may intensify thirst and none of which will serve as useful moisture sources for the body. Do not drink alcoholic beverages; the body processes alcohol as a food, and water is required in the process. In emergency situations in which vehicles are involved, radiator water may be available. However, ordinarily, this water contains coolants or similar agents with a basic ingredient of alcohol. Drinking water containing these agents can cause severe stomach cramps, pain, and possible death. Radiator or other polluted water and urine can be used for purposes other than drinking, however. Spread the liquid over the skin or use it to soak clothing; it serves briefly to reduce the body's sweat needs for evaporative cooling.

If one is preparing to walk to seek rescue, often one has some water available at the location of departure—be it water carried in a plane or auto or that in a waterhole. If water is available, the person preparing to walk should forcefully over-drink, thereby using the stomach as an auxiliary canteen capable of carrying one to two quarts of extra water. Originally thought to be detrimental to the human system, this forced drinking has been proven to be beneficial in survival situations. Another fallacy which has been dispelled relates to the amount of water an individual should carry when attempting to walk to find help. Formerly, the disadvantages of strain placed on the individual by carrying a large supply of water were believed to outweigh the advantages of the water itself. Not so, for water in an amount equal to one-third a man's body weight can be carried with only a 32 percent increase in effort. The cost in sweat of carrying water was found to be less than 1 percent per hour of the supply carried. Each extra quart carried and consumed can increase the hiker's expected attainable distance by five to seven miles in average summer weather. Lack of suitable containers probably most commonly limits the amount of water that can be carried.

Rationing one's water over an extended period of time does not increase one's survival time, as was once believed. Although one's morale may be boosted by knowing that the canteen is full, this knowledge does nothing for the body's physiological condition. Water in the stomach does a better job than water in the canteen. When one experiences thirst, the minimum amount of water necessary to quench that thirst should be drunk. In some cases, individuals have died of heat and dehydration while water remained in their canteens, so assiduously did they ration their scant supplies.

The human body expends a certain amount of water under certain conditions. It cannot be trained to do with less, nor can it be tricked into believing it is receiving water when it is not. Thus Adolph and associates found that the old trick of placing a pebble in the mouth might help an individual psychologically but certainly not physiologically.

Studies revealed that sweating rates of individuals are approximately proportional to two-thirds of the power of the body weight. Hence a 200-pound person sweats approximately 30 percent faster than a 130-pound person. This fact has practical applications for a party in difficulty in the desert. If a group of people is stranded with no water or only a very limited supply, and decides to send a member on foot for help, theoretically a larger person can endure longer in this quest if no water is available; however, if some water is available, a smaller person can make the same amount of water go further.

Water is vital to the human body. Neither heroics nor wishing will substitute for it. Plan your desert outings carefully, and be prepared with an adequate water supply. But if an emergency situation arises—if you are stranded in the desert due to an airplane crash or a disabled vehicle or are lost afoot—consider all factors of your situation carefully. Particularly consider your water supply or nonsupply, and ask yourself: How long can I survive if I stay where I am? What are the possibilities of my rescue in this location? How long can I survive if I walk? How far can I expect to walk? How far might I need to go to increase my chances of rescue? Answer yourself truthfully; you cannot deceive your body physiologically. Remember that a man at rest loses only half as much water as the man who walks. And since the rate of dehydration often determines survival time, the solution to your problem takes very careful consideration. Your life may well depend on your decision.

# CHAPTER XII

# Potentially Dangerous Desert Animals (and Some That Are Not)

WHEN LANDS hosting fearsome, dangerous, and venomous animals are mentioned, the desert is often popularly ranked second only to the tropical jungles as depicted in the movies and on television. This classification is unwarranted. The desert does contain a few species which are *potentially* dangerous to man. Most of these animals will not bother you if you provide them the same courtesy. In no way should their presence in the desert deter the outdoor enthusiast; but the hiker, camper, or backpacker who fails to take certain precautions against startling, upsetting, or damaging either himself or the animals that fall into this category, through an unneeded confrontation, is foolish and irresponsible. In addition to the potentially dangerous desert animals, we will also note some animals often considered to be dangerous which are not.

## *Centipede*

Their name indicates a hundred legs; however, centipede species vary in the number of legs they have. They are at least many-legged, with each pair of legs arising from a separate body segment. A large pair of pincerlike appendages, known as gnathosomes, are located in front of the legs and are used to inject venom into the prey. Over 3,000 described centipede species of varying sizes and colors—including yellow, red, blue, and combinations of these—are distributed throughout the world in both temperate and tropical climates; centipedes

FIG. 85. The giant desert centipede, *Scolopendra heros,* may attain a maximum length of 8 inches. It can inflict a painful, but not serious bite, if handled or molested.

are certainly not unique to the desert. The most impressive species present in the southwestern desert country is the giant desert centipede, *Scolopendra heros,* which occurs in Mexico and many of the southern states of the United States, including Georgia, Alabama, Kansas, Texas, and Arizona. *Scolopendra heros* may reach a maximum length of eight inches, has twenty-one pairs of legs, and is orange in color with a black head and tail. The last, or anal, pair of legs is modified for pinching or grasping. Prey may be attacked and grasped by these prehensile legs; the head is then rapidly curved backward and the venom claws are embedded in the prey, which is held immobile by other pairs of legs until the venom takes effect. Food consists of insects, spiders, worms, and similar items. Individual centipedes are solitary and nocturnal. They spend much time under stones and bark and in holes in the ground, preferring some moisture. In the desert they are observed primarily in the summer months, at night, and particularly after the moisture brought by summer rains has triggered insect abundance.

Desert centipedes may bite, or more correctly "pinch" with their gnathosomes, people who handle them or with whom they come into accidental contact, as they might in bedding left on the ground. The bite is reported to be a "painful inconvenience," but is ordinarily no reason for major concern. Application of an antiseptic to the bite is indicated to combat infection. If the animal has run across the skin, the many sharp-tipped claws may scratch the human skin, causing irritation and bacterial infection.

## Millipede

The nonvenomous millipedes superficially resemble centipedes. Their name implies that they are thousand-legged, which they are not; like the centipede, they are many-legged, with two legs per segment. Each time a millipede sheds, new segments and legs are added, therefore the number of legs varies over time for any one individual. As a group millipedes vary in size, but those commonly seen in our southwestern deserts are approximately four to seven inches in length. These species are dark brown or reddish brown to black in color. They are detritivores, consuming decaying organic material. Primarily nocturnal, millipedes spend much of their time underground, sometimes at a depth of more than two feet in the nests or burrows of other animals. They are not particularly fast moving and may, if threatened, roll up into a neat ball, rather well enclosed in the hard tergin covering their dorsal surface. They possess repugnatorial glands on each trunk segment; the chemical excreted from these glands varies from species to species and may include aldehydes, quinones, and phenols. Certain species have been identified as possessing hydrogen cyanide. Some have been reported to have secretions caustic to the skin; however, these reports are not from species in the area under discussion.

FIG. 86.    Millipedes of the southwestern deserts are 4 to 6 inches long, dark brown to black in color, and herbivorous. They are nonvenomous, but do excrete a substance which may temporarily stain the hands of human handlers.

Millipedes dwell primarily in moister habitats than the desert. They are seen in the dry desert environment after the summer rains when they emerge from under rocks and debris and from underground retreats in great numbers, and, by our standards and perhaps by their own as well, appear to revel in the moisture. At this time, children are likely to find that handled desert millipedes excrete from their repugnatorial glands a substance which temporarily stains the hands yellow-brown and gives them an unpleasant odor. These animals are essentially harmless. Rubbing the eyes with hands soiled by their secretion is not advisable, however. If the secretion does enter the eye, wash the eye with large amounts of water; contact a physician if discomfort is present.

## Whip Scorpion, or Vinegaroon

Whip scorpions belong to the class Arachnida (the scorpion, spider, mite, and tick class). Within it, they compose a separate small order, Uropygi; its members are also referred to as uropygids. These uropygids are certainly among the more menacing in appearance of the desert arthropods, yet they are not venomous. As a group, whip scorpions are found

FIG. 87. The whip scorpion, or vinegaroon, *Mastigoproctus giganteus,* may reach approximately 2½ inches in length and is dark gray to black. Though it appears ferocious, it is actually harmless to man.

throughout tropical and semi-tropical parts of the world. Some, such as *Mastigoproctus giganteus,* which occurs in the North American desert, live in dry environments, but most species prefer a moister habitat. *Mastigoproctus giganteus* ranges in the southern United States from the east to west coasts. It is one of the large species, up to approximately 13 inches in length. Dark gray to black in color, it normally walks on the last three pairs of long, jointed legs, using the first, even longer pair in a sensory-tactile function. The *pedipalps* (anterior appendages, lying on each side of the mouth) are extremely stout and heavy; they form formidable pincers used in seizing prey, which consists of small invertebrates. From the last segment of the abdomen arises a long, thin posterior appendage which is moved or whipped from one position to another, varying from straight up, to straight back, to a variety of intermediate positions. Neither it nor the jaws contain any substance of danger to man. When irritated, the animal elevates the end of the abdomen and sprays the attacker with a fluid secreted from a pair of large anal glands. In *M. giganteus,* this secretion is reported to be 84 percent acetic acid and 5 percent caprylic acid. When sprayed on a fellow arthropod, the caprylic acid effectively paves the way for the entrance into the arthropod victim's body of the acetic acid. The fluid may irritate human skin. Its repugnant odor is due to the acetic acid; hence the animal's common name, vinegaroon.

Whip scorpions are nocturnal, hiding in retreats during the day; in the desert they are seldom seen except during the warm summer rainy season. Some species do not mature until three years of age and may engage in courtship dances before mating. The female secludes herself in some retreat during egg laying. She remains there with the eggs attached to her body until they hatch and the young have undergone at least one molt; shortly after their dispersal, she dies.

## Sun Spider

The sun spider (*Eremobates* spp.), like the vinegaroon, is an arachnid. It belongs to the order Solifugae, which includes

FIG. 88. The sun spiders, or solpugids, *Eremobates* spp., are approximately 2 to 3 inches in length. Nonvenomous, they are not only harmless to man but are helpful as destroyers of insects.

approximately 800 tropical and semitropical species, with more than 100 species occurring in the southwestern United States. Many prefer an arid environment and are common in warm deserts of the world, where they hide under stones or in crevices, or burrow underground. Their tendency to have diurnal habits has earned them their common name, sun spider; a second name, wind spider, refers to their running speed. In the desert southwest they are most active from May through September.

Sun spiders are yellow or tan in color and may reach a length of 3 inches. They have two body sections. The first portion appears to be composed almost entirely of large pincers; the second is a fused abdominal section. Their most remarkable features are the two enormous *chelicerae* (anterior appendages), each composed of two pieces, which together form a pincer; these pieces articulate vertically. The first pair of legs is often held aloft or in front of the animal; they are used as tactile organs. The animal moves by means of the remaining three pairs. When mating occurs, a male finds a receptive female. Stroking or "dancing" occurs, after which the male flips the female on her back and, using his chelicerae, inserts a drop of sperm into her gonopore. This is stored in her body for future fertilization of her eggs. The female digs a burrow in which she deposits her eggs; no guarding of eggs or care of young takes place.

Sun spiders have voracious appetites and feed on all types of small animals, including arachnids, insects, and small lizards. They are nonvenomous and obtain food by seizing it, then killing it and ripping it apart with the chelicerae. Sun spiders are totally harmless to man; they are in fact helpful in destroying insects and certainly do not deserve the unwarranted fear man often feels toward them.

## Jerusalem Cricket

A totally harmless but impressive-appearing insect found in the desert as well as in other areas is the Jerusalem cricket, *Stenopelmatus fuscus*. These insects are shy, usually golden to dark brown in color, approximately 1½ to 2 inches in length, and have large, smooth, rounded heads. They may be active both diurnally and nocturnally. Other insects, roots, and decaying vegetation are among the items used for food. Following mating the female often devours the male. She deposits her white oval eggs in a depression in the ground.

The Navajo Indians reportedly apply to these insects a fitting common name which translates as "old man baldhead."

FIG. 89.  The Jerusalem cricket, *Stenopelmatus fuscus*, is a harmless, interesting insect up to 2 inches in length. It has often been erroneously considered dangerous to man and animals.

The top of the head has markings which, with imagination, can be seen to resemble a smiling face; hence another common name, "baby face." Since their legs are adapted for tunneling in sandy soil, the Jerusalem crickets are also sometimes referred to as sand crickets. Jerusalem crickets, like the sun spiders, are sometimes referred to as "niña de la tierra," or "child of the earth." Like a good many other unusual-looking animals, this one has suffered from a poor reputation, completely unfounded and perpetuated by superstitious, uninformed individuals who have in the past blamed this innocuous little insect for even the deaths of cattle and horses. In actuality the Jerusalem cricket's only protection against man, cow, or horse is its nipping jaws. This insect is not a true cricket, but a member of an insect family separate from, but closely related to, the family that includes the true crickets.

## Velvet Ant

Velvet ants, *Dasymutilla* spp., are not ants; rather they are wasps of the family Mutillidae, which resemble ants; they are often referred to as mutillid wasps. The males have wings, but the females are wingless and may be seen running over the

FIG. 90. Velvet ants are actually mutillid wasps. Often brightly colored, the females are wingless. As with other wasps, their sting can be painful.

THE DESERTS OF THE SOUTHWEST

ground in the summer. Approximately ⅛ to 1 inch in length, they are often striking in appearance; many have long, fuzzy hair over much of the body and are often brightly colored, varying from red, yellow, and orange, to white or silver, or occasionally displaying combinations of colors. The females seek nests of other wasps or sometimes of bees which are located in the ground. In these they deposit eggs. The young mutillid wasp feeds on the host larva or pupa and undergoes its own development in that location.

Velvet ants possess a powerful sting. Their often-bright color pattern is thought to serve as an *aposematic* or warning coloration, advertising their power to potential predators. Their stings have earned them the exaggerated common names of "cow-killers" and "mule-killers." They are not stock killers. But even man should observe their warning colors and take heed—watch, but do not touch, these wasps.

The desert is home to many other kinds of wasps, and to a rather bountiful array of ant and bee species. As in any other area where these insects abound, care should be taken, for one's comfort, to avoid being stung.

## Kissing Bug

Kissing bugs, *Triatoma* spp., are also commonly known as cone-nosed bugs, assassin bugs, bellows bugs, and walpai tigers. They are members of the family Reduviidae. Several species are present in the Southwest; they are similar in appearance to box elder bugs. One-half to one inch in length, these insects have an elongated cone-shaped head. Their mouth parts are of the piercing and sucking type and are folded beneath the head when not in use. Kissing bugs can be of concern to man; they may produce a painful bite and are carriers, at least in some parts of their range, of a serious illness, Chagas' disease.

Kissing bugs feed on the blood of their hosts, which may include man. Normally they live in rodent nests, particularly those of pack rats. By piercing and sucking, they feed on the rodents' blood. In early and midsummer, they often invade

FIG. 91. The kissing bug, *Triatoma* spp. (½ to 1 inch in length), produces a painful bite as it pierces human skin and consumes blood. In the early summer, these insects may invade and be serious pests in homes located in the open desert.

homes, particularly those located on the desert's edge around cities. This invasion is particularly likely where pack rat nests occur close to habitations. The kissing bugs hide in crevices and cracks of houses, emerging at night to feed on the blood of their sleeping human victim. These insects do not produce a venom, but enzymes in their saliva numb the bite area and stop the coagulation of blood while the bug feeds. These enzymes produce local reactions in the victims. The severity of the bite varies according to the susceptibility of the victim. Normally, a hard welt ½ to 3 inches in diameter develops. More sensitive individuals and those who have become sensitized through previous bites, may develop extensive swelling of the affected member, and some experience systemic symptoms such as nausea, rapid heart action, and increased rate of respiration, or may even enter anaphylactic shock, a very serious condition.

In southern Mexico and South America, *Triatoma* is host to a small flagellate microorganism which can, in its extended stage, cause Chagas' disease in humans. Symptoms of the disease are often delayed for long periods. The parasite may eventually invade the human blood system and migrate into tissues, commonly those of the heart, spleen, and lymph nodes. No cases of Chagas' disease have been recorded in the

THE DESERTS OF THE SOUTHWEST

United States. However, the same or a very similar trypanosome which causes Chagas' disease is known to be carried by *T. dimidiata* in rural areas in the state of Sonora, Mexico.

## Tarantula

The tarantula is the desert's largest spider, with a leg span of four or more inches. Heavy-bodied and hairy, light to dark brown in color, the various species which are found in our desert areas are classified in more than one genus. Tarantulas have often been needlessly feared and killed by man. In North America, tarantulas are not confined to the desert but are also found in other habitats; their eastern limit in the United States is the Mississippi River. They are, however, especially plentiful in the Southwest. Tarantulas live singly in burrows from which they venture for short distances for hunting, usually remaining within a few meters of their burrow, and quickly retreat underground if threatened with danger. Their primary food consists of insects, other arthropods, and lizards; in captivity they will eat mice, as they may also in the wild.

FIG. 92. Hairy, dark brown or black, the tarantulas in our deserts are unnecessarily feared. They are mild-mannered, and their bite is approximately equal to a bee or wasp sting where man is concerned. Some may have a leg span of 6 or 7 inches.

They tend to suddenly jump or pounce upon their prey, subduing it by injecting venom with their fangs. Digestive juices are then poured into the victim's body, and the liquefied nourishment is sucked into the spider's body.

Tarantulas are extremely long-lived. They do not reach sexual maturity until approximately ten years of age. Females have a tendency to eat their mates, if possible, and the males' longevity record following sexual maturity is not a good one, due both to this factor and to the fact that many of the males fall prey to predators in their search for mates. Females, which do not roam to the extent of the males, may live up to twenty years. Immature males and females are virtually indistinguishable until their last molt, when the males become apparent—they are darker than the females, who are often also heavier-bodied. The female lays her eggs on a silken sheet, which she then forms into a bag. Sometimes moving the bag from one location to another in the burrow, the mother watches over her eggs for as long as seven weeks until the spiderlings emerge. The young soon leave to establish their solitary burrows. They suffer a high mortality rate; ultimately, probably only one or two of the original group will survive.

Much of the year tarantulas are seldom or never seen by human observers. Those most often observed are males wandering in search of females. Summer is their most active period, when they tend to be nocturnal. They may also be observed after showers on moist, overcast summer days. Most often the tarantulas are observed crossing roads, and at night their eye shine may be seen reflecting in the car lights. Unfortunately a good many of the big spiders are killed by automobiles as the unsuspecting, long-legged creatures move slowly and deliberately across the blacktop. Other enemies include rodents, birds, lizards, some snakes, skunks, and javalinas. In its defense against such predators, the tarantula may tilt its body backward, displaying its fangs in a defensive attitude. In addition to their ability to bite, tarantulas have one unique feature—the fine, urticating, barbed, or venomous hair on their abdomens, which can be very irritating. If being attacked, as by a small mammal, the tarantula will work its hind legs rapidly and scrape loose a small cloud of the fine abdominal hair, brushing it at the intruder. When these hairs come into contact with the skin, eye, or mucous membranes of mammals, a disagreeable irritation results, and this diversion will often give the tarantula time to escape the predators.

One major predator of the tarantula is the tarantula hawk, *Pepsis* spp. This is a large, 1- to 1¾-inch, dark metallic blue, often orange- or red-winged, digger wasp, which uses the adult tarantula as a food source for its young. The female tarantula hawk searches for and finds an adult tarantula, usually a female (preferred because of her larger size), and paralyzes it by stinging the spider near the base of a leg, thus envenomating the prey. A series of stings may be necessary to completely subdue the prey. Once the spider is paralyzed, the Pepsis wasp drags the victim—eight to ten times her own weight—to a burrow or hole. There the wasp lays an egg on the tarantula, then exits, sealing the burrow. Inside, the spider, paralyzed but not dead, is gradually eaten alive, thereby providing the wasp's young with a source of fresh food for its entire larval period. Where humans are concerned, these wasps are not aggressive, but a sting from one can be exceedingly painful, reported to be many times more painful than that of a honeybee.

Tarantulas have in the past been inappropriately attributed with lurid attacks on unsuspecting people in Mexico, where they often were believed to be dangerous to horses, as shown by one common name "araña de caballo" (horse spider). The tarantulas in the North American desert areas are, in fact, virtually harmless to anything of horse, human, and even much smaller size. They do have venom but, for man, a tarantula bite is considered to be about equal in strength to a bee or wasp sting. The tarantulas actually are quite tractable and are sometimes referred to as the desert's "gentle giants." They are kept as pets by some individuals and can ordinarily be handled readily; the spiders will normally walk on the human hand or up an arm with no problem suffered by either human or spider, provided the spider is not confined in its actions or grabbed—which, after all, is better than a human could be expected to do if it were being handled by a spider many times its size!

## Africanized Honeybees

In recent years Africanized honeybees have become established in portions of the North American desert. They reached Arizona in 1993. Indistinguishable by sight from our familiar honeybees, the Africanized bees vary from them in being more excitable, more prone to attack, to do so in greater numbers, and to be more tenacious, pursuing a victim farther in an attack. They can pose a serious, even potentially lethal threat to animals and people.

Africanized honeybees nest in a variety of locations in urban areas including in the walls of buildings, in meter boxes, and in debris around homes, such as discarded vehicle parts and appliances. They may enter openings as small as 3/16 inch in diameter if there is a cavity behind the opening large enough for a nest. Thus they easily find sites for their nests in towns and cities. However, they may also be found away from these areas nesting in animal burrows, at the openings to caves, and in cavities in saguaros, in trees, or among rocks.

Africanized bees are sensitive to odors and to loud vibrations, such as those produced by lawn mowers or heavy equipment in use. In an attack they often target furry and dark-colored objects that resemble their natural enemies.

When hiking, never disturb a known bee colony. Wear light-colored clothing, including socks. Avoid having scents of any sort about you, including scented shampoo, soaps, perfumes, hair spray, or heavily scented gum. If on horseback, avoid using fly control products with a citrus odor on your horse. If hiking with dogs, keep them under control so they do not go bounding through brush.

If attacked, **RUN** and keep running. Do not fight or flail at the bees. Cover your face and head as much as possible, as these are targeted by the bees. If you have no other covering available, pull your shirt up over your head. Run for shelter—a vehicle, building, etc.—if any is available. Africanized bees can attain 12 to 15 miles per hour and may follow their target for more than a quarter mile.

## Black Widow Spider

"Black Widow" is the common name for several species of spiders of the genus *Lactrodectus*. Spiders of this genus have an almost worldwide distribution in tropical and temperate regions. They are found in every state in the continental United States and in portions of Canada, although they are more common in the southern rather than in the northern portions of the United States. They are one of the most easily recognized and best-known of our North American spiders, and are among the most venomous spiders known. The venom is a neurotoxin and can cause cramping, respiratory problems, nausea, muscular spasms in the abdomen and chest, fever, high blood pressure, headache, dizziness, and weakness. Progression of symptoms is rapid, but the effects

FIG. 93. Widespread in distribution, the black widow spider, *Latrodectus* spp. (approximately 1 inch in length), occurs throughout much of the temperate and tropical world. It is retiring and unaggressive, but extremely venomous; antivenin is available. These spiders are common around abandoned buildings, in piles of debris, or in undisturbed dark corners of garages and storage buildings. An adult female is readily recognized by the red marking on her abdomen, easily noted as she often hangs upside down from her web.

begin to regress after several hours. Envenomation may be particularly serious for small children, to people with hypertension or coronary problems, and for pregnant women. Frequently the human victim has not seen the spider and does not realize the cause of his illness. Fatal cases are rare.

Black widows spin their webs in crevices, under logs, in abandoned rodent holes, and in similar locations. They are less spiders of the desert environment than of man's environments, often being found in old buildings, woodpiles, and dark corners of garages and attics. You are, in fact, much more likely to encounter them around residences in the desert than in the desert wilderness.

A remarkable dimorphism is present in the sexes of the black widow; only the larger, dark females produce sufficient venom to be dangerous to man. Females are fairly large, ½ to ¾ inch in body length, and are a deep, shiny black or very dark brown in color. A globular abdomen displaying a red or orange hourglass marking on its ventral surface makes the female easily identifiable. Males are much smaller, less than half the size of the females, are medium brown to cream colored, and do not carry the red marking. The black widow spins a rather messy-appearing, ungeometric web in which prey is trapped. These spiders are solitary and active primarily at night. The females spin egg cocoons, white or light gray in color; the 300 to 500 eggs they contain hatch in approximately thirty days and the young disperse by ballooning.

Although potentially dangerous, these spiders are retiring and nonaggressive, probably normally biting a human only when the victim brushes against the spider or a similar contact is made. In one incident with which we are familiar, the human victim put his bare foot into a shoe which had been sitting in his garage for some time where it had, unfortunately, been appropriated by a black widow.

## Brown Recluse Spider

Spiders of the genus *Loxosceles* are distributed fairly widely in the United States; several species are represented,

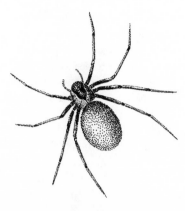

FIG. 94. Recluse spiders, *Loxosceles* spp. (approximately 5⁄16 inch in length), are also known as violin spiders after the darker marking on the upper side of the cephalothorax. These spiders possess a hemolytic venom. Their bite may produce a serious ulcerous condition which spreads outward from the site of the bite.

particularly in the southern and western states. The true brown recluse, *L. reclusa,* is not found in the Southwest; the *Loxosceles* species in this area have venom less potent than *L. reclusa,* but still powerful enough to be dangerous. Those in the Southwest are small to medium-sized spiders, approximately 5⁄16 inch in body length, are dark brown to fawn color, with a darker, violin-shaped mark on the upper side of the cephalothorax. This mark gives rise to one of their common names, "violin spider." Like black widow spiders, the recluse spiders are most abundant around manmade structures.

This spider possesses a hemolytic venom. When bitten, a person may feel little or no discomfort or may have a local stinging pain. Systemic involvement may occur within two to eight hours, in which case the victim may have chills, fever, joint pains, and nausea. Within twelve hours to a few days a lesion appears at the bite site and gradually increases in size. Over a period of days, the affected area centered about the bite becomes necrotic, tissue sloughs off, and a draining ulcer forms. The necrosis may continue to spread outward, destroying adjacent tissue due to the fact that the toxin remains in the

tissue at the site for a long period. Physicians may find it necessary to excise the bite area to remove the infecting source,
after which the ulcer begins to heal. If left unchecked, the
ulcer may continue to grow to a size several inches in diameter. In some cases the victim may have chills, fever, joint pains,
and nausea. Death is rarely associated with the bite of the
brown recluse.

As with the black widow, this spider is retiring, and man's
encounters with it are often connected in some way with moving stored materials such as bundles of unused clothing and
piles of debris, or otherwise disturbing the spider and its
large, irregular web. Ordinarily the primary problem associated with the bite of this spider is that of the ulcer. Its bite
does not present an emergency situation, inasmuch as several
hours may elapse before the first symptoms appear. Such a
bite, however, is a situation to be handled by a physician.

## Gila Monster

Worldwide, only two known species of venomous lizards
exist. The two species are members of the same genus and are
similar in appearance. The Mexican beaded lizard, *Heloderma
horridum,* occurs only in Mexico; its range in the Pacific

FIG. 95.    The Gila monster, *Heloderma suspectum,* is one of the
only two venomous lizards in the world. This lizard may reach a maximum length of 20 inches, is patterned with orange, to pink, to yellow, and black, beaded-looking scales. If cornered or handled it may
bite, chewing its venom into the victim. The bite of a Gila monster
should be considered a serious medical emergency.

drainage from the state of Chiapas northward into southern Sonora is such that it barely touches the Sonoran Desert's southern boundaries. Basically the Mexican beaded lizard is not a desert inhabitant, but rather is a resident in thornscrub and tropical deciduous forest.

The Gila monster, *Heloderma suspectum,* however, is a desert species occurring in extreme southwestern Utah, the southern tip of Nevada, southwestern New Mexico, Arizona, and Sonora, Mexico. A rather typical habitat of it is the saguaro forest of the Arizona Upland Division of the Sonoran Desert.

The Gila monster is a heavy-bodied lizard with an almost cylindrical body. The head is large, somewhat flattened, and equipped with strong jaws; it terminates in a rounded snout. Out of the generous-sized mouth flicks, snakelike, a black tongue. The animal has a large sausagelike tail which serves as a fat storage organ, changing from plump to depleted according to the animal's condition. The legs are short and appear set too far apart to support the lengthy body. The feet have strong curved claws. Average adult length (body plus tail) for the Gila monster is 14 to 18 inches; a specimen of 20 inches has been reported; these lizards may weigh up to two pounds. The Mexican beaded lizard is larger, a specimen 32 inches having been recorded. These two lizard species are covered over their dorsal surface with small, round, closely set scales. The Gila monster is patterned with contrasting markings of orange, pink, or yellow, and black; the Mexican beaded is similarly mottled and blotched in terms of yellow and black. The family name for these lizards is Helodermatidae, meaning "warty skin," and the combination of rounded scales and irregular color pattern gives these lizards a general effect of Indian beadwork.

Gila monsters are dormant during the coldest months, diurnal in moderate temperatures, and primarily nocturnal during the hottest months. Their irregular color pattern serves in dim light to conceal them. Against a dark background, the black portions of the pattern blend, and the light markings appear to be sticks, rocks, or the like. On a light background, the reverse occurs. The Gila monster retreats to burrows of other animals, digs its own, or enters pack rat nests or natural cavities. It is most common on the lower slopes of desert mountains, ranging onto the outwash plains, and may also be found in canyons and along washes where water, which it appears to need during its active period, may be available. An average of five eggs are produced by the mature female after the summer rains have begun. The eggs are buried in a shallow depression in sand or soft soil. There they overwinter and hatch the following April through June.

Gila monsters are thought to live to an age of twenty-five years. They hibernate from roughly November through February and are thought to spend 97 percent of their time underground. Their food consists of bird and reptile eggs and small mammals, such as young rabbits and rodents, which are killed by means of the lizard's venom.

The venom of these two lizard species is produced in modified salivary glands in the lower jaw. The venom is not injected by means of fangs, but is free flowing and is chewed into the wound by the grooved teeth. The Gila monster is famous for its tenacity; it hangs on tightly when biting. Modified teeth, which draw the venom by their capillary action, quickly become bathed in the venom and, as the lizard continues to chew, increasing amounts of venom enter the wound. Gila monsters have been reported to hang on as long as fifteen minutes. Obviously it is important to disengage the reptile from its human victim as quickly as possible if a bite does occur.

No human deaths appear to be uncontestably attributable solely to the bite of the Gila monster. Deaths have occurred in connection with such bites, but these appear to have been complicated by alcoholism, debility, or similar conditions. Since the 1940s, when more complete medical records have been kept, only one death related to a Gila monster bite has been recorded and in that case death was due to alcohol in conjunction with the bite. Symptoms and their severity following a bite are varied and depend upon many factors, such as the quantity of venom received, which depends somewhat upon the number of teeth engaged in the bite and the length of time they were engaged; the size of the lizard; the physical

THE DESERTS OF THE SOUTHWEST

condition and size of the victim; and other variables. Symptoms following a minor bite have been reported as consisting of pain and prolonged bleeding at the site, and sometimes nausea and faintness. More serious bites may cause severe pain, profuse bleeding, initial shock, low blood pressure, and edema.

Two other lizards are sometimes confused with the Gila monster. The nocturnally active gecko is occasionally thought to be a young Gila monster, and the chuckwalla—a large, rock-inhabiting, primarily vegetarian lizard—is sometimes confused with the adult Gila monster. Neither the gecko nor the chuckwalla have the beaded scales of the Gila monster, and neither is venomous.

The Gila monster deserves neither name—monster nor *suspectum*—nor does the beaded lizard deserve *horridum*. All of these names simply continue to contribute to a popular misconception and fear of these exceedingly interesting animals. They are not numerous and, unless they are caught, handled, or cornered, they make every attempt to avoid man. These lizards are somewhat deceptive, often appearing slug-

FIG. 96. The chuckwalla, *Sauromalus obesus*, is a large (5½ to 8 inches, snout-to-vent length), heavy-bodied, herbivorous lizard. The chuckwalla inhabits rocky sites, basking on top of the rocks, and wedging itself into crevices among the rocks when threatened.

gish and slow moving. If teased, cornered, or forced to bite, they then exhibit agility and speed, being capable of rapidly twisting the head about and grabbing the victim with unexpected rapidity, singleness of purpose, and tenacity. Many of the reported Gila monster bites have occurred as a result of human handling of the lizards (some of the alcohol-accompanied bites have taken place in this situation), and bites by captive animals have occurred through cloth bags in which the lizards were being held captive.

The Gila monsters pose almost no threat to the person who avoids them or simply observes them from a respectful distance. If a bite does occur, however, it is to be considered potentially dangerous, and immediate medical attention should be obtained. We wish also to note that the Gila monster is *protected by law* in the state of Arizona. These lizards are not to be killed, and they cannot be caught, sold, or kept as captives without a special permit. This law, passed in 1952, made the Gila monster the first venomous animal in North America to be protected by law and is certainly a commendable example of environmentally protective legislation.

## Scorpions

Scorpions are members of the class Arachnida and are among the oldest known terrestrial arthropods; they have changed little in the past 350 to 400 million years. Scorpions are found in many of the tropical, subtropical, and desert areas of the world. All scorpions are venomous; some are of great danger to man. In the North American deserts potentially lethal species are limited, but of importance.

Scorpions are eight-legged and have long anterior pedipalps greatly enlarged to form a pair of pincers for capturing and holding prey. The telson or "tail" consists of five segments and terminates in a bulbous base and sharp, curved barb that injects the venom hypodermically. The tail is articulated, allowing movement to the side or up over the body, bringing the barb beyond the head. In stinging, the scorpion raises the tail

FIG. 97. Note the comparative sizes of two scorpion species. The smaller specimen is *Centruroides exilicauda,* a potentially lethal species. At the right is the larger, nonlethal, giant hairy scorpion, *Hadrurus arizonensis.* Average adult size of the *Centruroides* is 2 to 3 inches; for *Hadrurus* it is approximately 4 to 6 inches.

over the body, curves it forward, and, with a stabbing motion, envenomates the prey. The pedipalps alone are generally used to subdue the prey; however, if difficulty is met, the prey is held by the pedipalps and envenomation is accomplished by use of the barbed tail. Scorpions are predacious in nature and eat spiders, beetles, flies, grasshoppers, worms, centipedes, sun spiders, black widow spiders, and sometimes other scorpions. Inasmuch as the principal purpose of the venom is to paralyze small invertebrate prey, the strength of the toxin in most species is not powerful enough to cause great danger to man. The sting of many nonlethal species is often equated to that of a yellow jacket or hornet.

Scorpions are secretive, usually hunting for prey at night. They are commonly found under loose bark on trees; in lumber piles, brick stacks, and firewood; under rocks; in abandoned buildings; in garages and attics; under houses; and in crevices. Their presence in shoes and bedding is not un-known. Scorpions require water and may be attracted to habi-tations for this reason.

In the desert southwest three species of scorpions are most common. *Centruroides exilicauda,* the bark scorpion, is the smallest in size, and is the species with potentially life-threatening venom. The striped tail or devil's scorpion, *Vejovis spinigeris,* is somewhat larger and heavier-bodied, darker col-ored, and has a striped tail, as is obvious from its name. The giant or desert hairy scorpion, *Hadrurus arizonensis,* is much larger and heavier than the others, reaching up to 5½ inches in length.

In the United States scorpions are more widespread than one might presume, being distributed over three-fourths of the nation; more than fifty species occur in the state of Ari-zona alone. Scorpions range across the southern states from Florida to California; they occur as far north as Washington and Montana and have been collected in southern Canada. In general they are not found in the New England and Great Lakes states. In the deserts under discussion, Arizona, south-ern California, Baja California, southwestern New Mexico, and Mexico have potentially lethal scorpions.

Scorpions are preyed on by lizards, some small snakes, pal-lid bats, elf owls, and grasshopper mice. They give birth to live young which, following birth, crawl up on the mother's back, where they remain for a few days until their first molt, follow-ing which they disperse. Scorpions fluoresce under ultraviolet light and can be observed in the desert on warm summer nights through use of a black light.

Because its venom is potentially lethal, the desert dweller or hiker should be able to identify *Centruroides exilicauda.* Unfortunately, to complicate the problem, *C. exilicauda* is not the largest scorpion in its range, being quite small by compar-ison to the desert hairy scorpion, and is not brightly marked, as is the black widow spider. Some of the points for identifica-tion include: (1) *C. exilicauda* is yellowish or greenish-yellow to straw color. (2) In size, *C. exilicauda* range from ½ inch in length at the time they leave the mother to an average adult length of 1½ inches. (3) These scorpions are "slender." The adult female's body at its greatest width is not wider than ⅜ inch; the male's is only ¼ inch or less. (4) The adult female's "tail" may be slightly more than ¹⁄₁₆ inch in diameter; the male's is even more slender. (5) The pincers are very slender, about six times as long as the broadest part. (6) Most important, *C. exilicauda* possesses a subaculear tooth. This very small tooth, or *tubercle,* located at the base of the stinger, may be discernible to the naked eye if it is silhouetted against the light, or may be seen with a hand lens.

Although the only potentially lethal scorpions which occur in the North American desert area belong to the genus *Centruroides,* this genus also includes nonlethal species. Most, although not all, members of this genus, whether poisonous or not, display the subaculear tooth. The only species of *Centruroides* in Arizona is *exilicauda.* Thus if one is stung by a scorpion in Arizona, which is identified as possessing the subaculear tooth, one is able to positively identify the species as *exilicauda* and the sting as potentially dangerous. In other areas, where nonlethal subaculear-toothed *Centruroides* occur, this determination is not valid.

One behavioral feature also helps to differentiate *C. exilicauda.* Nonlethal species are sometimes known as "ground scorpions"; they are often found on the ground or substratum. *C. exilicauda,* however, does not burrow and reacts negatively to gravity, thus is more often found clinging to the underside of its covering; it is often found hanging from the underside of

FIG. 98. A subaculear tooth is found at the base of the stinger of species of *Centruroides.* A hand lens may be necessary to determine its presence. This tooth, or tubercle, is one aid in identifying the lethal species, *C. exilicauda;* however, in some areas additional species of *Centruroides,* bearing the tooth, may be present.

rocks, boards, firewood, and bark. Keep this fact in mind when moving materials or picking up rocks. Stings commonly occur when people pick up objects without checking the underside and inadvertently touch or press the scorpion with their hands.

The study of *C. exilicauda* and the nonlethal species (perhaps in a natural history museum) is recommended homework for desert enthusiasts; the differences between them are easy to note. One common name for *C. exilicauda*, slender scorpion, notes one of its identifying characteristics. Another, bark scorpion, refers to its penchant for clinging to the underside of loose bark on tree trunk and limbs. This name denotes another trait that is advisable for the human firewood-gatherer to remember.

The sting of a *C. exilicauda* can be lethal, particularly to young children, the elderly, or adults with hypertension. The venom contains numerous neurotoxins. Symptoms that follow a scorpion sting aid in differentiating the lethal from the nonlethal. Reaction to the nonlethal sting is largely localized at the site with pain, swelling, and discoloration of the immediate tissues; in some cases, pain extends up the affected extremity. The sting of the lethal species may cause immediate severe pain at the site; this pain soon recedes; swelling and discoloration *do not* occur. Instead, the reaction is systemic, the venom being a convulsant neurotoxin (affecting the nervous system and leading in some cases to convulsions). The sting site tingles, prickles, and becomes hypersensitive. The presence of this sensation at the site proves one more means of identifying the sting of *C. exilicauda*. In testing, give a gentle tap to the sting site. If the victim immediately draws away, the sting is very likely to have been that of *C. exilicauda*.

Individuals vary in their sensitivity to the venom of the bark scorpion and some people may exhibit a more severe reaction than others. Symptoms which develop following a *C. exilicauda* sting may include the following: A numbness travels up the affected extremity; tightness develops in the throat; the tongue has a thick feeling; speech is slurred, the victim may drool, there may be abdominal pain and cramping, rapid eye movements, and the patient may exhibit fever and breathing difficulties. Great restlessness develops, which can lead in severe cases to seizures. Even after recovery, the original site of the sting often remains hypersensitive for from a few days to a week, and a slight bump to the sting site will initiate tingling or painful sensations in the area.

In 1998 the Arizona Poison and Drug Information Center in Tucson received reports of approximately 2,600 scorpion stings; its counterpart in Phoenix received approximately 5,000. And certainly not all stings in the state are reported. However, no deaths due to scorpion stings have been recorded in Arizona since 1965. In the 36 years previous to that, 75 people died as a result of bark scorpion stings in Arizona. More medical facilities and better treatment are credited for the improvement.

### AVOIDING UNNECESSARY CONFRONTATIONS WITH SCORPIONS

1. Remember that the potentially lethal species *C. exilicauda* tends to cling to the underside of objects, such as rocks, logs, and bark. Do not put your hands where you can't see. The common name, bark scorpion, advises you to be somewhat cautious about grabbing firewood without first checking for scorpions.

2. Scorpions need a certain amount of moisture and may be attracted to damp spots.

3. Learn to tell the difference between the lethal and nonlethal species.

4. The age-old rule has been to shake out your shoes before putting them on in the morning if they've been on the ground. We've never known anyone who found a scorpion by doing so, or failed to find one by not doing so, but shaking out your shoes doesn't hurt anything, may make you feel more secure, and will at least get rid of any sand or gravel in them. Anything left lying on the ground which can provide a hiding place for scorpions may harbor them. We recommend rolling up or elevating your bedroll above the ground when it's not in

use—at least, inspect and shake it out before you crawl in if it has been in a location where scorpions may have had access to it.

5. As with rattlesnake bites, the sting of a *C. exilicauda* will often affect small children more severely than adults. Take proper precautions for them. Don't frighten children, but teach them precautions. A common way in which children sustain bark scorpion stings is by picking up rocks and inadvertently touching the scorpion clinging out of sight on the underside.

## Arizona Coral Snake

The coral snakes are members of the family Elapidae, which includes the cobras, kraits, mambas, and other notorious Old World members. In the United States, two distinct genera of coral snakes occur: the *Micrurus fulvius,* or eastern coral snake, approaches the Chihuahuan Desert on its eastern borders but does not enter it; in Arizona, extreme southwestern New Mexico, and extending southward into Mexico to Sinaloa is found the western or Arizona coral snake, *Micruroides euryxanthus.*

FIG. 99. The western or Arizona coral snake, *Micruroides euryxanthus* (average of 15 to 20 inches in length), produces venom dangerous to man. However its small mouth size prevents it from easily biting a human. This coral snake has alternating rings of red, cream and black, each red ring bordered by the cream colored rings; all rings of color completely encircle the body, and the snout is black.

THE DESERTS OF THE SOUTHWEST

The highly venomous eastern coral snake is a large reptile, up to almost four feet in length. Fortunately the Arizona coral, although also highly venomous, is very small and retiring and is seen only occasionally. Average adult size of the Arizona coral is thirteen to twenty-one inches. The snake's body has a diameter not much greater than that of a human finger. The snake is strikingly beautiful. Shiny, waxy-looking, and appearing almost as though it were painted with enamels, the Arizona coral is marked by alternating, bright rings of red, white or cream, and black. Several other brightly colored, harmless snakes are often confused with the Arizona coral, including the long-nosed snake, the Sonora mountain kingsnake, the California mountain kingsnake, and the shovel-nosed snake. To differentiate the Arizona coral from look-alikes, remember that the coral has a blunt head that is black from the snout to behind the eyes, the color bands completely encircle the body, and the yellow or white bands occur on both sides of the red band.

Arizona coral snakes are secretive and nocturnal, retiring to sandy burrows or rock cover much of the time. They live in a variety of arid and semiarid regions within their range, including scrub, grassland, and the plains and lower mountain slopes within the desert; they appear to be partial to rocky desert areas with sandy soil. The Arizona coral has one peculiar trait, which is also displayed by certain hook-nosed snakes. If annoyed or molested, it everts its cloacal lining, producing an audible, sharp popping sound. Its food is thought to consist primarily of small lizards and snakes.

The venom of these snakes is essentially neurotoxic. The bite of the large eastern coral snake may prove fatal to human beings. No deaths have been reported from the bite of the Arizona coral snake, and very few bites have been reported. In keeping with its body size, the mouth of the Arizona coral is small. Additionally, these snakes have fixed, erect fangs (unlike the rattlesnake). These fangs are necessarily short; otherwise they would project beyond the snake's lower jaw. The opening through which the venom flows is not at the tip of the fangs, but rather at a higher level on the front face of the fang; for venom to be released from the fang opening into the victim, the fang must penetrate to a certain depth and the venom must flow into the victim; all of these factors prevent the Arizona coral snake from easily injecting venom into a human subject.

## Rattlesnakes

The rattlesnakes are a diverse and extremely interesting group of New World venomous snakes which have developed, as their first line of defense, the rattle, which is attached to the tail and which serves in essence as a warning to creatures that might injure the snake. As an evolutionary device, the rattle has great significance, and while still useful in a warning context today, certainly must have been even more significant in the past in the areas once shared by the rattlesnakes and large hoofed animals, such as the buffalo.

All rattlesnakes are venomous, and all rattlesnake bites should be considered of *serious significance* with proper measures immediately instituted (first aid measures are discussed in Chapter XIII). Rattlesnakes as a group are easily identified by the presence of the rattle, composed of hollow segments of keratin. However, a rattleless rattlesnake has evolved on Isla Catalina in the Gulf of California and, occasionally, a snake's rattle may have been broken off. Also, at birth rattlesnakes have but a single prebutton or button. It is the first of the loosely articulated rings which will form the rattle, but inasmuch as these very young individuals have but a single segment, no rattle sound is produced. Be advised, however, that even these young *do* possess venom.

Rattlesnakes occur from southern Canada southward to Argentina and range from sea level to near timberline. The majority of species are found in arid and semiarid areas, but some occur in marshes and forests. Through evolution, they have differentiated and vary greatly in size, color, patterns, and venom type and toxicity. All belong to one of two genera: *Crotalus* or *Sistrurus*. There are thirteen species of rattlesnakes in the western United States; eleven species or a total of seventeen species and subspecies are found in the state of Arizona. With more species of rattlesnakes than any other state, Arizona is the center of their radiation; as one moves away from this hub, less and less diversity is apparent.

In the United States, the rattlesnakes display extreme variations in size. The largest is the eastern diamondback, *C. adamanteus,* which may, in exceptional cases, reach eight feet in length; second largest is the western diamondback, *C. atrox,* of the southwestern United States and Mexico, a resident of the desert areas we are considering. It may occasionally reach seven feet in length. Dr. Laurence M. Klauber, authority on rattlesnakes, stated that the western diamondback is probably a greater hazard to man and domestic animals than any other snake in North America. The smallest species, also members of the *Crotalus* genus, inhabit the mountains and are among the smallest of all rattlesnakes. The species of *Sistrurus* are also relatively small; *S. catenatus,* known as the massasauga and found in some of the more eastern portions of the southwestern desert country, seldom reaches more than thirty inches in length.

Rattlesnakes are known as pit vipers because they possess heat-sensing pits located between the eyes and nostrils at the

FIG. 100. Pit vipers, the group including the rattlesnakes, have the most highly developed mechanism of venom injection among reptiles. The mouth opens widely; the large, hollow fangs in the upper jaw swing forward from their folded, resting position; the fangs stab and inject venom in the prey in one rapid, deft move.

anterior end of their snouts. The pits are capable of sensing radiant body heat from nearby potential prey and are a valuable sense organ. Rattlesnakes' sense of smell is good, their sense of sight moderately good, and they receive both airborne and earthborne sound frequencies. These snakes have hinged fangs, which are folded upward and stored along the upper jaw when not in use. As a rattler prepares to strike at prey, the mouth is opened widely and the fangs move forward. The two fangs have a slight backward curve. They sink into the victim's flesh and act as hypodermic needles, injecting venom, which flows in hollows through them from the venom ducts to an exit point near the tip of the fang. The fangs are immediately retracted, and the snake withdraws. The entire action is carried out with great rapidity. Dr. Charles Shaw, former Curator of Reptiles and Assistant Director of the San Diego, California, Zoo, stated that rattlesnakes have the most highly developed venom-injecting mechanism of all snakes.

Although very effective in defense, the venom is actually more a means of subduing prey to be used for food. The venom originates in modified salivary glands and also acts as a digestive agent once it is injected into the prey, which certainly accounts for some of its destructive properties when injected into a human victim. To state exactly the symptoms that will follow a rattlesnake bite is difficult due to the many species of rattlesnakes; the variations in makeup and strength of the various species' venoms; the size of the snake and hence amount of venom available to be injected; the amount of venom that the snake actually injects (in some cases, no envenomation occurs, or only a limited amount); the site of the bite; age, size, and condition of the victim; activity following the bite; and the first aid administered.

Rattlesnake venoms vary greatly; some contain as many as 130 ingredients; they may affect tissues, blood, the heart, the neurological system, or a combination of these. Symptoms which have been reported include the following: pain at the site; rapid occurrence of swelling and discoloration; swelling from the tip of an extremity which reaches the trunk in approximately twenty-four hours. (The rate of the advancement of the swelling and the amount is felt to be an indication of the seriousness of the bite.) Weakness and giddiness, respiratory difficulty, nausea and vomiting, circulatory disturbances, sometimes numbness and tingling of the face, lips, and other parts, and double vision and temporary blindness have also been reported.

In comparison to venoms of other rattlesnakes, that of the Mojave rattlesnake, *C. scutulatus,* in some cases displays a very high concentration of the neurotoxic factor, and its venom has been described as "unique." The bite of a Mojave is potentially much more serious than that of a western diamondback, a species with which it is sometimes confused. It is important, therefore, that desert enthusiasts learn to identify the Mojave, the bite of which may be more dangerous than that of most other rattlesnakes. The Mojave's range includes southern Nevada, eastern California, much of Arizona, extreme southwestern New Mexico, and thence southward to Puebla near the southern termination of the Mexican plateau. It is therefore found in much of the Chihuahuan, Sonoran, and Mohave Deserts.

Adult Mojaves reach a length of two to four feet. Among the key distinguishing factors for Mojaves are *whitish or light-colored scales sharply outlining brown diamonds or hexagons on the snake's back* (whereas the western diamondbacks similar markings tend to be flecked and obscure). The Mojave's tail has alternating dark and light rings with *the light rings significantly wider than the dark ones.* Slanting backward from the snake's eye toward the corner of the mouth is a dark streak which is bordered by light scales. Mojaves often, but not always, tend to have a green cast to their coloration. Their basic color varies from olive green to an occasional brown or yellowish. The Mojave is often found in open country where there is a sparse growth of mesquite or creosote bush; it occurs from sea level to 8,000 feet.

The Arizona Poison and Drug Information Center (APDIC) in Tucson, Arizona, is one of the nation's 75 poison centers. In 1997 APDIC responded to calls regarding approximately 170 rattlesnake bites. It is estimated that nationwide perhaps 8,000 people are bitten annually by rattlesnakes; of these only eight to fifteen die as a result of being bitten.

It has been found that about 25 percent of rattlesnake bites are "dry"—that is, the snake does not inject any venom. Another 25 percent of the bites receive only minimal amounts of venom; another 25 percent are severe, and the final 25 percent are potentially lethal and require antivenin. Handling or harassing rattlesnakes should definitely be avoided. An informal study revealed that approximately 90 percent of rattlesnake bites suffered by women or children are received on the foot or ankle. Of males over fifteen years of age approximately 90 percent of the bites occur on the hand or arm. Testosterone, sometimes aided and abetted by alcohol, is considered as a prime factor in at least some of these cases, which are sometimes referred to as "illegitimate," i.e., you really shouldn't blame the snake. Indeed, some experts estimate that up to 75 percent of all rattlesnake bites fall into the "illegitimate" category.

Rattlesnakes can be dangerous. Proper precautions should be taken to avoid being bitten, and a bite should be considered an emergency situation. However, worry regarding them

FIG. 101. The Mojave rattlesnake, *Crotalus scutulatus* (24 to 50 inches long), displays well-defined, light-edged diamonds down the back and tail with contrasting light and dark tail rings, the dark rings narrower than the light rings. Its ground color is a greenish-gray.

THE DESERTS OF THE SOUTHWEST

should not preclude enjoyment of the desert. As the foregoing statistics show, a desert hiker/camper is in less danger from rattlesnakes in the desert than he is from members of his own species on the highway while traveling to that desert.

The experienced desert hiker/camper/backpacker respects rattlesnakes as a part of the ecological community in which they live and for the ability they have to inflict a dangerous bite. These individuals realize that their chances of sustaining such a bite are very small and their chances of recovery very great. All would agree, however, that such a bite is to be avoided if at all possible. Certain precautions can be exercised to reduce the risk of serious encounters with rattlesnakes. Observing these precautions should become second nature to desert hikers and campers.

1. Wear protective clothing—boots and long pants—while hiking and after dark around camp (that is, don't leave camp for a bathroom break ill-protected at a time when rattlers are most likely to be moving about).

2. Keep your eyes open. Look where you step and where you put your hands. Never put your hands or feet where your eyes can't see. Estimates suggest that well over 90 percent of rattlesnake bites occur on the extremities.

3. Use a flashlight when walking in the desert and around camp on warm nights. Rattlesnakes do occasionally come into camp (no doubt unintentionally, or they may have been there first and you just didn't notice), notwithstanding human movement, noises, fires, and so on.

4. When walking, keep to clear areas as much as possible; most of the desert's surface is open, making this rule easy to follow. Rattlesnakes tend to rest under low plants and under or next to rocks, logs, debris, and the like.

5. Go around, rather than over, boulders, logs, and similar obstacles, if possible. If not, step on top of the object first to make sure a snake is not resting next to it on the far side.

Check the surrounding area before sitting down on a log or rock.

6. Resting rattlesnakes often coil themselves neatly and compactly, sometimes partially embedded in soft sand. Their coloration aids them well in blending into their background. The experienced hiker becomes adept at spotting the characteristic shape of a coiled snake.

7. Be careful in climbing rocky cliffs. Do not place your hands on a ledge above your eye level. Do not bring your face up to the same level as, and within striking distance of, a ledge which you have been unable to check by sight—snakes may be present.

8. Find a cleared area when crawling under a fence.

9. When moving logs, stones, and the like, you may want to use a stick or hook to turn over the object first to check for snakes and scorpions underneath. Gather firewood in the daytime when the surroundings are clearly visible.

10. Learn what rattlesnakes occur in the area and what they look like.

11. Remember that rattlesnakes are found in a variety of habitats, including the higher elevations of desert mountains. They range to 11,000 feet in the western United States and up to 14,000 feet in Mexico.

12. Become familiar with the habits of rattlesnakes. In hot weather, they will primarily be active nocturnally, but may also be encountered while resting in shade under logs or in similar locations during the day. They are likely to be found in areas where tumbled rocks, debris, abandoned buildings, and building material give them cover. They spend the winter denned up, often in caves or smaller rocky niches. They may sun themselves outside these on warm days, and be numerous in the surrounding area in spring and fall as they move toward or away from these locations. In cold weather, rattlesnakes are inactive, but even on cool days they may occasionally be unexpectedly encountered as they sun themselves in a warm, protected location. We found a sunning rattlesnake just inside the spacious entrance to a hole on a cool February day, and one of us was struck at by a rattler on a cold, windy Thanksgiving Day

when the snake was in the process of sunning in a protected niche out of the wind.

13. Remember that rattlesnakes do not always rattle before striking.

14. The advice often given is that if you hear a rattlesnake rattle close to you, stand still, locate the snake, and then move away; rattlesnakes will not chase you, and a calm, slow retreat is less likely to frighten or startle the snake into striking. Admittedly, such advice is easier to give then to follow. One's natural reaction to the sound of a nearby rattle or the sight of an uncomfortably close rattlesnake is to jump—which may prove to be a successful maneuver or may cause injuries. (One of the authors failed to follow this advice. While hiking over precipitous, loose rock she jumped away upon hearing a snake rattle from the location where she was about to place her hand. One broken leg later she could attest that a stay-calm, slow-retreat maneuver would have been a wiser move.)

15. Realize that you are responsible for young children you take into rattlesnake country. Do not unduly frighten them, but teach them proper precautions at an early age and oversee their activities while they are in the desert. Because of their smaller body size, children are more seriously affected by a rattlesnake bite than are adults. Placing children on cots or in a tent at night for sleeping is wise, if danger of rattlesnakes is present at that particular time and place.

16. Do not handle dead rattlesnakes nor allow children or dogs to do so. Reflexes allow the "dead" snake to inject poison for some time. The person or dog who handles a rattlesnake's head can be injected with the poison by inadvertently "stabbing" himself with the fang; more than one person has been bitten by a "dead" rattlesnake.

17. Respect rattlesnakes, but do not live in fear of them. Our family has been enjoying desert hiking and camping for more than forty years. During that time we have encountered more than a hundred rattlesnakes. Of those, two struck and missed. In other encounters three bites were sustained; two of these were due to human error while holding the snakes during scientific studies, and of the two, one was a dry bite; the

other required antivenin and hospitalization. Another unfortunate encounter was a result of ignoring rule number 7. A hand placed on an overhead ledge while rock climbing resulted in a serious bite.

## Copperhead Snake

The copperhead, *Agkistrodon contortrix,* is present in small portions of the Chihuahuan Desert. This snake, like the rattlesnakes, is a member of the family Viperidae and subfamily Crotalinae. The copperhead, too, is a pit viper, and is dangerously venomous, but the copperhead does *not* have rattles. The subspecies of the copperhead most likely to be encountered in the North American desert range is the Trans-Pecos copperhead, *A. c. pictigaster.* It is found primarily in Texas and attains an average maximum growth of two feet. Its ground color is a light hazel brown marked by broad, straight-edged crossbands of a coppery brown; these bands have narrow dark borders.

When alarmed, copperheads rapidly vibrate their tails and, although they lack a rattle, they may produce a noise by beating a tattoo with the tail against vegetation or the ground. The copperheads should be treated with the same respect as their

FIG. 102. The copperheads, *Agkistrodon contortrix* (2 feet in length, for the subspecies found in the desert), like the rattlesnakes, are members of the pit viper subfamily. The copperhead is found in only one of the four North American deserts—the Chihuahuan.

rattlesnake relatives; the copperhead's bite is similar in effect and severity.

## Rear-fanged Snakes

In addition to the venomous snakes already noted, a few small, venom-producing, rear-fanged snakes exist within the geographical range we are considering. All have a poorly developed venom-introducing means in which venom flows down grooves in enlarged teeth at the back of the upper jaw. The snake must "chew" with these fangs to embed them in the victim, allowing entry of the venom; inasmuch as the mouths of all these species are very small, these snakes find it difficult or impossible to envenomate man. Authorities state that the venom of these species found in the American West is probably not powerful enough in the small quantities that would be obtained by a bitten man to harm him, and that the effect would probably be no more serious than a bee sting. One of the authors, having been bitten as a child by a lyre snake, can attest that that particular bite caused no reaction whatsoever. These snakes should be considered essentially harmless to man and interesting. They include the black-headed snake, *Tantilla hobartsmithi;* vine snake, *Oxybelis aeneus;* lyre snake, *Trimorphodon biscutatus;* night snake, *Hypsiglena torquata;* and the western hognose, *Heterodon nasicus.*

The potentially dangerous animals of the desert should not be feared; in no way is the information given about them meant to induce fear. Rather it is hoped that the desert appreciator will *respect* these animals. Keep in mind that they should be respected not only on the basis of their potential danger to you, the human, but also—and primarily—on the basis that they are living things, each an important part of the ecosystem in which they live. True, some of them may be potential killers, but certainly none of these species is so successful in this regard as another desert dweller known as *Homo sapiens.*

# CHAPTER XIII

# First Aid in the Desert Environment

IN GENERAL the desert backpacker and camper risks incurring the same types of injuries as the person engaged in the same activities in other habitats: cuts, abrasions, sprains, fractures, and the like. However, the desert outdoorsman is particularly prone to two additional types of possible problems—those related to heat and dehydration, and the bites and stings of some of the desert's fauna.

We strongly recommend that all teens and adults who have not previously done so take a good first aid course. Knowledge thus gained may prove invaluable, not only in the out-of-doors, but also in the home and city.

## First Aid Kit

When camping or backpacking, carry a good first aid kit with you. Check it before leaving home; replace any missing items or outdated medications.

The following list identifies some of the items you should consider maintaining in your first aid kit. Decisions about the exact items to include should be determined in consultation with your physician, and should take into consideration the distance you will be from emergency support services and your level of training and experience. Discuss any preexisting medical conditions and special medications or potential first aid needs with your physician, as well.

Consideration should also be given to the size and exact configuration of your first aid kit. Items that may be needed immediately to mitigate serious symptoms or discomfort should be carried on your person, such as in a belt pack. Other items that should be readily available are useful for multiple purposes (combs, lighter, multitool pocketknife, penlight, antibacterial towelettes) as well as for first aid. Additional medications are suggested for comfort or treatment if access to emergency or medical care may be delayed. These items could be maintained in a nearby vehicle or an overnight backpack.

Communications, even from remote areas, can often be achieved via pocket-sized radios and cellular phones. It is highly recommended that these be available to access emergency response agencies, should an emergency occur.

SUGGESTED ITEMS FOR FIRST AID AND EMERGENCY RE-
SPONSE KIT (ITEMS NOTED BY ° SHOULD BE READILY
AVAILABLE AT ALL TIMES)

first aid booklet, including directions for medication uses, as provided by your physician
pocket-sized cellular phone and/or backpacker radio to contact base camp°
belt pack°
freezer-type zipper-lock plastic bags°
antibacterial towelettes°
waterless antibacterial soap or gel
Sawyer or other mechanical suction-type bite/sting extractor kit(s) (use of these is controversial, but if used, *two* kits are suggested)°
tweezers (pointed tip), good quality, particularly helpful for removing spines
small bottle of white glue (good for removing fine cactus spines)
small comb (good for removing cholla)°
needles
small magnifying glass or hand lens
scissors
multipurpose pocket knife/camping tool (includes tweezers, knife, scissors)°
pen°
penlight°

whistle°
chemical lightstick°
elastic bandages: assorted sizes
moleskin°
4-inch Ace bandage wrap
roll of 2-inch stretch roller gauze
roll of 3-inch stretch roller gauze°
roll of 1-inch adhesive tape°
Q-tips
lighter°
safety pins°
triangular bandage°
"Sam Splint"–types splinting rolls°
sunscreen (SPF of 36 or greater)°
thermometer (digital/battery type—**not** glass/mercury type)
disposable gloves (non-latex)°
pocket resuscitation mask with micropore filter/screen°
ice/chemical ice packs
aloe burn relief gel
itch relief gel, cream, or lotion
water purifying tablets or drops°
20 ml syringe (for wound cleansing/irrigation)
purified water (wound cleansing and back-up to drinking supply)°
high energy food bars°

*Over-the-counter preparations (consult with your doctor as to needs and uses):*
(medications are listed by generic names; you may want to compare with brand names which may be more familiar to you)
electrolyte replacement powder-drink mix (containing sodium, potassium, carbohydrates)°
liquid antiseptic, such as povidone iodine
antibacterial ointment, such as a triple antibiotic ointment
analgesic/anti-inflammatory medications, as aspirin, ibuprofen, or naproxen sodium tablets

mild laxative tablets, such as bisacodyl USP
antidiarrheal tablets, such as loperamide HCL
diphenhydramine capsules°
diphenhydramine ointment or gel
hydrocortisone ointment
antacid tablets
bismuth subsalicylate–type tablets
activated charcoal powder or slurry
epinephrine inhalation aerosol/unit dose inhaler°

*Prescription medications:*
oral antibiotic medication
"epi-pen" or epinephrine autoinjector kit (severe allergic
reactions)°
prescription-strength analgesia "painkiller" medications

Consideration should also be given to items around you
that could be used as splinting and evacuation devices: backpack stays, hiking poles, sticks, etc.—an emergency litter can
be constructed from two long, rigid poles and blankets.

## Mouth-to-Mouth Resuscitation

This chapter discusses only the specialized aspects of
desert-related first aid, with one exception: mouth-to-mouth
resuscitation. This skill is reviewed, below, as a reminder that
all individuals should know how to use this important life-
saving technique, which may serve them well in any environment. This review is not a substitute for the first aid and
cardiopulmonary resuscitation courses, which are highly recommended for everyone, and are particularly important when
traveling beyond the reach of timely access to professional
emergency responders.

1. Emergency medical system activation can now be
achieved from very remote sites using newer technologies.
Whenever possible, early access to emergency response agencies is very important. Once a patient is determined to be un-

responsive to a gentle tap or shout, send someone for help while you begin initiating resuscitation measures. Radio communication with base camp or cellular communication with emergency response agencies can sometimes be achieved from the trail, camp, or nearby hillside.

2. Rescuers should minimize exposure to possible infections by donning gloves and using barrier pocket masks and/or micropore screens.

3. Positioning of the patient to obtain an open airway is a top rescuer priority whenever a patient is not responsive. The relaxed tongue, fallen against the back of the throat, is the most common blockage of the patient's airway. The airway can be opened by turning the patient on his back, while supporting his head and neck in line with his spine. Then tilting the head back and gently lifting under the chin. If you suspect the patient may have fallen or injured his neck or spine, attempt first to open his airway by lifting only on his chin.

4. Next, determine if the patient is breathing by looking for the chest to rise and fall with air movement, listening for the sounds of breathing, and feeling for his breath/air movement on your cheek as you lean your cheek near his mouth and nose.

5. If there is not any evidence of a fall or traumatic injury, and the patient is breathing, roll him on his side while awaiting evacuation. If the patient is determined **not** to be breathing on his own, recheck the positioning of his head and neck. Next use your pocket mask to cover his mouth and nose and give two slow breaths. If you do not have a pocket mask, pinch his nostrils and make a tight seal around his mouth with your mouth; exhale your breath into the patient, watching for his chest to rise. (As the size of the patient decreases, so does the amount of air to be delivered. Gauge your ventilations to the size of the patient and the rise and fall of his chest).

6. Pause and allow for the patient's lungs to deflate (chest to fall) between your breaths. Continue by ventilating the patient one slow, full breath every five seconds.

7. The mouth-to-mouth resuscitation should be continued during evacuation and until the patient revives, or until trained personnel are available to assume care of the patient.

# Heat-Related Illnesses

As we have discussed, the desert's warm climate requires the human body to cool itself more frequently for greater periods of time than in most other climates. Man in the hot desert environment cools his body primarily by means of evaporation of perspiration from the body's surface. Therefore, the maintenance of adequate water input and salt intake is of the utmost importance. E. F. Adolph and A. H. Brown state that man in a temperate climate loses two to three liters of water per day, half of it in urine. In the desert, losses range as high as eleven liters daily, up to 90 percent of it through perspiration. Douglas H. K. Lee, writing in *Adaptation to the Environment,* provides even higher figures: eight to twelve liters of water daily in sweat; one liter as urine; and .75 liter from the respiratory tract. All of the body parts do not lose water equally; the blood serum concentrates more than twice as much as the liquids of other parts of the body. Thus plasma and blood volume diminish greatly; the heart's stroke volume diminishes; stress is placed on the entire circulatory system; and an accelerated pulse rate and elevated body temperature result. Additionally, quantities of sodium chloride are lost from the body in the sweat, causing further body complications.

Man can acclimatize to the *heat* to some extent; that is, his body makes adaptive changes over a period of time when continuously or repeatedly exposed to heat stress. A man whose body has so adapted is thus able to work longer and more efficiently under hot conditions than can a newcomer. Body mechanisms in this process may include a decrease in heat production (as elimination of nonessential movements), increase by the body of blood volume and extracellular body fluid during the early acclimatization period; gradual drop in pulse rate; reduction of the chloride concentration in sweat; and finally an ability to some extent to physiologically "tolerate" or "put up with" distresses that were very unwelcome and upsetting when first encountered.

For the most part, individuals in the desert, especially those acclimatized to the heat, need not take salt tablets or otherwise supplement their salt intake beyond the amount desired with their food. Individuals involved in moderate to heavy labor in heat, however, may, even if acclimatized, feel the need to consume some extra salt. The outdoorsman who suddenly subjects himself to strenuous exercise in the heat, particularly if he is not acclimatized, may need extra salt. Douglas H. K. Lee recommends that the sedentary, acclimatized individual in a hot, dry environment need take no additional salt beyond that provided by a normal diet; the acclimatized individual in a hot, dry environment undertaking moderate to heavy labor may need to add seven grams of salt to his normal intake; the unacclimatized individual undertaking heavy labor in the same environment may need to add fourteen grams of salt to the normal diet; and an unacclimatized individual undertaking moderate to heavy work in a very hot environment may need twenty-one grams more salt than is provided by his normal diet.

The disorders related to heat stress are derived from a deficiency of salt or water or both. They result from an imbalance in intake as compared to output in the commodity of sweat.

1. **Heat cramps.** Heat cramps may affect people engaged in strenuous or semi-strenuous activities in hot environments. Loss of large quantities of sweat creates an imbalance in the electrolyte ratio. If electrolyte intake is insufficient to remedy this imbalance, heat cramps may occur. At times these cramps may result from drinking iced drinks too fast or in too-large quantities. Prevention includes sufficient ingestion of extra salt—either with food, water, or as tablets—whenever heavy work is to be carried out in heat.

SYMPTOMS OF HEAT CRAMPS

a. Muscle cramps in arms, legs, and abdomen
b. Pain accompanying cramps
c. Faintness
d. Profuse perspiration

## FIRST AID MEASURES FOR HEAT CRAMPS

a. Remove patient to cool place.
b. Give patient water with electrolyte powder added. Water replacement should include balanced electrolyte replacement to avoid severe imbalances of sodium, potassium, and other essential body electrolytes, which are lost through sweating, vomiting, or diarrhea. Only if electrolyte solution is not available, use salted drinking water (one teaspoon salt to one quart water).
c. Apply manual pressure to the cramped muscles.
d. Remove patient to hospital if more serious problems are indicated.

2. **Heat exhaustion.** Heat exhaustion also occurs in individuals involved in strenuous activities in hot environments. The body, in its attempt to lose heat, transports quantities of blood from the body core to the vessels in the skin. The pooling of the blood in the peripheral vessels combined with the amount pooled in the lower extremities when standing sometimes provides an insufficient blood return to the heart and brain, thus leading to physical collapse.

### SYMPTOMS OF HEAT EXHAUSTION

a. Weak pulse
b. Rapid and usually shallow breathing
c. Generalized weakness
d. Pale, clammy skin
e. Profuse perspiration
f. Dizziness, headache, confusion
g. Unconsciousness

### FIRST AID FOR HEAT EXHAUSTION

a. Remove patient to cool place.
b. Keep patient lying down.
c. Remove as much of patient's clothing as possible.
d. Administer cool water with electrolyte powder added.

Water replacement should include balanced electrolyte replacement to avoid severe imbalances of sodium, potassium, and other essential body electrolytes, which are lost through sweating, vomiting, or diarrhea. Only if electrolyte solution is not available, use salted drinking water (one teaspoon salt to one quart water).

e. Remove body heat by convection, but do not chill.
f. Remove to medical help if any more serious problem is indicated.

3. **Heat stroke.** Heat stroke is a *true emergency* and, if prompt action is not taken, the victim may die. Heat stroke is a catastrophic disturbance of the heat-regulating mechanism of the brain. It is associated with high fever and collapse, and may result in convulsions and unconsciousness. Heat stroke is often related to direct exposure to sun, poor air circulation, age (over forty), poor physical condition, alcoholism, and obesity.

Symptoms of heat stroke are generally very different from heat exhaustion. A rise in skin temperature, along with increased skin blood flow, can result in a red or "flushed" appearance. The patient's skin is often dry, due to dehydration, inability to sweat, or rapid evaporation in an arid environment. The presence or absence of sweating is not a reliable indicator of heat stroke. It is important to realize that about half of the patients who succumb to heat stroke under exertion have persistent sweating; wherein exertion causes heat to accumulate faster in the body than it can be eliminated. Rapid recognition of the condition and rapid cooling are essential to avoid permanent injury or death.

SYMPTOMS OF HEAT STROKE

a. Sudden onset of condition
b. Hot, flushed, dry skin
c. Dilated pupils
d. Full and fast pulse
e. Breathing fast at first, graduating to shallow and faint
f. Confusion, early loss of consciousness

g. Muscle twitching possibly leading into convulsions

h. Body temperature elevated to 105° to 106° F. or higher

a. Remove patient to cool place.

b. Remove as much clothing as possible.

c. Assure an open airway (see the discussion of mouth-to-mouth resuscitation earlier in this chapter).

d. Reduce body temperature promptly by fanning the patient, dousing patient's body with water or, if possible, by wrapping patient in wet sheet, or all of the above.

e. Consider utilizing ice enclosed in a cloth or chemical ice packs at necks, armpits, and groin or other locations where blood vessels lie close to the skin to assist in rapid cooling, but do not chill to the point of causing the patient to shiver.

f. If convulsions should occur, protect the patient from injury by padding around the patient and moving objects away that the patient could bump up against.

g. Transport to a medical facility immediately.

## Desert Dehydration

Dehydration often plays a role in heat-related illnesses. However, an individual may also die of non–heat-related dehydration. A characteristic series of desert dehydration symptoms occur through a series of water deficits, based on a percentage of the victim's body weight. In its early stages dehydration acts mainly by reducing the blood volume, often promoting heat exhaustion. Dehydration in its later stages causes disturbances of cell functions, which reinforce one another with progressive deterioration of the individual's body. Until an irreversible point has been reached, dehydration is usually readily rectified by replacement of the body's water. A person active in the desert can suffer from early stages of dehydration, reducing his ability to work well or maintain a positive emotional state, without being fully aware that dehydration is affecting him other than that he is perhaps suffering a degree of thirst. Thirst becomes apparent at approximately a 2 percent loss of body weight, or even earlier.

According to Adolph and associates:

1. A 1 to 5 percent loss of body weight due to dehydration produces:

    a. Thirst
    b. Vague discomfort
    c. Economy of movement
    d. Anorexia (lack of appetite)
    e. Flushed skin
    f. Impatience
    g. Increased pulse rate
    h. Increased rectal temperature
    i. Sleepiness
    j. Nausea

2. A 6 to 10 percent loss of body weight due to dehydration produces:

    a. Dizziness
    b. Headache
    c. Dyspnea (labored breathing)
    d. Tingling in the limbs
    e. Absence of salivation
    f. Cyanosis (bluish skin caused by deficient oxygenation of blood)
    g. Indistinct speech
    h. Inability to walk

3. An 11 to 20 percent loss of body weight due to dehydration produces:

    a. Delirium
    b. Spasticity
    c. Swollen tongue
    d. Inability to swallow
    e. Deafness
    f. Dim vision
    g. Painful urination
    h. Shriveled skin
    i. Numb skin

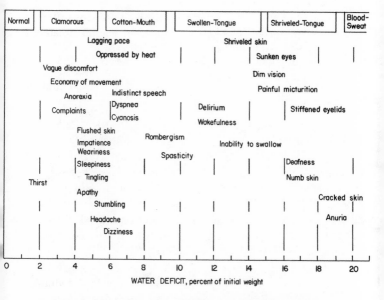

FIG. 103. Signs and symptoms characteristic of desert dehydration.° Each sign is located at the water deficit at which it is usually first noted.

° Reprinted from *Physiology of Man in the Desert*, courtesy of E. F. Adolph.

    j. Bloody cracked skin
    k. Anuria (absence or defective excretion of urine)

## Dehydration Exhaustion

Dehydration exhaustion occurs at a 5 to 10 percent deficit.

### SYMPTOMS OF DEHYDRATION EXHAUSTION

1. Vague discomfort
2. Feeling of heat oppression
3. Restlessness

4. Sleepiness
5. Inclination to sit or lie down
6. Muscular fatigue
7. Rising body temperature
8. Accelerated pulse
9. Tingling limbs

Experimentally, subjects suffering from dehydration exhaustion, when given all the water they wanted, usually drank copiously. Given sufficient water, these men regained their initial body weight in twenty-four hours or less. They suffered no obvious aftereffects from their dehydration. Adolph, et al., state that a man can undergo a water deficit so extreme as to be unable to walk or stand, yet will recover his walking ability within a few minutes after receiving water, with almost complete recovery in six to twelve hours.

At a 12 percent loss, an individual cannot recover without assistance, and a person dehydrated to this point, Adolph and associates state, must be given water intravenously, intraperitoneally, by stomach tube, or through the rectum.

Death occurs at a 15 percent to 25 percent body-weight loss, those occurring at the higher deficits in cool atmospheres. In hot environments, death occurs at a lower percentage of weight loss and is probably due to heat stroke.

FIRST AID FOR SERIOUS DESERT DEHYDRATION

a. Provide water and electrolyte replacement for patient.
b. Prevent overheating of patient.
c. Transport to a medical facility.

## Cactus-Related Problems

The cylindrical joints of the cholla cactus may at times pose a problem for the unwary desert explorer. These spine-studded joints are easily removed from the plant by simply brushing against it or are particularly plentiful on the ground

FIG. 104. To remove cactus joints easily, insert the teeth of a comb between the cactus and the impaled object. Pull the comb up-ward and outward.

beneath the plant where pants legs and footwear may pick them up. So readily do these joints attach themselves to ani-mals and humans that one species is known as the "jumping cholla." Jump it does not, but to the impaled individual it may seem to have done so. If one attempts to remove these joints from his body or clothing by use of bare hands, he simply transfers the problem to the hands. Attempts to remove a joint with a stick may be successful, or may simply roll the joint into an adjoining portion of the victim. The simplest means of removal is that using an ordinary pocket comb. In-sert the teeth of the comb between the cactus and the indi-vidual or object impaled. Holding one end of the comb, flip the joint *outward, away from you,* being careful not to toss it against an onlooker.

Cactus spines can cause rather intense pain, which may persist for several minutes or longer. For example, after slip-ping and falling while descending a mountain and in the process having firmly embedded the spines of a cholla joint in one hand while breaking the fall, one of us can state that the pain radiates up the arm and persists for a half hour or more in a severe case. Medical help is ordinarily not needed unless a person has been severely impaled in many parts of the body, as in a major accident, or if numerous spines are broken off in the body.

Prickly pear cacti have, in addition to the usual spines, very tiny hairs or spines called *glochids,* which are difficult or impossible to see once embedded in the human skin. These glochids are not dangerous, but are very annoying. The minute tips of glochids protruding from human skin cause irritation when rubbed or touched. The afflicted skin area can be rubbed with sand; the glochid tips are thus broken off, reducing the constant irritation; the flesh-embedded glochid portions are gradually dissolved by the body. Small spines, particularly glochids, may also be removed using white liquid glue. Coat the affected area with the glue. Once dried, the glue can be peeled off, carrying the spines or glochids with it. Adhesive tape can be used for the same purpose.

Prevention is the best cure for cactus spine problems.

## Sunburn

Sunlight is intense in the desert. Do not underestimate it or overestimate your skin. Even possession of a tan is not total insurance against sunburn, for tanned skin may burn if exposure is sufficiently intense and prolonged. Be prepared to prevent sunburn with preparations of your choice or based on your doctor's recommendation. Prevention is certainly best, but just in case—also be prepared with medication to treat sunburn.

## Special Rules for First Aid Treatment of Various Poisonous Bites and Stings

In no way is the following first aid information intended to alarm the desert explorer. Venomous bites and stings from the desert's inhabitants are relatively infrequent. The recovery rate from even the most severe of these, with proper medical assistance rendered when needed, is extremely high.

*Severe systemic reactions to bee stings may appear within fifteen minutes and include:*

1. flushing of the skin; hives
2. upper airway obstruction due to accumulation of fluid in the throat; bronchial spasms
3. bowel spasms
4. circulatory collapse, shock, hypotension, fainting, loss of consciousness.

On an average, human beings can sustain up to approximately ten Africanized honeybee stings per pound of body weight before the venom becomes life threatening. Victims who succumb from massive bee attacks usually die due to cardiac arrest, respiratory complications, or bleeding disorder.

*First aid for Africanized honeybees stings includes:*

1. If a victim has sustained 15 or more stings or is showing a severe reaction to one or more stings, they should seek **immediate** medical treatment.
2. When a bee stings, it leaves its stinger in the skin and venom continues to enter the wound for a short time. Stingers should be removed promptly; most sources recommend that you scrape them out using your fingernail, a dull knife blade, credit card, or other straight-edged object. Pulling them out with tweezers or fingers may squeeze more venom into the wound. Unless allergic, adult humans usually tolerate several stings without long-term complications. However, **if stung multiple times, if allergic by history, or if an allergic reaction occurs, transport immediately to a medical facility.** Do not delay transport in order to remove stingers.

## BLACK WIDOW BITE

*Symptoms of black widow bite include:*

1. Two tiny red marks may identify site of entrance of chelicera.
2. Severe local pain becomes increasingly severe within about thirty minutes.
3. Pain and muscular rigidity spreads through the body, settling in the abdomen and legs.

4. Other symptoms may include nausea, vomiting, muscle spasms, headache, dizziness, weakness, restlessness, anxiety, breathing difficulties, high blood pressure.

*First aid for black widow bite:*
1. Cool compresses may be used at the site.
2. Keep the patient quiet.
3. Elevate the bitten limb to heart level.
4. Mild pain relievers may be given.
5. Check with your doctor or local poison control center, or transport patient to medical facility immediately if severe reaction occurs, or the patient is a child, elderly, pregnant, or has high blood pressure. (Antivenin is available for administration by medical personnel, but is rarely used due to complications that may arise from its use.)

## ARIZONA BROWN SPIDER BITE
## (ALSO SOMETIMES REFERRED TO AS THE BROWN RECLUSE SPIDER)

*Symptoms of Arizona brown spider bite include:*
1. Little or no pain is felt at the site; patient may not be aware initially of bite.
2. Pain and swelling may develop at the site within two to eight hours after bite.
3. Other symptoms which sometimes occur include chills, nausea, vomiting, fever, and generalized skin rash.
4. Within twelve hours to several days, necrosis of the site may occur.

*First aid for Arizona brown spider bite:*
No first aid measures are needed. A physician should be seen promptly if a bite occurs, or if an individual suspects from evident symptoms that one may have occurred.

## SCORPION STING

All scorpions have venom, and all can produce a sting that will be accompanied by some degree of discomfort or pain; however, most are not usually dangerous. Symptoms resulting from stings of most species can be classified as localized and not systemic. Human reaction to the sting of most species consists of a sharp burning sensation lasting from a few minutes to half an hour. The stings of other species produce pronounced swelling, with or without slight discoloration; yet other species' venoms may cause a highly discolored swelling and a burning sensation. With some of these venoms, pain may travel some distance from the site of the sting, as from a hand as far as the armpit. Local application of an ice cube may provide some relief. Unless the victim displays an unusually severe reaction, the pain produced by these ground scorpion stings is usually approximately equal in intensity to a wasp or bee sting. One species, however, *Centruroides exilicauda,* can produce symptoms throughout the body, or systemically. *The potentially dangerous* C. exilicauda *sting may cause initial pain, but no swelling or discoloration at the site. Symptoms for* C. exilicauda *stings can become systemic, affecting primarily the nervous system. The systemic effect is most pronounced for those who are very young (under age three) and the elderly.*

*Symptoms of* Centruroides exilicauda *sting include:*

1. Pain at the time of the sting and radiation of pain when sting site is "tapped"
2. Prickly, tingling, numbness at site that may progress to other portions of the body
3. Extreme restlessness or "thrashing" movements
4. Possible convulsion-like movements
5. Roving, uncontrollable eye movements
6. Respiratory difficulties
7. Drooling
8. Difficulty in speaking
9. Tightness of throat

*First aid measures for* Centruroides exilicauda *sting:*

1. Use ice wrapped in cloth on site immediately.
2. Consult a doctor or local poison control center.
3. Young children, the elderly, and people with respiratory problems are most susceptible to systemic symptoms from *C. exilicauda* stings. Transport them and any other patient exhibiting serious reactions to a medical facility.

The *C. exilicauda* scorpion is found in Arizona, Baja California del Norte, northern Sonora, southeastern California, extreme southeastern Utah, and southwestern New Mexico. Related scorpions of the genus *Centruroides* are found in Mexico. Some of these may also produce serious systemic symptoms and/or death in humans. Supplies of locally produced antivenin may be stocked in specified hospitals and clinics in Arizona and Mexico, but this product is not routinely used due to complications that may arise from its use.

## GILA MONSTER BITE

The bite of a Gila monster is potentially dangerous. However, this reptile's bite is a natural defensive mechanism; most bites to humans have occurred when the lizards were being teased or handled, which should never be done.

*Symptoms of Gila monster bite include:*
1. Local pain
2. Prolonged bleeding
3. Low blood pressure
4. Shock
5. Swelling
6. Weakness
7. Dizziness

*First aid for Gila monster bite:*
1. Remove the lizard from the bite as rapidly as possible, since the lizard continues to chew venom into the victim while it remains attached. It may be difficult to disengage the reptile, which hangs on tenaciously once it has obtained a firm grip. It is suggested that you place the animal so that all four of its feet are on the ground; it will usually disengage and run away.

2. Loosely immobilize the extremity.

3. Transport the patient to an emergency department without delay.

4. Keep the patient quiet.

5. If lacerations or puncture wounds have resulted from the bite, cleanse the area well.

6. Patient may be encouraged to drink water if transport time to the hospital is lengthy.

7. An icebag may be used.

RATTLESNAKE BITE

Severity of rattlesnake bite is dependent upon many factors including size of snake; amount of venom injected (bites are sometimes received without injection of any venom or with only a limited amount delivered); type of venom; species of snake; location of bite; depth of bite; age, size, and physical condition of victim (due to their small size, children are often in more danger from rattlesnake bite than are adults); individual susceptibility to venom; activity of victim following bite; first aid treatment; and medical aid received.

Rarely, bites are received directly into a blood vessel, in which case generalized systemic symptoms—changes in heartbeat and respiration, shock, and unconsciousness—may occur almost immediately. However, in the majority of cases the venom is injected under the skin and usually not to any great depth into muscle.

*Symptoms of rattlesnake bite include:*

1. Pain at the site

2. Rapid onset of swelling and discoloration extending toward the heart. (This swelling may extend from the tip of an extremity to the trunk in approximately twenty-four hours. The amount and rate of advancement of swelling is an indication of the severity of the bite.)

3. Weakness

4. Respiratory difficulty

5. Nausea and vomiting

6. Low blood pressure, thready pulse

7. Shock

8. Central nervous system depression

9. Subnormal temperature

10. Numbness and tingling of face, lips, other body parts

*First aid for rattlesnake bite:*

1. Do not panic.

2. Keep patient quiet.

3. The use of mechanical suction extraction devices is controversial. If used, they should be applied over puncture marks and suction should begin immediately. *Such use should not delay transport.* If extraction device(s) cannot be placed within the first three minutes, their usefulness is greatly diminished. If the bite was delivered by a large snake, the suction cup, if of a small size, may cover only one puncture. It is in this event that a second extractor is useful in order to simultaneously cover and suction from the second puncture.

4. *Loosely immobilize bitten part at or below the level of the heart.* If not immobilized, keep movement of the bitten limb to a minimum; muscular action increases the spread of the venom.

5. **The victim should be transported to a hospital immediately.** Definitive care will be administered at the hospital, including evaluation regarding need for antivenin. However, many bites are sustained some distance from medical help in which case the following first aid measures should be considered.

6. Remove all rings, constricting jewelry, or clothing near affected area.

7. If some doubt exists as to whether the patient was bitten by a venomous snake, or whether or not envenomation has occurred, watch the bite for the first three to five minutes. If during this time pain occurs and swelling appears at the site, assume that envenomation by a poisonous snake has occurred. *Pain and swelling* at the site are signs of a rattlesnake bite; the bite of a nonpoisonous snake or a poisonous snake which has not injected venom will not produce swelling. *With a pen or marker time-mark the progression of swelling up an extremity,* if it occurs; the progressive rate of swelling provides medical personnel with an indication of the severity of the bite.

8. If some distance from a vehicle, transport the victim by litter, if possible. Prevention of as much activity as is possible on the victim's part is important.

9. If the snake species is known, the information may prove useful to hospital personnel, but do not delay leaving

the field in order to identify the species of snake. Do not capture the snake. Do not take the snake to the medical facility.

## RATTLESNAKE VENOM

Rattlesnake venoms are mixtures made up of a wide variety of elements in different quantities. The venom's primary purpose is primarily to help immobilize and secure the snake's prey. With proper medical support most people can absorb these toxins and suffer few long-term complications.

The elements that may be present in rattlesnake toxins in varying amounts can be generally divided into three types. Hemotoxins exert serious effects on the blood and break down blood components, leading to severe bleeding. Necrotoxins break down tissues, leading to swelling, poor healing, and possible long-term complications with the extremity. Neurotoxins primarily affect the victim's nervous system, affecting respiratory and essential bodily functions.

Due to its size and abundance, the western diamondback, *Crotalus atrox,* is considered a dangerous species. However, the sidewinder, *Crotalus tigris,* has venom considered very toxic. The venom of a Mojave rattlesnake, *Crotalus scutulatus,* is considered particularly dangerous. This snake attains a good size, is capable of delivering a quantity of venom, and some populations of the species have a special type of particularly dangerous venom. Whereas rattlesnake venom most commonly is primarily hemotoxic, it has been found that in some cases the Mojave's is neurotoxic, or it may be both. Those Mojave populations with venom type A have what is known as "Mojave toxin," which immobolizes prey by neuromuscular blockade. Mojave rattlesnake venom A has the largest quantity of this Mojave toxin, and the lowest median lethal dose values of any North America crotalid venom. Mojave rattlesnakes with venom type B lack the Mojave toxin. Studies have revealed that those Mojaves with venom B are located primarily around and in the area between Tucson and Phoenix. Mojaves with venom A are known from southeastern Arizona, west-central Arizona, southeastern California, and extreme southern Arizona. Mojaves with a combination of both A and B venom are known from south-central Arizona from near the Mexico-Arizona border, ranging north in a fairly narrow band to above Phoenix. In some additional crotalid species Mojave toxin has been found, although not in the quantity present in certain Mojave rattlesnake populations. These species include *Crotalus tigris, C. viridis concolor, C. horridus,* and *C. atrox.*

What you do not do in dealing with a rattlesnake bite is important, and advice in this matter has changed greatly in recent years:

1. Do not use a cut-and-suck method to extract venom.

2. Do not apply a tourniquet. (Even a constricting band, loose enough to insert fingers between it and the extremity, is controversial. If used, do not allow it to become constricting when swelling of the extremity occurs. These methods have caused loss of limb/extremity.)

3. Do not use ice or cryotherapy (immersion in ice). This potentiates the toxicity of the venom and has contributed to loss of limb.

4. Do not use electroshock. This has caused extreme injury and loss of life.

5. *Do not* administer any drugs or alcohol.

6. *Do not* follow directions in outdated snake bite kits which advocate cut-and-suck methods. Additionally, many of these kits are old and the suction devices are weak. If mechanical suction is used, a Sawyer-type extractor is recommended.

7. **Do not delay transporting victim to a medical facility.**

Antivenin for rattlesnake bite is available to be administered by medical personnel when needed. The antivenin currently in use has, at times, caused side effects in the form of serum sickness due to a delayed allergic response to the horse serum used. Currently a new antivenin known as Crotab is being tested and is expected to be on the market in the near future. Therapeutic Antibodies, Inc., is the developer. This new product is prepared by immunizing sheep with rattlesnake venom, and the sheep serum is purified to extract key antibody fractions. The venoms of four North American crotalids are used to immunize the sheep: *Crotalus atrox* (western diamondback), *C. adamanteus* (eastern diamondback), *C. scutulatus scutulatus* (Mojave rattlesnake with venom A), and *Agkistrodon piscivorus piscivorus* (eastern cottonmouth). Limited use of Crotab in trial studies has shown it to be highly effective, with less complications due to serum sickness.

For most rattlesnake-bite victims, intelligent first aid and immediate transport to a medical facility, followed by knowledgeable medical services, results in recovery with only minimal problems in injured extremities. Death is rare. One recent study found that mortality from severe, complicated rattlesnake envenomation has a low incidence of approximately 1.4 percent. In other words, chances for recovery from rattlesnake bite are approximately 99 in 100, and those, you must admit, are good odds.

CHAPTER XIV

# Desert Survival Skills

IN ANY desert emergency, decide on an intelligent course of action to be taken. Give yourself time to think this situation out calmly and rationally. Talk to yourself, if you are alone, to help restore calmness. If you are in a group, discuss your situation with one another. To let one person take charge may be the best plan. Consider all possibilities open to you. In deciding upon a plan, *consider all alternatives in terms of physiological cost.* Once a decision is made, set your plan into action and stick with it unless additional unforeseen factors make it necessary and truly advisable to change it.

# The Vehicle in an Emergency

When a survival situation must be faced, very often a vehicle or aircraft is present. If you have any hope that rescue operations may be undertaken, remaining with the machine is considered the best plan. If you have a contact who knows where you were going and when you were to return, *as you should have,* rescue should be imminent. A vehicle is easier for the rescuers to see than is an individual. Additionally, the vehicle provides many advantages and resources important to survival and rescue. Take stock of the resources you have. Determine how to use them effectively.

1. Food or water supplies, or both, may be present in the vehicle.

2. The mirrors (rearview and side) may be used for hand-held signaling devices.

3. Seat covers, upholstery, cool cushions, and so forth may be used to provide shade or may serve in many other ways.

4. Seat cushions may be removed from the vehicle. Sit or lie on them in shade, elevating the body above the high surface temperatures.

5. Floor mats may serve a variety of purposes.

6. The glove compartment may provide matches, maps, and other papers for starting fires. Often it holds a flashlight, which can be used for night signaling.

7. Tools may be used for many purposes, such as digging, breaking open barrel cacti, obtaining gas from car for starting fires.

8. Hub caps may be used for digging, signaling, and as containers for use in solar stills.

9. The tires can be burned as signals.

10. Oil from the engine is useful in producing quantities of black smoke in signal fires. Oil may also be used under the eyes to reduce glare, or on the lips to prevent cracking. (Do not cover large body areas with oil, for this covering prevents evaporative cooling.)

11. Gas is useful in building fires. It can be siphoned from the gas tank, or fittings around the engine may be loosened,

allowing the gas to drain into a container or onto rags or pieces of upholstery.

12. The cigarette lighter may be used in starting fires. (This technique is somewhat difficult, and very fine, dry tinder is needed.)

13. Sparks to be used in starting fires may be obtained from the vehicle's battery.

14. Dismounted headlights, powered by the vehicle's battery, can be used to signal at night.

15. Flares are often carried in vehicles; use these for signaling.

16. The vehicle provides shade outside in which to rest during the day and protection within during cooler night temperatures.

17. The vehicle may, and should, hold a first aid kit.

18. Never drink radiator water. Coolant and antifreeze chemicals render it poisonous. It may be spread on the skin, or clothes may be soaked in it to aid in body cooling.

Leave your vehicle and hike to help only if you feel there is no hope of rescue in your present situation; or you know exactly how far and where to hike for certain rescue, and you know you have sufficient water to take you to your destination. Refer to the figures and tables on water needs in Chapter XI. Do not underestimate your water needs nor overestimate your ability to survive dehydration. Remember that in average summer weather a healthy hydrated man can walk approximately ten miles per gallon of water during the day and approximately twenty miles per gallon at night. If water is available, carry all you can with you. If you decide to walk to help, leave clear, obvious signals or notes as to the route you are intending to follow in order that rescuers may follow you if necessary.

## Direction-finding

In determining direction in your hike to help, you should always have a compass with you in the desert and know how to use it before you arrive there. Additionally, you should have maps of the area in which you are hiking or camping. You should make a consistent habit of noting landmarks in your camp and as you hike. The openness of the desert's terrain grants excellent visibility of the many landmarks, provided by the numerous low mountain ranges. These ranges are distinctive, if one takes the time to study them and get them firmly in mind. Their appearance changes with variations of light and shadow during different times of day and as you change your location and angle toward them; take these factors into consideration.

You *should* have compass, maps, and the like. If you are without a compass, confused regarding directions, and must hike to help, use common sense to determine direction.

1. The sun rises in the east (depending upon the time of year and your distance north of the equator, the sun will rise a little to the north or the south of true east), and it sets in the west (again, a little to the north or south according to the season). With your right hand to the morning sun and your left to the setting sun, you are facing north. In the desert, most days are sunny; the sun's location and movement are easily observed.

2. During the day you can use a watch to determine direction, if the watch is set on actual sun time, not daylight savings. Hold the watch on a horizontal plane. Point the hour hand at the sun. SOUTH will be located in the smallest angle between the symbol 12 and the hour hand.

3. If the day is cloudy, hold a stick upright on the center of the watch. Align the faint shadow the stick will cast over the hour hand. NORTH will be halfway through the small angle between the shadow and the symbol 12.

4. East can be determined during midday hours by use of a shadow. Select an object at least three feet in height which will cast a shadow with a definite projection. On the ground, mark the point where the shadow tip is located. After fifteen minutes, mark the shadow tip again. Draw a line from the first mark through the second mark. This line points EAST.

5. At night you can locate Polaris, the North Star, which is

never more than approximately one degree from the Celestial North Pole. Locate the Big Dipper. The two stars, called the pointers, located on the outer edge of the bowl of the Dipper (the portion of the ladle farthest from the handle) point almost directly to the nearby North Star. The North Star is thus opposite the open top of the Dipper.

6. If you are walking toward help and there is any possibility of becoming disoriented while resting, mark your direction of travel with rocks, equipment, or the like before falling asleep.

## Walking Out

If you are walking to help, walk toward a known travel route, an inhabited area, or, if nearby, toward the coast. Walk slowly and steadily. Rest approximately ten minutes out of each hour. When resting it is often advisable to prop your feet up, unlace your boots. Adjust or change your socks, which become compacted after a period of hiking; feet may then begin to shift in the boots, causing blisters. Even dirty socks will provide a good change as they are likely to be less compacted after having been given a "rest."

While walking, be alert to signs of water, food, civilization, or rescue efforts. If possible, be prepared to signal to rescuers with mirror, flashlight, firearm, whistle. Unless in your specific situation you have reason to believe differently, it is normally considered best to move downhill toward lower elevations in your search for help. If you find a road, it is advisable to stay on it; by following this sign of civilization, your chances of reaching help should be much improved.

Remember that night walking is most economical from the standpoint of water. However, also remember that walking in the early evening and morning when there is some light is advantageous in certain ways. You have less chance of missing possible water, food, or signs of human habitation when some light is available. Also with improved vision, your chances of avoiding accidents are improved. Remember that in the sum-

mer the cooler night hours are the favored times for rattlesnake activity. Watch for snakes insofar as possible, and take
precautions (for example, check before you sit down to rest).

When walking, take the easiest route; avoid obstacles if
possible. Attempt to go around steep gullies and hills. If you
must ascend a steep incline, zig-zag up, for a straight assault
exacts a greater cost in sweat and energy. When climbing,
place your entire foot on the ground; when descending an incline, bend your knees and take your time. Do not use undue
speed, which may cause loss of control. Falling or a similar accident will only compound the problems you already face. If
possible, avoid walking for long distances in sand, as this walking is most fatiguing. If you must hike over sand, place your
body weight well forward and keep your knees bent. If it is
necessary to travel through dunes, follow the firm valley floors
between the dunes as much as possible.

Distance in the desert is deceptive. Do not overestimate
your ability to reach a particular point which can be seen in
the distance. It is recommended that one unfamiliar with this
desert-distance deception estimate the distance to a point and
then multiply the figure by three for a more accurate estimate. Underestimating distance can be dangerous; so, too,
can underestimating your ability to cope and falling prey to
panic.

## Basic Survival Techniques

Certainly whether resting while hiking toward help or
while awaiting rescue, follow all suggestions which will serve
to prolong your survival time:

1. Remain quiet. Undertake no unnecessary activity or
movements.

2. Take advantage of the coolest microclimate available to
you—rest in shade, elevate yourself several inches above the
ground surface.

3. Avoid strong breezes, if possible, as these unnecessarily
increase evaporation of perspiration and heat gain from convection.

4. Remain clothed. Wear a hat if available, or improvise one. Wear sunglasses if available. If not, and glare bothers you, improvise slit goggles, or blacken under eyes with small amounts of engine oil or soot.

5. Drink water as needed to prevent fuzzy thinking and serious dehydration. Remember it is the water in your body that will save your life, not the water in your canteen. Ration your sweat, not your water.

6. Do not drink urine, blood, or seawater. Use urine on skin or clothing to provide cooling. If near the coast, soak clothing in seawater for cooling.

7. Do not eat unless water supplies are available; if limited water supplies are available, consume carbohydrates, rather than proteins.

8. Do not talk any more than necessary. Do not smoke, and keep your mouth closed to prevent evaporation of moisture.

9. Do not substitute alcohol for water. Its use not only results in fuzzy thinking, which can be extremely dangerous in an emergency situation, but also requires large amounts of water for the alcohol's digestion. (In July 1964, five men in an Arizona labor camp, drinking wine on a Sunday afternoon when the temperature was 119° F., died from a combination of exposure to high temperature and humidity levels plus alcohol consumption. That same year, four other men died in Arizona under similar circumstances.)

## Signals

Take any feasible signal measures available to help rescuers find you. These may be either sound or sight signals. In signaling, three is the number signifying an emergency.

**Sound signals** include the following:

1. If you have a firearm, you can signal with three evenly spaced shots. Do not fire indiscriminately, and do not fire unless you think someone is in the area. If hunters are shooting in the area, three shots may not be recognized as a call for help. In this case, if you believe people are in the vicinity, fire after dark when no hunter would be firing.

2. Banging on metal provides a far-reaching sound. You can improvise; for example, you can hit a hubcap with a tool.

3. Yelling or calling is not advised unless searchers are close, as a large amount of energy is required.

4. A whistle is a very good sound signal. It can be heard for a long distance and is an unusual, attention-getting sound in the wilderness.

**Sight signals** are the most effective to employ. Many types might be used:

1. Every hiker should carry a signal mirror which can be used in an emergency. A regular small mirror can be used; however, a signal mirror, which is made to be sighted through the center, is best. Made of metal or glass, it is small, lightweight, and may save your life. It is considered to be one of the most effective means of signaling.

When using a signal mirror, sight through the hole, holding the mirror about three inches in front of your face. Sight toward the target, as a plane's cockpit, looking in the mirror reflection for the spot of sunlight shining on your face. At this point, adjust the angle of the mirror until the spot of sunlight lines up with the hole. When you have done this, your flashes will be directly on target. This method can be used to signal

FIG. 105. Hold the signal mirror in front of your face. Sight the target through the hole. The spot of light coming through the hole will fall on your face or shirt and be reflected on the rear of the mirror. Adjust the mirror until the light spot in the mirror disappears through the sighting hole while you continue to sight your target through the hole.

　　　THE DESERTS OF THE SOUTHWEST

searchers on foot, in vehicles, or in aircraft many miles away. The signal is amazingly intense, almost blinding. Once you have targeted in on a plane's cockpit, flash the plane periodically, but do not keep the light flashing into the cockpit constantly as it can seriously interfere with the pilot's ability to see.

The foregoing method works well if the angle from the sun to the target is ninety degrees or less. If it is more than ninety degrees, the following method must be employed: In slightly outstretched hand, hold the mirror at an angle so that it catches the sun. A light spot will fall on the palm of your hand. Sight the target through the hole, then adjust the angle of the mirror so that the reflection of the light spot on your hand coincides with the hole in the mirror and disappears. This method may be used when the sun is as much as approximately 180 degrees away from the target.

The only disadvantage in using an ordinary mirror is that perfect sighting is more difficult to accomplish. By holding your hand in front of the mirror and catching the reflected light, you can get a general idea of where the flashes are most intense and can adjust your aim by catching the reflected light on your surroundings. You may be able to scratch off a small portion of the mirror backing to allow a sighting hole. Many women carry mirrors in their purses and mirrors attached to vehicles can be used when a signal mirror is not available. A tin can lid can also be employed; in this it is simple to punch a sighting hole through the center.

To flash a mirror along the horizon consistently throughout the day is advisable in an emergency situation, even though the effort may appear to be futile. The energy required is little, and the flashes seen for great distances may well attract attention. Flash toward the sound of an aircraft, even though you may be unable to see the plane itself.

2. If you have a flashlight, use it to signal at night, if you have reason to believe that rescuers are nearby. Dismount vehicle lights and use these for night signaling when it appears their use may be effective. Remember your battery power is limited. Chemical light sticks can provide a night signal. If these are routinely carried, replace them annually to make

sure they are operable, if needed. Battery-operated mini strobe lights can also be used. These are available at sporting goods stores, are small and easily carried.

3. Raise the hood and trunk lid of your vehicle to signal trouble.

4. Make your site as obvious as possible. Spread objects around that are not in use—blankets, tarps, extra clothing, parachutes, and so on.

5. You may wish to use the International Ground-Air Emergency signals. Make these signals in a large size on the ground. Use available materials—strips of blanket, aluminum foil, parachute, rocks, and the like. Those signals most commonly needed are the following:

   a. Require doctor—use a single straight line, as **I**
   b. Unable to proceed—use **X**
   c. Need food and water—use **F**
   d. Am proceeding in this direction—use arrow pointing in direction taken
   e. All is well—use **LL**
   f. No—use **N**
   g. Yes—use **Y**
   h. Not understood—use two of the capital letters **L**, back to back

THE SIGNAL FIRE

All of the foregoing signals are effective in their own right; however the signal fire is used more often than any other. Both the bright blaze and the smoke it emits are chances to attract attention. If possible, maintain three fires in a triangle—the recognized distress signal. In an emergency situation have a fire prepared for lighting, if possible, or keep a fire going to which material may be quickly added. In some parts of the desert, long-lasting fuel may be difficult to find, and one should weigh the energy required and the possible value to be derived from a constant large fire as opposed to a small fire, which can be increased if rescuers are thought to be in the area. At best, as a minimum measure when awaiting rescue, keep a plentiful supply of fuel around and keep at least coals burning at all times.

If the country in which you are situated is generally dark colored, attempt to build a fire which gives off a light-colored smoke. If you are in light-colored country, try to get a dark-colored smoke. Very black smoke probably has the best visibility, especially to aircraft. Green branches, if available, can be collected and thrown on hot coals or flames, when great amounts of light-colored smoke are desired. If you are stalled with a vehicle, one of the best fuels for smoke signals is your spare tire. By pouring engine oil over the tire and igniting it, you should be able to produce a large amount of billowing black smoke visible for many miles.

A signal fire may also consist of a bucket of sand soaked with gasoline and lit (very carefully) when possible rescuers are in the vicinity.

You should always carry waterproof matches with you. However, if you do not have these, alternatives are possible. In order to start a fire with a spark or series of sparks, prepare tinder carefully. Tinder should consist of very fine, very dry, readily flammable material, such as the underbark of the cottonwood tree, bird or mouse nests, small dry grass, frayed bits of cotton cloth, or the like. When building any fire, start with tinder, then work your way up through a series of increasingly larger sticks until you reach the size you need for your particular purpose.

1. Start your fire with a cigarette lighter, if any member of your party has one.

2. Use the cigarette lighter from your vehicle.

3. Damp wooden matches can usually be dried by stroking them twenty to thirty times through the dry hair on your head.

4. Bright sunlight can be directed through a hand lens or other magnifying glass from your first aid kit, or any convex lens, to start a flame.

5. If you have a live storage battery in your vehicle, you can produce a spark from it. Direct this spark into fine tinder.

6. Use flint and steel to strike a spark. The steel is struck against flint or agate. Iron pyrites may be substituted for steel. If you have no flint, find a piece of hard rock from which you

can strike sparks when it is struck with steel (use a knife blade, tool, or the like). Strike with a downward scraping motion so that the sparks fall on the tinder placed below them. As the tinder begins to smolder, fan or blow it gently until a flame is present.

## Finding Water

If you are stranded in the desert, regardless of the circumstances, your foremost concern is very likely to be water. A good general rule to follow in emergency situations is: *If you have a sufficient water supply, or if you have found a water source, stay where you are and await rescue.* However, if your water supply is very low or absent and rescue seems far distant, your decision may be to attempt to locate a source of water. Hopefully, you will have a good map of the area which will designate probable water. Lacking this, other possibilities may be explored. Remember in all cases, however, that the energy and moisture required to search or dig for water must be determined to be small in comparison to the expected reward.

1. Tanks which hold water for varying lengths of time are found in almost all desert areas. These basins are natural rather than manmade. Located in the bottoms of stream and arroyo beds, they are usually hollowed out of rock; however, dirt tanks may also be present. Tanks are essentially depressions in the bed which are impermeable to water. Hence, as it rains and the arroyos or washes become active, these tanks fill with water. The water may be retained for varying periods of time, particularly if the tanks are partially protected by being located in shade, or in some other way. Some members of the animal population of an area stake their lives on these tanks where they occur; normally they are fairly dependable water sources. Tanks can be located in a number of ways, but usually a combination of methods is best. First, scan the land for 360 degrees. Because the desert land is open, one can determine the slope of the land and ascertain where the main drainage is located. As the smaller streambeds converge, the size of the

common drainage gradually increases. In the larger runoff channels, the water has often eroded its path down to the bedrock, which is the perfect material for forming the tanks. By following these major streambeds downhill, you have a good chance of finding a tank.

Since local animals depend on these water sources, many animal trails lead to or from these natural cisterns. Watch for trails and follow them. The correct direction can be determined by finding a junction of two trails; follow the direction indicated by the arrow formed by the joining of the two trails. Birds flock to these waterholes; listen for their calls or watch their flights in the early morning and evening hours. Doves often fly toward water in the early morning and evening.

2. Animal trails and bird flights may also lead you to manmade watering sources. Watch always for windmills and also for watering troughs to which ranchers may haul water by vehicle for their stock.

3. In some cases, water may be found at the base of cliffs either on the surface or not far underground, for some time following rains. Occasionally springs may be located; lava and

FIG. 106. For some months following a rain, in occasional locations water may be found by digging at the base of rock cliffs, particularly lava cliffs.

limestone tend to have larger springs than other types of rocks. Limestone caverns often contain pools or dripping springs. Be careful not to venture past the cavern's lighted areas as you can easily become disoriented.

4. Moisture often condenses at night on cool objects, such as metal or stones. This moisture may be collected just after sunup, for example, by soaking it up in a handkerchief and wringing it out. Airplane wings or similar surfaces may provide such moisture. If you possess a piece of canvas, scoop out a depression in the ground, cover the bottom with the canvas, and line the basin with pebbles taken from about a foot below the surface (which are less dry than those found on the ground surface). Dew may collect on the rocks during the night and trickle down onto the canvas. (Consider carefully, though, the energy and moisture required to prepare this dew trap in relationship to expected returns.)

5. Look for indicator plants which grow only where they can obtain water supplies. Sycamores, cottonwoods, willows,

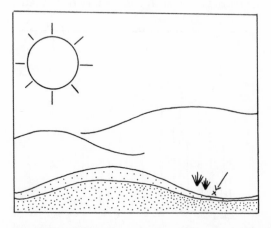

FIG. 107. When digging for water in sand dunes, pick the lowest point between dunes. Along a beach, dig in the first depression behind the first sand dune. The top sand layer may be underlain by wet sand. If you hit wet sand, dig no deeper, for below the freshwater layer may be one of saltwater. Prepare a hole in the damp-sand layer and wait for water to seep in.

THE DESERTS OF THE SOUTHWEST

hackberry, tamarisk, and cattails are examples. You may have to dig to find the moisture.

6. If you are along a sandy beach, either on the seashore or along a dry lake, the best place to dig for water is in the first depression behind the first sand dune. This spot is the most probable place for rainwater to collect. If you hit wet sand, cease digging; if conditions are right, water will seep out of the sand into the hole you have dug. The primary water is usually fresh; however, if you dig deeper, the lower water may contain salt. If you are among the sand dunes, rain water will collect in the lowest point between the dunes. At these points, dig down three to six feet; if the sand becomes damp, continue digging. However, if in lower layers the sand becomes dry, you have passed the water-bearing layer and should discontinue digging.

7. If you locate mud flats, find the lowest point and wring out any damp mud in a cloth to collect water. Check the water to determine its salinity. If it is too disagreeable, do not drink it.

8. Small upwellings of freshwater occur along some beaches. Occasionally these upwellings are found on the Gulf of California coast where underground freshwater floats above saltwater. Where the freshwater is exposed, a *pozo,* or "coyote well," is formed. Animals take advantage of these "wells," as can man if he locates them, although the water tends to be rather saline. Pozos are small, often consisting of a small basin only a few inches in diameter. These "wells" are often surrounded by a small ring of green succulent vegetation, which helps one to identify such a site.

9. If you come upon a dry desert streambed, dig at the lowest point on the outside of a bend in the bed. At this point, water sinks and accumulates as the stream dries up. Watch for damp spots in dry streambeds and dig there. Watch also for holes dug in streambeds by coyotes seeking water. Often water seeps into these holes, and man as well as coyotes and other animals can benefit from the water source.

10. If you locate an open water supply such as a tank or the like, *purification of the water is always advisable.* If it is dirty, strain it through a cloth. Purify it by boiling it for five minutes;

FIG. 108. If you are digging for water in a dry streambed, dig at the lowest point on the outside of a bend in the channel.

by using purification tablets according to directions; by using two to three drops of tincture of iodine per quart of water (let stand for thirty minutes); or by adding two to four drops of household bleach per quart of water. Admittedly, in a desperate situation, the above methods may be unavailable to you, and the water, polluted or unpolluted, may be literally your lifesaver.

11. Certain desert plants may constitute a possible source of emergency moisture. Particularly the cacti, which soak up moisture supplies as sponges would when moisture is present, may be important to man in a survival situation. Several species of barrels are present, depending on the area you are in. These cacti are globular to short cylindric in form, and usually unbranched, although a few species produce a clustered group of several stems. Barrel cacti are heavily spined, and some species have in each cluster a main spine that is strongly hooked, closely resembling a large fishhook. Moisture does not simply flow out of this cactus. The best means of obtain-

ing moisture from the barrel cactus is to break the cactus open, using a heavy knife, rock, or tool, such as the jack in your vehicle. The pulp inside, which holds the moisture, may be pulverized to obtain the liquid (use tool, rock, or the like), or you can chew on the pulp extracting the moisture and then spitting out the residue. Do not swallow the pulp; it can make you ill. Smaller plants tend to contain the most moisture. These cacti are "accordion-pleated" to allow for expansion with water supply. A well-filled plant with its pleats expanded will contain more moisture than a shriveled, tightly pleated specimen. The barrel cactus is the only one from which acceptable moisture in any quantity can be obtained. The saguaro, although large, does not contain potable moisture.

Consider carefully the cost in terms of heat and dehydration that it will cost you to attempt to obtain a limited amount of water from a barrel cactus. Barrel cacti pieces may serve you better used in a solar still.

12. If the materials are available, you may wish to construct one or more solar stills for obtaining water. Essentially, the solar still is a simple device which can distill drinkable

FIG. 109. Depending upon the species, certain barrel cacti, *Ferocactus* spp., may reach 9 to 12 feet in height, although most species range from 2 to 4 or 5 feet tall. These cacti are usually solitary, unbranched, and globular to short cylindric in form. In an emergency, they can be cut open by man and the inner pulp mashed to obtain limited moisture.

water, using as its source soil, fleshy plants such as cacti, or polluted waters such as body waste. The functioning pieces of the solar still are a piece of clear plastic film about six feet square and some type of fairly broad-mouthed container with which to collect water. The solar still is constructed by scooping out a bowl-shaped hole in the soil. The hole should be about thirty-six to forty inches in diameter and about eighteen to twenty inches in depth. Dig the sides down straight at first, then taper them to the center to provide a slanting ledge on which to place plant material. At the center of the hole, dig a small, deeper depression approximately the size of the container. Place the container securely in this bottom-most part. The container may be a pan, bucket, hub cap, or the like. A trough may be dug around part of the perimeter of the still, at about mid-depth, as a site in which to place polluted water. Lay the plastic sheet over the top of the cavity and hold it in place with a rim of rocks and soil. In the center of the plastic, place a small-sized rock (no larger than your fist). The rock, weighting the plastic down in the center, causes an inverted cone of plastic to be formed, with the tip of the cone directly above the container. With sunlight shining through the plastic, water is evaporated from the soil and from materials placed in the still; the air becomes super saturated and water condenses on the underside of the cooler plastic. The drops of water then flow to the low point of the cone and drip into the container below. (If the plastic is very smooth and slick, you may need to roughen it a bit by rubbing it with sand or some other abrasive so that the water drops are not shed from its surface above the tip of the cone.)

The plastic must be held firmly against the ground surface by the ring of sand, soil, and rocks so that no moisture is allowed to escape from the still. Each time the plastic is removed, a half hour to an hour or longer is required, once it is replaced, to get the still into operation again. Therefore, do not remove the plastic any more frequently than is absolutely necessary. The use of a plastic tube 4 to 6 feet in length, ¼ inch in diameter, as a part of the still is helpful. Securely place one end of the tube in the water container (if you have tape, tape it in place). Bring the other end of the tube to the ground surface and out beyond the edge of the plastic and dirt rim. Use this tube as a straw for sucking the moisture up from the container without disturbing the distillation process. When the plastic tube is not being used to remove water, tie the end of it shut or otherwise seal it.

The location of the still is important. If the soil is going to be your only source of water, the still is best placed in a streambed or depression in which rainwater collects, so that you are making use of the soil with the highest water concentration. In general, a clay-type soil is usually better than a sand type, as clay normally holds more water for longer periods. Following long dry spells, the water yield from soil alone may be quite small. If cactus or polluted water is to be used as the still's primary source of moisture, the still can be placed in almost any convenient spot. However, always make sure its lo-

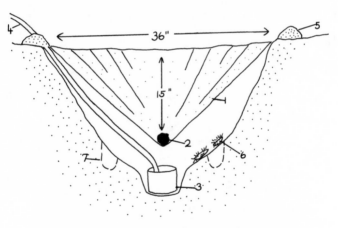

| | |
|---|---|
| 1 = plastic film | 5 = dirt or sand to hold plastic in place |
| 2 = small rock | and to seal it to the ground surface |
| 3 = water container | 6 = cut pieces of cactus |
| 4 = plastic tube | 7 = trough for waste liquids |

FIG. 110.  In the solar still, water from the soil, plant parts, human waste, and other materials condenses on the underside of a plastic film and drips into the container. Water can be sucked up through the plastic hose to avoid disturbing the condensation process.

cation receives maximum sunlight. Be very careful that polluted water, cactus parts, or soil do not touch the inner portion of the plastic sheet or the collection container, polluting the water. When using succulent plant material, be sure the plants have been chopped open to some extent. In the still, do *not* use radiator water, which contains chemical contaminants.

## Finding Food

The need for food in a survival situation is far less pressing than the need for water. If water is in short supply or lacking, one should eat nothing; digestion of food intensifies the need for water. Man can survive a mere few days without water; he can survive for several weeks without food—not, admittedly, entirely in comfort. In actuality, a person undergoing a water deficit usually does not feel hungry.

Inasmuch as this chapter is concerned with survival in an emergency situation in the desert, and not with wresting a living from the desert wilderness, we do not recommend foraging for and eating foods growing wild in the desert.

Relatively few people are ever actually required to face an emergency-survival situation in the desert. With respect for the desert and the conditions it imposes, and with proper preparation for enjoyment of the arid land, one is far safer exploring the desert than exploring many American cities. Advice for the desert enthusiast is *Do not get caught in an emergency situation if preplanning and good sense can avoid it.* But if you do find yourself in trouble, remember:

1. *Do not panic.*
2. *Think. Your brain is your greatest asset.*
3. *Neither underestimate nor overestimate either desert conditions or your abilities to cope with them and the situation in which you find yourself.*
4. *Consider all alternatives from the standpoint of physiological costs.*
5. *Follow the rules for survival.*
6. *Do not give up.*

One should depend on preparation and intelligent action in desert exploration, rather than miracles. But when only sheer determination remains and the object is survival, don't discount the miraculous, backed by resolve.

May you never need desert survival information. May all your desert exploration be "rewarding travel in an unfrequented land."

# Bibliography

Adolph, E. F. and Associates. *Physiology of Man in the Desert*. New York: Hafner Press, 1969.

Alcock, John. *In a Desert Garden: Love and Death Among the Insects*. New York: W. W. Norton, 1997.

Alcock, John. *Sonoran Desert Spring*. Chicago: University of Chicago Press, 1985.

Alcock, John. *Sonoran Desert Summer*. Tucson: University of Arizona Press, 1990.

Aschmann, Homer. *Central Desert of Baja California: Demography and Ecology*. Riverside, CA: Manessier, 1967.

Austin, Mary. *Land of Little Rain*. Albuquerque: University of New Mexico Press, 1974.

Benson, Lyman. *The Cacti of Arizona*. Tucson: University of Arizona Press, 1974.

Benson, Lyman. *The Cacti of the United States and Canada*. Stanford: Stanford University Press, 1981.

Benson, Lyman, and R. A. Darrow. *Trees and Shrubs of the Southwestern Deserts*. Tucson: University of Arizona Press, 1981.

Bowden, Charles. *Blue Desert*. Tucson: University of Arizona Press, 1986

Bowden, Charles. *Killing the Hidden Waters*. Austin: University of Texas Press, 1977.

Bowers, Janice E. *A Full Life in a Small Place and Other Essays from a Desert Garden*. Tucson: University of Arizona Press, 1993.

Bowers, Janice Emily. *100 Desert Wildflowers of the Southwest*. Tucson: Southwest Parks and Monuments Association, 1989.

Bowers, Janice Emily. *Seasons of the Wind: A Naturalist's Look at the Plant Life of Southwestern Sand Dunes*. Flagstaff, AZ: Northland Press, 1986.

Bowers, Janice Emily. *Shrubs and Trees of the Southwest Deserts*. Tucson: Southwest Parks and Monuments Association, 1993

Brown, David E. *Biotic Communities: Southwestern United States and Northwestern Mexico*. Salt Lake City: University of Utah Press, 1994.

Brown, David E. and Neil B. *Gila Monster: Facts and Folklore of America's Aztec Lizard.* Silver City, NM: High-Lonesome Books, 1991.

Brown, G. W., Jr. *Desert Biology,* Vols. I and II. New York and London: Academic Press, 1968 and 1974.

Broyles, B. and R. S. Felger, eds. "Dry Borders." *Journal of the Southwest* 39 (3–4): 303–860 (1998)

Buchmann, Stephen L. and Gary Paul Nabhan. *Forgotten Pollinators.* Washington, DC: Island Press, 1996.

Coyle, Jeanette and Norman C. Roberts. *A Field Guide to the Common and Interesting Plants of Baja California.* New York: Natural History Publishing Company, 1976.

Cunningham, Richard L. *50 Common Birds of the Southwest.* Tucson: Southwest Parks and Monuments Association, 1990.

Dahl, Kevin. *Wild Foods of the Sonoran Desert.* Tucson: Arizona-Sonora Desert Museum, 1995.

Dodge, Natt N. *Flowers of the Southwest Deserts.* Tucson: Southwest Parks and Monuments, 1985.

Dunbier, Roger. *The Sonoran Desert: Its Geography, Economy, and People.* Tucson: University of Arizona Press, 1968

Dykinga, Jack W. and Charles Bowden. *The Sonoran Desert.* New York: Harry N. Abrams, 1992.

Ernst, Carl H. *Venomous Reptiles of North America.* Washington, DC: Smithsonian Institution Press, 1989.

Ferris, Roxana. *Death Valley Wildflowers.* Death Valley, CA: Death Valley Natural History Association, 1983.

Findley, Rowe. *Great American Deserts.* Washington, DC: National Geographic Society, 1972.

Fischer, Pierre C. *70 Common Cacti of the Southwest.* Tucson: Southwest Parks and Monuments Association, 1989.

Fradkin, Philip. *A River No More: The Colorado River and the West.* Tucson: University of Arizona Press, 1984.

Friederici, Peter. *Strangers in Our Midst: The Startling World of Sonoran Desert Arthropods.* Tucson: Arizona-Sonora Desert Museum, 1997.

Gehlbach, F. R. *Mountain Islands and Desert Seas: A Natural History of the U.S.–Mexican Borderlands.* College Station: Texas A&M University Press, 1981.

Glinski, Richard L., ed. *The Raptors of Arizona.* Tucson: University of Arizona Press, 1998.

Hanson, Jonathan, and Roesann Beggy Hanson. *Desert Dogs.* Tucson: Arizona-Sonora Desert Museum, 1996.

Hanson, Roseann Beggy, and Jonathan Hanson. *Southern Arizona Nature Almanac.* Boulder, CO: Pruett Publishing Company, 1996.

Hare, Trevor. *Poisonous Dwellers of the Desert: Description, Habitat, Prevention, Treatment.* Tucson: Southwest Parks and Monuments Association, 1995.

Hartmann, William K. *Desert Heart: Chronicles of the Sonoran Desert.* Tucson: Fisher Books, 1989.

Hastings, James R., and Raymond M. Turner. *The Changing Mile.* Tucson: University of Arizona Press, 1965.

Humphrey, Robert R. *The Boojum and Its Home.* Tucson: University of Arizona Press, 1974.

Jackson, Donald Dale, and the editors of Time-Life Books. *Sagebrush Country.* New York: Time-Life Books, 1975.

Jackson, Donald Dale, Peter Wood, and the editors of Time-Life Books. *The Sierra Madre.* New York: Time-Life Books, 1975.

Jaeger, Edmund C. *Desert Wild Flowers.* Stanford: Stanford University Press, 1969.

Jaeger, Edmund C. *Desert Wildlife.* Stanford: Stanford University Press, 1961.

Jaeger, Edmund C. *The North American Deserts.* Stanford: Stanford University Press, 1957.

Johnson, William Weber, and the editors of Time-Life Books. *Baja California.* New York: Time-Life Books, 1972.

Kearney, T. H. and R. H. Peebles. *Arizona Flora.* Berkeley and Los Angeles: University of California Press, 1964.

Kirk, Ruth. *Desert: The American Southwest.* Boston: Houghton Mifflin Company, 1973.

Klauber, Laurence M. *Rattlesnakes: Their Habits, Life Histories and Influence on Mankind.* Berkeley: University of California Press, 1997.

Krutch, Joseph Wood. *The Desert Year.* New York: The Viking Press, Inc., 1963.

Krutch, Joseph Wood. *The Forgotten Peninsula.* New York: William Sloane Associates, 1961.

Krutch, Joseph Wood. *Voice of the Desert.* New York: William Morrow & Co., Inc., 1955.

Laney, Nancy R. *Desert Waters: From Ancient Aquifers to Modern Demands.* Tucson: Arizona-Sonora Desert Museum, 1998.

Lazaroff, David Wentworth. *Secret Lives of Hummingbirds.* Tucson: Arizona-Sonora Desert Museum, 1995.

Leopold, A. Starker. *Wildlife of Mexico: The Game Birds and Mammals.* Berkeley: University of California Press, 1957.

Leopold, A. Starker, and the editors of *Life. The Desert.* New York: Time Inc., 1961.

Lowe, C. H., C. R. Schwalbe, and T. B. Johnson. *The Venomous Reptiles of Arizona.* Phoenix: Nongame Branch, Arizona Game and Fish Department, 1986.

Lowe, Charles H. *Arizona's Natural Environment: Landscapes and Habitats.* Tucson: University of Arizona Press, 1964.

Lowe, Charles H. ed., *The Vertebrates of Arizona.* Tucson: University of Arizona Press, 1964.

MacMahon, James A. *Deserts.* New York: Alfred A. Knopf, 1998.

McClaran, Mitchel, and Thomas R. Van Devender, eds. *The Desert Grassland.* Tucson: University of Arizona Press, 1995.

Miller, Alden H. and Robert C. Stebbins. *The Lives of Desert Animals in Joshua Tree National Monument.* Berkeley: University of California Press, 1964.

Nabhan, G. P. *Saguaro: A View of Saguaro National Monument and the Tucson Basin.* Tucson: Southwestern Parks and Monuments Association, 1986.

Nabhan, G. P. and A. R. Holdsworth. *State of the Desert Biome: Uniqueness, Biodiversity, Threats, and Adequacy of Protection in the Sonoran Region.* Tucson: The Wildlands Project, 1998.

Nabhan, Gary. *Gathering the Desert.* Tucson: University of Arizona Press, 1985.

Nabhan, Gary P. *The Desert Smells Like Rain.* San Francisco: North Point Press, 1982.

Nabhan, Gary Paul. *Counting Sheep.* Tucson: University of Arizona, 1993.

*A Natural History of the Sonoran Desert.* Tucson: Arizona-Sonora Desert Museum; Berkeley: University of California Press, 2000.

Nesbitt, Parul H., Alonzo W. Pond, and William H. Allen. *The Survival Book.* New York: Funk and Wagnalls Inc., 1969.

Niethammer, Carolyn. *American Indian Food and Lore.* New York: Collier Books, 1974.

Olin, George. *House in the Sun: A Natural History of the Sonoran Desert.* Tucson: Southwestern Parks and Monuments Association, 1994.

Olin, George. *Mammals of the Southwest Deserts.* Tucson: Southwestern Parks and Monuments Association, 1982.

Peterson, Roger Tory. *A Field Guide to Western Birds.* Boston: Houghton Mifflin Company, 1961.

Peterson, Roger Tory and Edward L. Chalif. *A Field Guide to Mexican Birds.* Boston: Houghton Mifflin Company, 1973.

Phillips, Allan, Joe Marshall, and Gale Monson. *The Birds of Arizona.* Tucson: University of Arizona Press, 1964.

Pinau, Merlin. *A Field Guide to Desert Holes.* Tucson: Arizona-Sonora Desert Museum, 1999.

Polis, G. A. ed. *Ecology of Desert Communities.* Tucson: University of Arizona, 1991.

Reisner, Marc. *Cadillac Desert: The American West and Its Disappearing Water.* New York: Penguin Books, 1986.

Robichaux, R., ed. *Ecology of Sonoran Desert Plants and Plant Communities.* Tucson: University of Arizona Press, 1999.

Russell, Findley E. *Snake Venom Poisoning.* Philadelphia: J. B. Lippincott Company, 1980.

Ryan, R. Mark. *Mammals of Deep Canyon; Colorado Desert, California.* Palm Springs, CA: The Desert Museum, 1968.

Schmidt-Nielsen, Knut. *Desert Animals: Physiological Problems of Heat and Water.* New York: Oxford University Press, 1964.

Sellers, William D., Richard H. Hill, and Margaret Sanderson-Rae. *Arizona Climate: The First Hundred Years.* Tucson: University of Arizona Press, 1985.

Shaw, Charles E. and Sheldon Campbell. *Snakes of the American West.* New York: Alfred A. Knopf, Inc., 1974.

Shreve, Forrest and Ira L. Wiggins. *Vegetation and Flora of the Sonoran Desert,* 2 vols. Stanford: Stanford University Press, 1977.

Small, Arnold. *The Birds of California.* New York: Winchester Press, 1975.

Smith, Robert L. *Venomous Animals of Arizona.* Tucson: College of Agriculture, University of Arizona, 1997.

Stebbins, Robert C. *Field Guide to Western Reptiles and Amphibians.* Boston: Houghton Mifflin, 1985.

Stebbins, Robert C. and Nathan W. Cohen. *A Natural History of Amphibians.* Princeton: Princeton University Press, 1997.

Sutton, Ann and Myron Sutton. *The Life of the Desert.* New York: McGraw-Hill Book Company, 1966.

Trimble, Steve. *The Sagebrush Sea: A Natural History of the Great Basin.* Reno: University of Nevada Press, 1989.

Turner, Raymond M., Janice E. Bowers, and Tony L. Burgess. *Sono-*

ran *Desert Plants: An Ecological Atlas.* Tucson: University of Arizona Press, 1995.

Werner, Foyd G. and Carl Olson. *Learning About and Living with Insects of the Southwest: How to Identify Helpful, Harmful and Venomous Insects.* Tucson: Fisher Books, 1994.

Zwinger, Ann Haymond. *The Mysterious Lands.* New York: Truman Talley Books/Plume, 1989.

# INDEX

# ABOUT THE AUTHORS

PEGGY LARSON has lived in the American Southwest for more than forty years. A retired librarian, she is currently Archivist for the Arizona-Sonora Desert Museum. She is the author of many books about the natural world, including *All About Ants, Lives of the Social Insects, Deserts of America,* and *Caving.* She lives in Tucson.

LANE LARSON, coauthor of Sierra Club's *Caving,* is owner of Caiman Enterprises, which sponsors scuba trips to the Sea of Cortez and river-running expeditions in Mexico and Alaska. He is co-owner of Ecoscapes, Inc., which fabricates artificial rockwork for museums, zoos, aquariums, and private firms.

MEASURING SCALE IN CENTIMETERS AND MILLIMETERS

1

2

3

4

5

6

7

8

9

10

11

12

13

14

15

16

17

18

MEASURING SCALE IN INCHES

1

2

3

4

5

6

7